WITHDRAWN FROM THE LIBRARY UNIVERSITY OF WINCHESTER

D1354611

KA 0288185 3

# THE LIGHT IN THEIR EYES

*Creating
Multicultural
Learning
Communities*

*Sonia Nieto*

Trentham Books
Stoke on Trent, England

Teachers College, Columbia University
New York and London

UNIVERSITY COLLEGE
WINCHESTER

371.97 0288 1858
NIE

Published by Teachers College Press, 1234 Amsterdam Avenue, New York, NY 10027

Published in Great Britain and Europe by Trentham Books Limited

Copyright © 1999 by Teachers College, Columbia University

All rights reserved. No part of this publication may be reproduced or transmitted in any form or by any means, electronic or mechanical, including photocopy, or any information storage and retrieval system, without permission from the publisher.

*Library of Congress Cataloging-in-Publication Data*

Nieto, Sonia.
    The light in their eyes : creating multicultural learning
communities / Sonia Nieto.
       p.    cm. — (Multicultural education series)
    Includes bibliographical references (p.   ) and index.
    ISBN 0-8077-3783-6 (cloth : alk. paper). — ISBN 0-8077-3782-8
(pbk. : alk. paper)
      1. Multicultural education—United States.  2. Children of
minorities—Education—United States.  I. Title.  II. Series:
Multicultural education series (New York, N.Y.)
LC1099.3.N55  1999
370.117—dc21                      98-51677

ISBN 0-8077-3782-8 (paper)
ISBN 0-8077-3783-6 (cloth)

Printed on acid-free paper
Manufactured in the United States of America

06 05 04 03 02 01 00 99     8 7 6 5 4 3 2 1

For Jazmyne, Monique, August, and Marcus:
The new generation

# Contents

# Series Foreword

THE NATION'S DEEPENING ethnic texture, interracial tension and conflict, and the increasing percentage of students who speak a first language other than English make multicultural education an imperative as we enter a new century. The 1990 Census indicated that one of every four Americans is a person of color. About one of every three Americans will be a person of color by the turn of the century.

American classrooms are experiencing the largest influx of immigrant students since the turn of the twentieth century. More than eight million legal immigrants settled in the United States between 1981 and 1990 (U.S. Bureau of the Census, 1994). A large but undetermined number of undocumented immigrants also enter the United States each year. The influence of an increasingly ethnically diverse population on the nation's schools, colleges, and universities is and will continue to be enormous. In 50 of the nation's largest urban public school systems, African Americans, Latinos, Asian Americans, and other students of color made up 76.5% of the population in the 50 school districts combined in 1992 (Council of Great City Schools, 1994). In some of the nation's largest cities and metropolitan areas, such as Chicago, Los Angeles, Washington, DC, New York, Seattle, and San Francisco, half or more of the public school students are students of color. In California, the population of students of color in the public schools has exceeded the percentage of White students since the 1988–89 school year.

Students of color will make up about 46% of the nation's student population by 2020 (Pallas, Natriello, & McDill, 1989). Fourteen percent of school-age youth live in homes in which English is not the first language (U.S. Bureau of the Census, 1994). Most teachers now in the classroom and in teacher education programs are likely to have students from diverse ethnic, cultural, and racial groups in their classrooms during their careers. This is true for both inner-city and suburban teachers.

An important goal of multicultural education is to improve race relations and to help all students acquire the knowledge, attitudes, and skills needed to participate in cross-cultural interactions and in personal, social, and civic action that will help make our nation more democratic and just. Multicultural education is consequently as important for middle-class White suburban students as it is for students of color who live in the inner city. Multicultural education fosters the public good and the overarching goals of the commonwealth.

The major purpose of the Multicultural Education Series is to provide preservice educators, practicing educators, graduate students, and scholars with an interrelated and comprehensive set of books that summarizes and analyzes important research, theory, and practice related to the education of ethnic, racial, cultural, and language groups in the United States and the education of mainstream students about ethnic and cultural diversity. The books in the series provide research, theoretical, and practical knowledge about the behaviors and learning characteristics of students of color, language-minority students, and low-income students. They also provide knowledge about ways to improve race relations in educational settings.

The definition of multicultural education in the *Handbook of Research on Multicultural Education* (Banks & Banks, 1995) is used in the series: "Multicultural education is a field of study designed to increase educational equity for all students that incorporates, for this purpose, content, concepts, principles, theories, and paradigms from history, the social and behavioral sciences, and particularly from ethnic studies and women studies" (p. xii). In the series, as in the handbook, multicultural education is considered a "metadiscipline."

The dimensions of multicultural education, developed by Banks (1995) and described in the *Handbook of Research on Multicultural Education*, provide the conceptual framework for the development of the books in the series. The dimensions are *content integration, the knowledge construction process, prejudice reduction, an equity pedagogy,* and *an empowering school culture and social structure.* To implement multicultural education effectively, teachers and administrators must attend to each of the five dimensions of multicultural education. They should use content from diverse groups when teaching concepts and skills, help students to understand how knowledge in the various disciplines is constructed, help students to develop positive intergroup attitudes and behaviors, and modify their teaching strategies so that students from different racial, cultural, and social class groups will experience equal educational opportunities. The total environment and culture of the school also must be transformed so that students from diverse ethnic and cultural groups will experience equal status in the culture and life of the school.

Although the five dimensions of multicultural education are highly interrelated, each requires deliberate attention and focus. Each book in the series focuses on one or more of the dimensions, although each book deals with all of them to some extent because of the highly interrelated characteristics of the dimensions.

John Siraj-Blatchford, a scholar who specializes in science and multicultural education at the University of East London, raises this important question, "What is a multicultural atom?" He responds by describing it as an atom that students from diverse racial, ethnic, and cultural groups can understand because of the modifications that the science teacher makes in instruction. Siraj-Blatchford's insightful question and response indicate that an important dimension of multicultural education is equity pedagogy. This dimension necessitates that teachers change their instruction in significant ways so that students from diverse racial, ethnic, and cultural groups will experience academic success when learning essential science, math, reading, and writing knowledge and skills.

This informative book by Sonia Nieto, one of the leading theorists in multicultural education, focuses on ways in which teachers can modify their teaching in order to increase the academic achievement of students from those racial and ethnic groups that are experiencing massive failure in the nation's schools, and consequently in society. As Nieto points out, modifying instruction to improve the academic achievement of groups such as African Americans and Latinos will benefit all students because underachievement exists within all segments of the school population.

This is a significant and timely book. The fact that an important goal of the multicultural education project is to improve the academic achievement of students is lost in many schools because multicultural education too often is conceptualized as special units and lessons for holidays and celebrations, or is viewed as oppositional to academic achievement and serious learning. Nieto describes how academic achievement and content knowledge are important parts of the multicultural project. I recommend this book highly to all educators who want to improve our schools and to create a more caring and humane society.

James A. Banks
Series Editor

## REFERENCES

Banks, J. A. (1995). Multicultural education: Historical development, dimensions, and practice. In J. A. Banks & C. A. M. Banks (Eds.), *Handbook of research on multicultural education* (pp. 3–24). New York: Macmillan.

Banks, J. A., & Banks, C. A. M. (Eds.). (1995). *Handbook of research on multicultural education*. New York: Macmillan.

Council of Great City Schools. (1994). *National urban education goals: 1992–1993 indicators report*. Washington, DC: Author.

Pallas, A. M., Natriello, G., & McDill, E. L. (1989). The changing nature of the disadvantaged population: Current dimensions and future trends. *Educational Researcher, 18*(5), 4, 16–22.

U.S. Bureau of the Census. (1994). *Statistical abstract of the United States* (114th ed.). Washington, DC: U.S. Government Printing Office.

# Acknowledgments

MOST OF THE HUNDREDS OF STUDENTS I have been privileged to teach in the past 25 years have been teachers, and they have given me much food for thought since I began my career as a teacher educator. As I struggled through the writing of this book, their presence was very evident to me. I want to thank them for giving me the inspiration to write something that might be of help to other teachers. I especially want to thank the students and former students who allowed me to include their contributions in this book: *Patty Bode, Maria Botelho, Elizabeth Capifali, Karen McLean Donaldson, Bill Dunn, Mary Ginley, Deborah Leta Habib, Tom Hidalgo, Lizette Román, David Ruiz, Ann Scott, and Youngro Yoon Song.* They are all talented teachers or teacher educators who have thought long and hard about what schools should be like and about the role of multicultural education, critical pedagogy, and social justice in creating those schools. I'm sure you will agree with me that their words, most of which were written in journals when they took class with me as long as 10 years ago, bring the issues that I address in these pages to life. They also demonstrate in a powerful way what it means to have the courage to be teachers of all our students.

It was Ann Scott who encouraged me to add in the book more descriptions of actual events and anecdotes from my classes, and Mary Ginley suggested that I include excerpts from the journals of teachers who've taken my classes over the years. I want to thank them both for these perceptive recommendations and for their feedback on a very rough draft of the manuscript that I asked them to read. I also want to thank Ann Scott and Elizabeth Capifali for help in tracking down some references. Lori Mestre, reference librarian at the W. E. B. Du Bois Library at the University of Massachusetts, provided tremendous help with my bibliography and with hard-to-find data. Patricia Ramsey gave me thoughtful and critical feedback on the first complete draft of the book. Jim Banks, the series editor, read the manuscript with his usual keen eye and gave me valuable suggestions. Their advice, I know, helped to improve the book considerably. At Teachers College Press, Brian Ellerback was a supportive and careful editor whose counsel I have appreciated greatly. Finally, I want to thank my husband and *compañero*, Angel, for reading every word I write and for helping me make sense of the world.

# Introduction

To think of history as possibility is to recognize education as possibility. It is to recognize that if education cannot do everything, it can achieve some things.

—Paulo Freire, in Freire & Macedo, "A Dialogue"

I BEGAN THINKING about what it might mean to develop a multicultural perspective on student learning many years ago when it became clear to me that much of what takes place in classrooms and schools in the name of multicultural education is little more than window dressing. I clearly remember a student teacher telling me of her experience at a faculty meeting where teachers were discussing whether they should "do" multicultural education. Although most claimed to be interested in it, the teachers said they did not have time to include multicultural education during the fall but would leave it instead for the spring semester, when it would happily coincide with Black History Month and other "ethnic" celebrations. As I was beginning to see, to "do" multicultural education in many cases and for many teachers and schools meant simply to include, quite often in a shallow way, a segment of curriculum on some aspect of diversity.

In other schools, multicultural education is approached in different, although not necessarily more adequate, ways. "We do multicultural education here," I would be told when visiting a school, but the only signs I could see of it were a few posters of children with brown faces or, if it happened to be January or February, a bulletin board with a saintly looking Dr. Martin Luther King, Jr., engulfed in clouds with the words "I HAVE A DREAM" above, and with students' compositions of their own dreams below. In December, a school might have an assembly program on "Win-

ter Festivals of Light" in which Christmas, Chanukah, Kwanzaa, and Indigenous solstice celebrations were included. In more self-consciously
progressive schools, there even might be evidence of curriculum about
the civil rights movement or the internment of the Japanese during World
War II. In other cases, schools have mission statements that include "developing tolerance toward others," or slogans such as "Celebrating Diversity" that serve as the school theme. These are gestures that indicate some
degree of attention to multicultural education, but such efforts are at best
incomplete; at worst, they serve to camouflage the massive failure of
schools to improve education for students who traditionally have been
impeded from experiencing academic success.

Curiously missing from discussions in most schools that claim to "do"
multicultural education are statements having to do with *student learning.*
This situation was brought out dramatically to me one day many years
ago when I was talking with a friend about a multicultural education
initiative being implemented in a nearby urban school system. The reservations she had about the project were evident in the question she asked
about it, a question remarkable in its simplicity: "But are the kids learning?" she wanted to know. Several years later, another friend struck a
similar theme as we were discussing the value of multicultural programs.
Of the children who took part in such programs, she asked impatiently,
"But can they do math?"

These questions should not be read as conservative knee-jerk reactions to multicultural education. Both of these women have spent their
professional lives promoting educational equity and they have whole-
heartedly supported multicultural education for many years. Nonetheless, their questions demonstrate plainly the underlying discomfort that
even proponents of multicultural education feel about the direction it often takes. Although multicultural education began as a reform movement
with a powerful commitment to educational equity and an unequivocal
stance against racism, in most places it is implemented as curriculum and
practices that are little more than ethnic additives or cultural celebrations.
My friends' questions disclosed a concern that schools, in their enthusiasm to provide students with positive role models, to boost self-esteem,
and to diversify the curriculum (all sorely needed, no question about it),
were neglecting their fundamental role: to promote student learning. I
have thought about these questions many times since, and they are the
reason for this book.

There are other equally vital concerns related to what and how
students learn. Such questions as, "Can they think critically?" "Can they
create?" "Do they know how to ask the right questions?" "Have they
learned how to learn?" and "Do they care about others besides them-

selves?" are also basic to a broad-based conception of learning. But in posing the seemingly mundane but deeply profound questions they asked, my friends were reminding me of the reason that multicultural education had come about in the first place: It was not to promote human relations, to help students feel good, or to preserve their native languages and cultures. These are important goals, to be sure, but there is reasonably unanimous agreement by the major theorists in the field that these purposes are secondary to the primary objective of advancing student learning (Banks & Banks, 1995b; Gay, 1996). When multicultural education reaches actual schools, however, the theory and practice often become disconnected (Gay, 1995a; Grant & Millar, 1992). These secondary objectives need to be placed in the service of the primary goal of education: to promote the education and achievement of all students, but particularly of students who too often are dismissed as incapable of learning and who consequently end up as the dismal statistics of school failure.

## GOALS AND FOCUS

It is my contention that questions such as, "But can they do math?" are profoundly *multicultural questions* because they strike at the very heart of access to learning, and this is where educational inequities are most visible. I believe that student learning needs to become once again the primary objective and focal point of multicultural education. Consequently, *my purpose in this book is to suggest how teachers' practices, attitudes and values, and schools' policies and practices, can promote student learning*, especially for students who have not benefited from their schooling. More often than not, these are students who live in poverty, and they are primarily students of American Indian, African American, Latino, and sometimes Asian background (usually referred to as "minority students").

These students (whom I will call *bicultural students* or *students of color\**)

------

\* My focus in this book is students who usually are designated as "minority," but given the negative connotation of this term, I have opted to use instead the terms *people of color* and *bicultural* (Darder, 1991), depending on the situation. It seems to me that these terms emphasize what students from these groups *have* rather than what they are *missing*, as is usually the case when terms such as *minority, deprived, disadvantaged, at risk*, or even more consciously politically charged words such as *disempowered* or *dominated*—terms that I use and that I believe are accurate although incomplete because they emphasize only victimization—are used. However, for a number of reasons, I do not consider any term to be completely satisfactory (see a more detailed explanation of my use of terminology in Nieto, 1996).

are the primary focus of this book. By highlighting students of color I do not mean to dismiss the importance of multicultural education for students from majority backgrounds. Indeed, as I have made clear elsewhere (Nieto, 1996), multicultural education benefits *all* students. The case even can be made that multicultural education *especially* benefits majority-group students, who may develop an unrealistic and overblown view of their place in the world because of the unbalanced and incomplete education they have received in the school curriculum in particular and in the larger society in general. That is, although the schooling of bicultural students often has failed to include their histories, discourses, and cultures, majority-group students also have been miseducated to the extent that they have been exposed to only majority discourses.

I define multicultural education as embedded in a sociopolitical context and as antiracist and basic education for all students that permeates all areas of schooling, and that is characterized by a commitment to social justice and critical approaches to learning (Nieto, 1996). My definition is an expansive one, comprising not only race, ethnicity, and language but also gender, social class, sexual orientation, ability, and other differences. Students from the majority culture certainly are included in this definition. But for those whose race, social class, and gender differ from the majority, educational failure is multiplied. Because these are the students who have borne the brunt of devastating educational failure, I have chosen to focus especially on them; moreover, when schools are made better for them, they become better for everybody.

## MULTICULTURAL EDUCATION AS A PERSONAL, COLLECTIVE, AND INSTITUTIONAL TRANSFORMATION

Multicultural education, and all good teaching, is about *transformation.* I do not refer to just individual awareness but to a deep transformation on a number of levels—*individual, collective,* and *institutional.* Each of these levels is needed to foster student learning. That is, although multicultural education is on one level a personal awakening and call to action, or what Paulo Freire (1970a) called *conscientizao,* it is more than this. Developing a multicultural perspective also means learning to work with colleagues in collaborative and mutually supportive ways; it means challenging conventional school policies and practices so that they are more equitable and just; and it means working for changes beyond the four walls of the school. In this sense, multicultural education is a journey: beginning with their personal transformation, teachers can move on to create more productive ways of working with others, and from there to challenge the policies and practices of the schools in which they work.

I believe there are lessons to be learned from teachers themselves about where they began, what helped them change, and how their practice changed as a result. For this reason, I have included examples of teachers' own accounts throughout this book. Most of them are from the journals that I require students to keep; others are from essays or case studies they have written. Many of the students were already teachers, and others were preparing to teach. Most were graduate students, some are now teacher educators in their own right, and some remain classroom teachers. The point of including their reflections is not to suggest that one course can do it all, or to imply that they were changed forever by one experience. Rather, just as in a previous book I used the words of students to illuminate major issues in multicultural education (Nieto, 1996), I believe that the reflections of teachers can have a profound impact on educational theory and practice.

## THE LIGHT IN STUDENTS' EYES AND THE LIVES OF TEACHERS

In thinking about why learning needs to be more centrally connected with multicultural education, an image came to me: the light in students' eyes when they become excited about learning. There is nothing quite as dazzling as this sight. Once we have seen the look of discovery and learning in students' eyes, we can no longer maintain that some young people—because of their social class, race, ethnicity, gender, native language, or other difference—are simply unmotivated, ignorant, or undeserving. The light in their eyes is eloquent testimony to their capacity and hence their right to learn, and it equips educators with the evidence and courage they need to defy the claim that some students are more entitled than others to the benefits of education. But student learning is not simply a personal discovery, but also a social act; it is also deeply connected with the beliefs and daily practices of teachers.

The power of individual learning should not be overstated or idealized. That is, the simple fact that one or two students discover learning will not change the fundamental conditions in schools, nor will it guarantee that the thrill of learning will extend automatically to other young people. In a dialogue with Ira Shor, Paulo Freire used a similar metaphor, that of "illumination" as learning, in the following way: "Liberation is a social act. Liberating education is a social process of illumination" (Shor & Freire, 1987, p. 109). Although individual learning may initially be a satisfying psychological experience, teachers can help it become the basis for a more social and collective conception of learning and consequently for a truly empowering education. In writing this book, I have come to see "the light in their eyes" as a powerful metaphor for learning because it can illuminate the work of teachers and it can be a beacon for the learning of others.

The connection between those moments when we see the light in the eyes of students and the lives of teachers is a crucial one. If it were not for these moments, few of us would remain in teaching. I also have seen "the light in the eyes" of teachers and prospective teachers many times. I have participated with teachers in reflecting and learning about the power and the limits of education; with them, I have considered the tremendous chasms that exist between the rhetoric of equality and the reality of oppression; I have listened as they have described fundamental changes they have made in their beliefs, or their teaching, or both; and I have continued my own transformation as a teacher and a learner. I have seen changes in the eyes and expressions of my students that reflect the more profound changes taking place inside. It is these experiences that have convinced me that unless and until teachers undergo a personal transformation, little will change in our schools.

But in spite of the fact that I believe individual teachers can make an immense difference in the lives of their students, I also understand that the ability of teachers to effect change is constricted by the broader societal context. That is, teachers work in real schools that often contradict the very ideals upon which the educational system is based, ideals such as equal access, fair play, and meritocracy. In order to resolve these contradictions, teachers sometimes develop an uncritical and idealized brand of hope that does not take into account the broader context. Bram Hamovitch (1996) has described this as a "conservative ideology of hope," the simplistic notion that upward mobility and success are equally available to all students. Because schools teach and support the ideals of equality and fair play, they also may promote an uncritical hope that is not reflected in reality. This stance can result in scapegoating those young people who are in greatest jeopardy of educational failure. In the program he studied, for instance, Hamovitch analyzed how teachers used the ideology of uncritical hope to deny the destructive effects of deep-seated inequities in society and schools and to blame students and their parents entirely for academic failure. An uncritical hope is neither useful nor liberatory.

Given the arduous demands and few material rewards of teaching, it is clear that those who enter the profession do so with a profound belief in children and in their ability to learn. But even in the best of circumstances, teaching is a demanding job, and most teachers do not work in the best of circumstances. In addition to grim conditions in many schools, teachers also need to contend with difficult individual and family situations. Many children today live in circumstances so difficult that they would have been unthinkable even a decade or two ago, conditions including abject poverty, disrupted families, homelessness, neglect, violence, and drug abuse. The effects of institutional discrimination and injustice also have a visible impact on the daily lives of many young people. These conditions, whether individual, familial, or societal, cannot be dismissed as if they did not influence student learning.

In spite of tremendous challenges, some teachers remain enthusiastic and creative, convinced that they can make a difference in the lives of their students. But there are also many enthusiastic and creative teachers who, after 2 or 3 years in difficult teaching situations, lose their idealism and end up dejected and demoralized. Because enthusiasm and creativity can dissipate in short order, in and of themselves they are not the answer to ensuring that teachers remain hopeful, effective, and committed. To maintain their initial hope and enthusiasm, teachers also need to develop different and more effective ways of working with their colleagues, and schools need to undergo a parallel institutional transformation.

## MY OWN JOURNEY

As a teacher educator, I have struggled with a number of questions for many years: How can teachers retain the hope and commitment with which they began their careers? How can they become both critical and hopeful without falling into the extremes of romanticism or despair? Why do some teachers continue to approach each day with determination and courage? Where does their profound belief in students come from? How have they developed and maintained a multicultural vision grounded in social justice and hope? These questions are at the heart of this book.

Perhaps my own journey as a teacher can help explain why I took these questions on. I began my teaching career working primarily with Puerto Rican and African American youngsters in economically devastated urban neighborhoods in New York City, first in a junior high school and later in a bilingual elementary school. As a novice teacher, I was convinced that I could make a dramatic difference in the lives of my students. I thought that through hard work and dedication, I could change their lives. Not only did I believe in the myth of education as the "great equalizer" (this despite—or because of?—my own experience as an "exception" to the widespread failure of most other Puerto Rican students in New York City), but I also was convinced that individual teachers could turn students' lives around by sheer willpower. I would bring students home with me, take them to visit museums they never knew existed, and bring them to other educational and cultural centers where they could discover new worlds just minutes away from their homes. I believed that in this way their previous academic failure miraculously would be turned into success. I like to think that I did in fact influence the lives of some of my students, but after a few years, I realized that something was missing. For most of the students whom I taught, in spite of my best intentions and efforts college was out of the question and even high school graduation was an unfulfilled dream. Many of my students dropped out before even reaching high school, too many of the girls became mothers at 14 or 15, and most faced a future of poverty and dashed hopes.

Given my own experiences growing up in a struggling, working-class family in a poor Puerto Rican neighborhood in New York City, I thought I knew firsthand about inequality. But my work as a teacher with students whose lives were far more difficult than mine had ever been, opened my eyes to the impact of daily and unrelenting oppression. Although I continued to work hard and to believe in my students, it was becoming clearer than ever to me that we teachers worked under severe limitations that made our jobs difficult and at times impossible. I saw that successful student learning was not simply a matter of positive individual interactions between teachers and students. Rather, structural conditions and policies outside the control of most educators—including societal stratification through institutional racism, sexism, and social class oppression, and discriminatory policies of schools—prevented many of my students from learning. My ideas shifted somewhat, and for years I saw the structures of schools and society, rather than the influence of teachers, as the primary reason for student failure. The natural optimism I had always had as a teacher was giving way to a more restrained view of the limits of teachers' influence.

These ideas coalesced further when I was a graduate student in education and took an economics course taught by Samuel Bowles and Herbert Gintis in which they used their now classic book *Schooling in Capitalist America* (1976) while it was still in manuscript form. Although the course was one of the most exhilarating educational experiences I had ever had because we discussed many empowering and thought-provoking "big ideas," paradoxically the atmosphere in the class also was imbued with a sense of despair. The professors themselves remained hopeful about education in spite of the depressing results of their powerful study: that the nature and outcomes of students' educational experiences were tied largely to their fathers' income and social class. However, others in the course, most of them students of economics, were cynical about the promise of education. I did not share their dismay, and it became clear to me that the two or three of us in the course who were teachers shared an attitude quite different from the others: As teachers, we knew that we could not set foot in a classroom if we did not conceive of education as a hopeful enterprise.

I believe in the power of teachers because I have seen the tremendous good or harm they can do for their students. Yet, because teachers are not disconnected from society but deeply embedded within it, they relate in complicated ways with the political ideologies that surround them. I have come to understand how individual beliefs, institutional norms, and political ideologies interact with and create one another in complex and contradictory ways. That individual teachers can profoundly influence the lives of their students is not at issue here. Who among us does not have a story about "the teacher who made a difference"? There are too many such stories to dismiss the power of teachers; however, there are too many examples of student failure in spite of teachers' best efforts and intentions to believe that teachers alone can change the world.

Although I am no longer the Pollyanna of years ago, neither am I the skeptic that I thought I had started to become. This is because at the same time I was studying about the limits of educational reform from an economics point of view, I was studying the theories of liberation and utopian hope through the writings of Paulo Freire (1970b, 1973). I saw that the marriage of hope with critique was not only possible but in fact indispensable for true learning to take place. As educators who believe in and work with students, it seems to me that an attitude of hope and critique is our only option.

## OVERVIEW OF BOOK

In this book I will consider a range of issues that are directly related to a sociopolitical perspective on multicultural education, student learning, and teacher transformation. In Chapter 1, I propose five principles concerning learning, the social context, and diversity. Chapter 2 will focus on the ways in which unequal access manifests itself in schools in the United States, and the responses of groups and individuals to inequality. Chapter 3 concerns culture, characteristics that help define it, and the links between language, culture, and learning. Chapter 4 begins with the question, "Who does the accommodating?" to highlight the kinds of institutional adaptations that schools need to make to promote learning among all students. The important role of critical pedagogy and empowerment in learning is the subject of Chapter 5, and several examples of how teachers have used students' identities, experiences, and strengths are discussed. Chapter 6 focuses on the personal and collective transformation of teachers, with several stories of how these have taken place. The book concludes with a consideration of major themes and with implications for school reform with a multicultural perspective.

# THE LIGHT IN
# THEIR EYES

# CHAPTER 1

# Learning, the Social Context, and Multicultural Education

The point is clear: the way we define thinking exerts a profound impact on the nature of our schools, the role that teachers play in the world, and the shape that society will ultimately take.

— Joe Kinchloe and Shirley Steinberg,
"A Tentative Description of Post-Formal Thinking"

WHAT DOES IT MEAN to learn, especially as it pertains to schools? And how is multicultural education related to learning? These are the basic questions that I hope to address in this chapter. I begin with the premise that *context* is always implicated in learning. Hence, a comprehensive view of learning needs to include multiple factors: curricular and pedagogical approaches, strategies, programs, and policies, and also less tangible factors such as the ideologies, attitudes, and behaviors of teachers and students. All of these factors can promote or impede student learning.

In its most restricted sense, learning can be thought of as the mastery of a series of skills leading to good grades and high scores. Given this conception of learning, if students do well on tests and other measures of their command over a particular subject, they are thought to have "learned." In fact, learning often is defined simply as academic achievement, and it is difficult to separate one from the other. There are a number of problems with this notion of learning. For one, students are treated only as "subject matter learners" (McCaslin, 1996), and little attention is paid to other aspects of schooling that can influence their educational experiences. A focus on *learning as achievement* also assumes that test scores are always accurate and complete reflections of learning, or that tests actually promote learning. Yet we know that these assumptions are far from true: When learning is defined primarily through standardized test scores, learning is restricted by narrowing the curriculum and pedagogy and reducing teacher motivation (Darling-Hammond, 1994). In addition, standardized tests are exorbitantly expensive and inequitable and they provide little insight into the reasons for students' actual failure to learn (Ascher, 1990; Darling-Hammond, 1994). Equating learning with grades and grade point averages is equally limiting because it brings up questions of inequitable access and opportunity to learn, and it denies the enormous variability in prior learning experiences among students of different backgrounds. It also fails to appraise the quality of thinking that produced a particular grade, or students' own views concerning whether or not they have learned.

The goal of this chapter is to consider student learning from a comprehensive perspective. Specifically, I will address the sociocultural and sociopolitical contexts of learning. In the process, I hope to advance a conception of learning that departs from the purely psychological frame of reference that focuses on individual growth and development. It is not my purpose in this chapter to discuss developmental theory as it relates to diversity or multicultural education; that has been done admirably by other authors (Derman-Sparks & ABC Task Force, 1989; Kendall, 1996; Ramsey, 1998). Instead, I will consider issues other than developmental concerns that can impinge on learning. In what follows, I will propose five interrelated principles that consider learning from a sociocultural and sociopolitical perspective. These principles are also highly consistent with multicultural education as I defined it in the Introduction.

## LEARNING FROM A COMPREHENSIVE SOCIOCULTURAL AND SOCIOPOLITICAL PERSPECTIVE

The discussion that follows is based on the assumption that learning develops primarily from the social relationships and the actions of individuals that take place within particular sociopolitical contexts. That is to say, learning emerges from the social, cultural, and political spaces in which it takes place, and through the interactions and relationships that occur among learners and teachers. As is clear from the quote at the beginning of this chapter, how one views learning can lead to dramatically different curricular decisions, pedagogical approaches, relationships in classrooms and schools, and educational outcomes. Joe Kinchloe and Shirley Steinberg (1993), in an important critique of traditional learning theories, have proposed what they call *postformalism* to challenge the constraints of formal thinking *à la* Piaget:

> The modernist conception of intelligence is an exclusionary system based on the premise that some people are intelligent and others aren't. . . . Intelligence and creativity are thought of as fixed and innate, while at the same time mysterious qualities found only in the privileged few. (p. 298)

My point of departure is that school conditions and climate, in conjunction with the attitudes and beliefs of educators that undergird that climate, can foster or hinder learning. This means that student cognition exists within a context that is broader than the talents, inclinations, and capabilities of individual learners. This is not to diminish the role of personal talents and abilities, which are always at play in learning; it is simply to underscore that the social and political context is always implicated as well.

The five principles of learning that will be addressed below are: *learning is actively constructed; learning emerges from and builds on experience; learning is influenced by cultural differences; learning is influenced by the context in which it occurs;* and *learning is socially mediated and develops within a culture and community.*

## Learning Is Actively Constructed

Constructivism has come to be largely accepted, at least in theory, as an important way of understanding the process of learning. The basic proposition underlying constructivism has been well articulated by Duffy and Jonassen (1992): "Learning is an active process in which meaning is developed on the basis of experience" (p. 21). But this proposition is not apparent in many classrooms and schools, where learning continues to be thought of as direct instruction through transmission rather than mutual discovery by students and teachers. At its crudest level, learning is thought of as the reproduction of socially sanctioned knowledge. How students replicate and represent the dominant attitudes and behaviors deemed important in a specific society, as these are reflected in the curriculum, is often the yardstick used by teachers to determine whether or not students have learned. The most extreme manifestation of this notion of learning is what Paulo Freire (1970b) called "banking education," that is, the simple depositing of knowledge into students who are thought of as empty receptacles. Freire (1985) challenged the notion of learning as a passive enterprise when he defined the act of studying as a process in which knowledge is actively constructed: "To study is not to consume ideas, but to create and re-create them" (p. 4). *Learner agency* is thus at the heart of the active construction of knowledge.

Learning as the reproduction of socially sanctioned knowledge often is verbally repudiated by teachers and theorists alike, but it continues to exist in many schools and classrooms, and it is the basis of such ideas as teacher-proof curriculum, the need to cover the material in a given subject, and the endless lists of skills and competencies that every student should know (Hirsch, 1987). The contradiction between the assertion that learning is actively constructed and the reality that it is transmitted by teachers and passively accepted by students was evident even near the beginning of the twentieth century when John Dewey (1916) asked:

> Why is it, in spite of the fact that teaching by pouring in, learning by a passive absorption, are universally condemned, that they are still so entrenched in practice? That education is not an affair of "telling" and being told but an active and constructive process, is a principle almost as generally violated in practice as conceded in theory. (p. 38)

The existence of this contradiction probably is based on many reasons, not the least of which is a basic distrust among the public that teachers and students have the ability to construct meaningful and important knowledge. This distrust is especially apparent in low-income schools with students from diverse cultural and linguistic backgrounds. In these schools, teachers have been taught that their primary responsibility is to "teach the basics" because students are not thought to have either (1) the innate ability or (2) the experiential background of more privileged students. In either case, it is assumed by educators, teacher educators, and the public at large that some students have not developed the necessary skills to benefit from more cognitively demanding work. In this view of learning, there is a logical process from concrete to abstract thinking, and from lower-level to higher-level skills. Yet, according to cognitive psychologists, this proposition about how learning takes place is highly debatable (Means & Knapp, 1991).

An equally significant reason for the contradiction between the verbal support of learning as knowledge construction and the reality of "teaching as telling" is the widely accepted idea that learning is primarily habit formation. According to Jerome Bruner (1996), this idea privileges drill as "the true pedagogy" (p. 5), and, as a result, the most widely adhered to "folk pedagogy" in practice is that learning is essentially the acquisition of "propositional knowledge." That is, learning takes place when students are presented with facts, principles, and rules that they memorize, remember, and apply. Knowledge is, in this view, a canon. Although this conception of learning certainly makes it easier to decide what knowledge is of most worth, it is based on erroneous or incomplete notions about learning. Bruner (1996) adds:

> Its principal appeal is that it purports to offer a clear specification of just what it is that is to be learned and, equally questionable, that it suggests standards for assessing its achievement. (p. 55)

Conversely, according to Bruner, when learning is thought of as emanating from reflection and discourse, dialogue is favored as a pedagogical approach. As a result, teaching becomes much more complex when learning is based on the idea that all students have the ability to think and reason. It is no longer simply a question of transmitting important knowledge to students, but rather of working with them so that they can reflect, theorize, and create knowledge. According to Bruner, "The child, in a word, is seen as an epistemologist as well as a learner" (p. 57).

The above discussion should not be read as promoting an either/or conception of knowledge, but rather as suggesting that learning is more complex than simply providing students with facts and information. Nor am I suggesting that drill and memorization in and of themselves should be rejected, because I believe they can be helpful tools in learning. What I am suggesting instead is that teaching facts, or having students memorize lists, or focusing on drills as the *end* rather than as one *means* of learning does a disservice to the immense potential for learning shared by all human beings.

Another idea related to the concept of learning as knowledge construction is the development of "habits of mind," a term coined by Deborah Meier (1995) and her colleagues. "Habits of mind" reflect the kind of thinking and learning usually reserved for graduate school students; rarely are children, especially poor and bicultural children, expected to perform to such high levels. But according to Meier (1995):

> All kids are indeed capable of generating powerful ideas; they can rise to the occasion. It turns out that ideas are not luxuries gained at the expense of the 3 R's, but instead enhance them. And it turns out that public schools, in new and different forms, are the best vehicle for nourishing the extraordinary untapped capacities of all our children. The question is not, Is it possible to educate all children well? but rather, Do we want to do it badly enough? (p. 4)

According to this view, students can develop important "habits of mind" by considering such thoughtful questions as: How do we know what we think we know? Whose viewpoint are we viewing? How is one thing connected to another? How else might it have been? And, finally, what difference does it make (Meier, 1995)? These questions invite the use of evaluative tools other than standardized tests, especially portfolio or other performance assessments, to determine that learning has taken place. Given this idea of learning, it is unlikely that learning as "banking" would take place. Instead, the focus on reflective questions invites students to consider different options, to question taken-for-granted truths, and to delve more deeply into problems.

## Learning Emerges from and Builds on Experience

That learning needs to build on experience is a taken-for-granted truism. This characteristic of learning is based on the idea that it is an innately human endeavor accessible to all people. Hence, it begins with the assumption that everyone has important experiences, attitudes, and behaviors that they bring to the process of education. Yet some students are placed at a serious disadvantage for learning when it is assumed that they have not had the kinds of experiences that prepare them for academic success. This is particularly true for those students who have not been raised within "the culture of power" or who have not explicitly learned the rules of the game for academic success (Delpit, 1988), primarily bicultural students and those who live in poverty. The experiences of these students tend to be quite different from those of more socially advantaged students, and it becomes evident when they go to school. In a word, students from socially and culturally dominant groups generally begin school with the kind of knowledge that will place them at an advantage to learn in that setting; they have more of the *cultural capital* (Bourdieu, 1986) that it will take to succeed in school.

Pierre Bourdieu (1986) has described how different forms of cultural capital help maintain economic privilege, even if these forms of capital are not themselves strictly related to economy. Cultural capital is evident through such intangibles as values, tastes, and behaviors and through cultural identities such as language, dialect, and ethnicity. Some manifestations of cultural capital have more social worth, although not necessarily more intrinsic worth, than others. If this is true, then youngsters from culturally subordinated communities are a priori placed at a disadvantage relative to their peers from the cultural mainstream. Understanding this reality means that the issue of power relations is a fundamental, largely unspoken, aspect of learning.

I do not mean to suggest that all children might not benefit from the kinds of experiences that prepare them for school learning. For instance, middle-class families tend to prepare their children for the kinds of literacy experiences they will encounter in school, and this no doubt gives the children an early boost in their school learning. Exposing children to books at an early age, reading to them at bedtime, and having a print-rich environment could benefit all children. And while it is important to make all parents aware of the tremendous advantages their children might enjoy if they were to participate in experiences such as these, the truth is that not all children will have the benefit of early literacy activities. This is no reason to give up on their potential, however, as if the first 5 years of their lives were devoid of any experiences that might benefit their learning. This means that teachers need to build on what the children *do have*, rather than lament about what they *do not have.*

As a young child in a working-class family where no one had even graduated from high school, I do not remember any books or reading activities taking place in our apartment; the only reading matter available was the daily newspaper that my father, who never completed fourth grade, brought home every day. The Sunday newspaper was our big treat, but aside from the funnies, I do not recall reading anything before starting first grade. But this does not mean that we had no experiences with literacy. I remember sitting around our kitchen table listening to stories in Spanish of Juan Bobo or of "jíbaros" (greenhorns or peasants newly arrived from Puerto Rico), or tall tales of family exploits. I also recall my mother repeating the rhymes and riddles (in Spanish) that she herself had learned as a child, and my aunt telling us scary stories (in English) in the dark. These too were literacy experiences, and although they generally were not known or acknowledged by my schools, they could have been used to extend my learning. The point is that not all parents have the access or the predisposition to provide these experiences, but their children should not be penalized or considered incapable of learning by their teachers. All children have had *some* experiences that can help them learn.

It is also relevant to consider the impact of teachers' attitudes concerning the cultural capital that their students bring to school, and teachers' subsequent behaviors relative to this cultural capital. For instance, an intriguing study by Francisco Ríos (1994) sought to uncover teachers' thinking about their students of color and the classroom practices that resulted from their thinking. Through interviews, Ríos found that only one teacher of 16 thought that her students even *wanted* to learn. Nevertheless, when he asked teachers to describe the theories that guided their pedagogy, he discovered that many of their ideas were related more to control and discipline of students and to students' social behaviors than to academic achievement. In fact, only one of the principles mentioned by teachers, "providing options for learning," had anything to do with learning in any substantive way. It is clear, then, that teachers' thinking about the identities, previous knowledge, and experiences of their students relates very directly to the kinds of practices and climate they create for learning.

That students come to school as a *tabula rasa*, or blank slate, no longer is widely accepted as a self-evident truth. That is, virtually all children develop many cognitive abilities before even setting foot in a school building, and these include at least one language, among numerous other skills. Children come to school as thinkers and learners, aptitudes that usually are acknowledged as important building blocks for further learning. Yet there seems to be a curious refusal on the part of many educators to accept as valid the *kinds* of knowledge and experiences with which some students come to school, and this is particularly the case with students from low-income and bicultural backgrounds. For instance, speaking languages other than English, especially those languages considered to have low status, generally is thought of by teachers as a potential detriment rather than a benefit to learning. Likewise, while traveling to Europe to ski is considered culturally enriching, the same is not true of traveling to Haiti to visit family. The reason that these kinds of experiences are evaluated differently by teachers, and in fact in the general society, has more to do with their cultural capital than with their educational potential or intrinsic worth. But when students' skills and knowledge are dismissed as inappropriate for the school setting, schools lose a golden opportunity to build on their students' lives in the service of their learning.

### Learning Is Influenced by Cultural Differences

Learning also is influenced by the particular individual personalities of students and by the values of the cultures in which they have been raised. Usually, however, it is primarily individual differences that are considered to affect learning, and intelligence and achievement tests as well as other measures of students' individual abilities are used to determine why they are successful or unsuccessful at learning. On the other hand, teachers ordinarily do not take into consideration students' cultural identities to help them understand how their students learn. In this instance, teachers and other educators may assume that learning is just an individual psychological process, not a cultural or social one.

The refusal to acknowledge the impact of cultural differences on learning may be due to many factors. For example, given the stated ideals of equality and fair play in our society, it is assumed that ethnic, racial, cultural, and other differences should play no part in our understanding or treatment of people. Worthy as this ideal may be in the abstract, in reality the unfortunate result is that teachers commonly learn to think of differences only in negative terms. In addition, their refusal to acknowledge culture may lead to obscuring real differences in cultural values that may influence student learning. Minds do not function in purely theoretical spheres; on the contrary, they work in contexts that are characterized by individual, cultural, economic, social, and political realities. If teachers and schools want to help all students learn, they need to be aware of what all of these realities are and of how they may influence learning.

Another reason that cultural differences usually are not taken into account may be an understandable reluctance on the part of educators to consider culture as *determining* the learning capabilities of students. In fact, when culture is thought of as a fixed and tangible set of qualities that *controls* how learning takes place, the unfortunate result may be, for example, long lists of the supposed cultural values of specific ethnic or racial groups. These lists, often presented to teachers in workshops or included in textbooks on teaching, purport to describe the cultural values that are the basis for the attitudes and behaviors of *all* people from a particular group. Although such lists can be useful as a basis for understanding some broad-based cultural differences between groups, as the basis of pedagogy they are fairly useless and even dangerous. This is because such lists can perpetuate the notion that culture is passive, fixed, and equally distributed among all members of a group (this will be discussed in more depth in Chapter 3). In summary, the aversion that teachers may feel to focusing on the cultural differences of their students, if it results in static thinking of this kind, is certainly reasonable. However, culture is never fixed or passive, nor is it manifested in the same way in each person. What is needed is a different way to appreciate how culture may influence learning.

A more conceptually sophisticated understanding of the influence of families of culturally diverse backgrounds on the learning and cognitive development of their children has been developed by a number of psychologists. For instance, Patricia Greenfield (1994) reviewed two value themes that are the basis of this line of research. These value themes characterize and contrast European American culture with that of African, Asian, Latin American, and Native American societies. One value is an individualistic, private, or independent orientation versus a collective, social, or interdependent orientation; the other is the contrast between the early socialization goal of maximizing educational development that is found in what she calls "commercial societies" versus the socialization goal of infant survival and childhood subsistence skills that is more typical of both hunting/gathering and agricultural societies. Greenfield has suggested that when people move from their homeland, they take these "cultural scripts" with them, and the outcomes in child development based on these contrasting values are quite different from one another.

Although Greenfield does not claim that either of these values exists in any pure form, she suggests that the nature of the value in its idealized form has important implications for the socialization process and the character of social relations. Cultures that tend to stress interdependence usually emphasize such values as family responsibility, respect for elders, and cherishing of the extended family. Children's learning often takes place simply by being around adult family and community members who are carrying out essential tasks. Given the physical closeness of such families, they often favor instruction that teaches by osmosis and observation. In contrast, families and cultures that favor independence often value individualization, separation, and self-creation, and consequently they tend to instruct through verbal teaching. This also happens to be the preferred approach in most Western schools, and it reflects the child-rearing practices of most mainstream, European American families.

The problem becomes evident when school-based literacy contradicts the previously learned value of interdependence that generally is preferred in the homes of children of backgrounds other than European American. In this situation, according to Greenfield (1994), "schooling undermines the family as an educational institution" (p. 15). As a consequence, there is a genuine value conflict between the "independence script" needed for academic success and the "interdependence script" needed for social and family success. Accordingly, multiple perspectives on development need to be advanced so that educators move away from a deficit explanation of academic achievement. In order to do this, educators need to begin with a knowledge of the values and the cognitive socialization in the cultures of origin of students.

Howard Gardner (1983) has challenged the relationship of culture, affect, and cognition through his theory of "multiple intelligences." He has suggested that intelligence, rather than a unitary concept, can be thought of as multiple skills, aptitudes, and abilities that are manifested differently in individual people. Part of the reason for the differences in how intelligence is manifested, although certainly not the entire explanation, is how children are socialized into their particular families and cultural groups. Viewing intelligence in this way not only opens up the possibility that learning is more complex and multifaceted than the usual focus on abstract thinking, but it also suggests that other ways of thinking—whether related to ethnicity, gender, or other differences (Belenky, Clinchy, Goldberger, & Tarule, 1986; Irvine, 1997)—may be just as legitimate. A more extensive discussion of the interplay between culture and learning is found in Chapter 3.

## Learning Is Influenced by the Context in Which It Occurs

Learning cannot be separated from the context in which it takes place because minds do not exist in a vacuum, somehow disconnected from and above the messiness of everyday life. The way we learn, what we choose to learn, the opportunities and resources available for learning, and the social and political status of our identities all influence how and the extent to which we are successful learners. We have already considered how individual differences and cultural values may influence learning. In what follows, we will explore how the social, political, and economic context also affects learning.

Piagetian developmental theory as developed in the first half of the twentieth century has been the basis for much of the thinking that has guided teachers' ideas about learning in the past several decades (Piaget, 1951). Piaget's theories revolutionized how cognition came to be viewed by educators and psychologists and what could be expected of young people as they progressed in their learning. Nevertheless, it also has been suggested that these theories do not pay enough attention to the enormous impact of *context*. Jerome Bruner (1996) has stated that Piaget's theories "left very little room for the enabling role of culture in mental development" (p. xiii). Piaget's theories also have been criticized as falling within a mechanistic world view that is oblivious to questions of power relations. According to Joe Kinchloe and Shirley Steinberg (1993), the "meaning-making frameworks" brought to school by children who are not from White, mainstream backgrounds are very often disregarded or thought to be developmentally inappropriate by teachers and schools:

> Because developmentalism fails to ground itself within a critical understanding of power relationships of dominant and subordinate cultures, it has often privileged White middle-class notions of meaning and success. (p. 300)

According to Kinchloe and Steinberg, cognitive development is never static but always interactive with the environment.

It is especially significant that teachers grasp the influence that social and political context may have on learning because this realization can alter how they perceive their students and, consequently, what and how they teach them. That is, if teachers believe that intelligence and learning are somehow divorced from context, then they can conclude that the political and economic realities of their students' lives have nothing to do with how they learn or how successful they are in their learning. Teachers can, in a word, believe that they and the schools in which they work inhabit an "ideology-free zone" in which dominant attitudes and values play no role in learning.

An ethnographic study by Nancy Commins (1989) of four bilingual Mexican American students provides a graphic example of the influence that the social and political context can have on learning. In the study, Commins found that the children were reluctant to speak Spanish because they perceived it to be the language of "the dumb kids." The children did not create this perception; on the contrary, they were quite correct in recognizing that Spanish had a low status in the context of their school and they acted accordingly. Even if the bilingual program in the school was an excellent one, these youngsters no doubt would have wanted no part of it or of any of the baggage associated with it. They understood that the "bilingual kids," simply by virtue of speaking Spanish, were perceived as less intelligent than other children. As a consequence, the very language that they spoke, the language with which they communicated with their families and that gave them part of their identity, carried with it a sign of shame and disrepute. The four Mexican American children refused to use what could have most helped them: their native language, the primary medium they had for learning. This refusal to use their native language needs to be seen as directly shaped by the political and social status it has in the school and the broader society.

Research by Claude Steele (1992) concerning what he has called *stereotype stigma* adds an important dimension to this discussion. Although his research focuses on the education of African Americans, Steele believes that stigmatization also affects working-class Whites, Hispanics, and women. Steele defines stereotype stigma as "the endemic devaluation many blacks face in our society and schools. This status is its own condition of life, different from class, money, culture" (p. 68). Additionally, Steele insists that stereotype stigma is tied intimately to school achievement among Blacks, and that this connection has been vastly underappreciated in explicating academic success or failure. On the other hand, if the situation is understood and accepted by educators, then they can develop strategies to make Blacks less racially vulnerable.

Through this stance, Steele counters head-on the theory that Black culture does not sustain the values and expectations critical to education or that it fosters an "oppositional culture" to academic success (Ogbu, 1992). On the contrary, in his investigation, Steele found that neither culturally specific learning orientations nor socioeconomic disadvantage adequately explained Black students' poor achievement. In addition, he found that disadvantage in background preparation is also not a full explanation for poor achievement; for instance, Black students at one prestigious university dropped out even when they had the *highest levels* of preparation. Steele's conclusion was that something else depresses the academic achievement of Blacks at *every level* of preparation. The "something else," Steele claims, is their inability to identify with school, which leads to their not being treated as valuable members of the school community.

Given the plethora of negative messages that devalue the lives of African Americans both in school and out on a daily basis, it is difficult for many young Blacks to identify with school and to consider academic achievement something worth striving for. As a result, many Blacks, according to Steele, develop the stance of "not caring," of de-emphasizing school achievement as a basis for their self-esteem, thus protecting themselves from the psychic alienation that makes them vulnerable to devaluation. The process may happen in elementary, secondary, or even postsecondary school. For instance, Steele cites research that he and his colleagues did at a predominantly White college in which they found that Black students' attitudes related to disidentification with school were actually more accurate predictors of grades than even academic preparation as seen through SAT scores and high school grade point averages. According to Steele:

> To make matters worse, once disidentification occurs in a school, it can spread like the common cold. . . . Thus pressure to make it a group norm can evolve quickly and become fierce. Defectors are called "oreos" or "icononegroes." One's identity as an authentic black is held hostage, made incompatible with school identification. (p. 75)

Steele's theory illuminates once again the importance of *context* in influencing learning. That is, in reviewing those situations in which learning among traditionally underachieving students has improved dramatically, Steele found one factor that consistently was linked to improvement: the reduction of racial vulnerability. As we shall see throughout this book, when the context in which students learn is a caring and supportive one as well as respectful of their identities, students by and large learn. On the other hand, when they are asked to give up their identities for an elusive goal that they may never reach because of the negative context in which they must learn, students may be quite correct in rejecting the trade. This will be discussed in more depth in Chapter 4.

## Learning Is Socially Mediated and Develops Within a Culture and Community

In the past several decades, a great deal of attention has been focused on cognition as a sociocultural process. Lev Vygotsky (1978), a Russian psychologist in the first decades of the twentieth century, was a catalyst for the development of this viewpoint. Suggesting that cognition is rooted in social interaction, Vygotsky went far beyond the behaviorist notion of learning as a response to a particular stimulus. Instead, he suggested that development and learning are firmly rooted in, and influenced by, society and culture. In a word, development and learning are *mediated by* culture and society.

The idea that cognition is social and cultural action takes learning out of the passive arena in which it often is located. Cognition described as social and cultural implies agency on the part of the learner; no longer is the learner simply acted *upon,* but she *acts, responds,* and *creates* through the very act of learning. Paulo Freire (Shor & Freire, 1987) expressed it in more poetic terms when he described the act of reading: "I say that reading is not just *to walk on the words,* and it is not *flying* over the words either. Reading is re-writing what we are reading" (p. 10).

No longer is it possible to separate learning from the cultural context in which it takes place, or from an understanding of how culture and society influence and are influenced by learning. According to Jerome Bruner (1996), this view of cognition "takes its inspiration from the evolutionary fact that mind could not exist save for culture" (p. 3). Bruner (1996) goes on to say:

> Culture, then, though itself man-made, both forms and makes possible the workings of a distinctly human mind. On this view, learning and thinking are always *situated* in a cultural setting and always dependent upon the utilization of cultural resources. (p. 4)

This was precisely the point made by Paulo Freire (1970a) when he described literacy education for adults not as the teaching of mechanistic techniques for deciphering language, but as *cultural action for freedom,* because through literacy adults could learn to read both the word and the world and therefore become actors in the world. Learning implies both *action* and *interaction* because it develops within the social and cultural conditions of society, which themselves are created by human beings.

Vygotsky and others who have advanced the sociocultural foundation of cognition (Cole & Griffin, 1983; Scribner & Cole, 1981) have provided a contextualized framework with which to view schools and learning. That is, schools and other learning institutions organize themselves in particular ways, and these ways are more or less comfortable and inviting for particular individuals. Never neutral, institutional environments are based on certain views of human development, of what is worth knowing, and of what it means to be educated. When young people enter schools, they are entering institutions that have already made some fundamental decisions about such matters, and in the process some of these children may be left out through no fault of their own. A cogent description of how learning conditions are created and sustained in schools, and the influence that such conditions may have on student learning, is provided by Ellice Forman and her associates (Forman, Minick, & Stone, 1993):

> [E]ducationally significant human interactions do not involve abstract bearers of cognitive structures but real people who develop a variety of interpersonal relationships with one another in the course of their shared activity in a given institutional context. . . . For example, appropriating the speech or actions of another person requires a degree of identification with that person and the cultural community he or she represents. Educational failure, in this perspective, can represent an unwillingness to subordinate one's own voice to that of another rather than an inability to learn. (p. 6)

These ideas of how social and cultural issues influence learning are a radical departure from viewpoints that consider learning to be largely unaffected by context. Such viewpoints automatically assume that children who do not learn a specific skill have low intelligence, or that they are suffering from some psychological disorder or cultural inferiority. In their early research with the Kpelle children of Liberia, Michael Cole and his associates (Cole, Gay, Glick, & Sharp, 1971) took a very different approach:

> If there is a general principle to be gleaned from the method upon which our work is based, it derives from our belief that the people we are working with always behave reasonably. When their behavior appears unreasonable, it is to ourselves, our procedures, and our experimental tasks that we turn for an explanation. (p. xv)

A Vygotskian perspective provides a hopeful framework for thinking about learning; that is, *if learning can be influenced by social mediation, then conditions can be created in schools that can help most students learn.* Particularly significant in this regard is the notion of the *zone of proximal development* or ZPD. In his work, Vygotsky (1978) described the ZPD as "the distance between the actual developmental level as determined by independent problem solving and the level of potential development as determined through problem solving under adult guidance or in collaboration with more capable peers" (p. 86). If one accepts the ZPD as a reasonable explanation of how learning takes place, one also accepts a number of assumptions that derive from it, namely, the following:

1. Schools have a role to play in making learning accessible to students.
2. Teachers' actions can influence whether and to what extent children learn.
3. All children can learn if given the opportunity to interact socially and appropriately with others.

According to Henry Trueba (1989), if we accept Vygotsky's theory of the ZPD, then failure to learn cannot be defined as individual failure but rather as systemic failure, that is, the failure of the social system to provide the learner with an opportunity for successful social interactions. In order to change academic failure to success, appropriate social instructional interventions need to occur in the learning context. Extending this idea further, Díaz, Flores, Cousin, and Soo Hoo (1992) proposed that because teachers are always *sociocultural mediators,* their acceptance and validation of the cultural symbols used by their students of diverse backgrounds may positively influence student learning.

One of the ways that learning is socially mediated is that it depends on the relationships established between learners and teachers. Michael Cole (1985) has insisted that *social relations* and how these are internalized by learners are a crucial part of cognitive development. Jim Cummins's (1996) theories concerning the negotiation of identity and the significant role this process plays in learning are particularly appropriate to mention here. According to Cummins, the ZPD needs to be understood beyond purely cognitive parameters and expanded into the realm of affective development and power relationships; otherwise, it can become another empty technique. He states: "Teacher-student collaboration in the construction of knowledge will operate effectively only in contexts where students' identities are being affirmed" (p. 26). This is a further reminder that the nature of the relationship between students and teachers is key to understanding whether and how learning takes place.

## AN UNLIKELY CONTEXT FOR LEARNING

Unraveling the mystery of how particular conditions and beliefs interact to support or thwart learning is difficult at best. A good example can be found in research concerning the relative success of African American and other students of color in Catholic schools, or what has come to be known as "the Catholic school effect" (Bryk, Lee, & Holland, 1993; Irvine & Foster, 1996). In general, African American students in Catholic schools achieve far greater academic gains than they do in public schools, in spite of the fact that generally the pedagogy and curriculum of Catholic schools can be characterized as traditional and Eurocentric. Paradoxically, those African American students who have been described as most "at risk"—the most economically disadvantaged students and those who start with the worst academic records—have had the highest rates of achievement in Catholic school.

How can these results be explained? In most Catholic schools, curricula are not specifically geared to African American or other students of color, and generally the pedagogy is far from culturally relevant. Furthermore, the level of education, income, and occupational status of the parents of African American students in Catholic schools are for the most part inconsistent with what generally is expected of high academic achievement (York, 1996). And yet many students have thrived in ways that can only be dreamed about in most public schools. Not surprisingly, more African American families than ever (most of whom are not themselves Catholic) pin their hopes for their children's academic futures on Catholic schools: In the 1970s, students of color represented just 8.2% of Catholic school enrollment, but by 1990, the percentage had risen to over 22%, higher than for any other group when religious preference is taken into account (Foster, 1996).

It is important not to romanticize the benefits of Catholic schools because the experiences of African American and other students of color in those schools have not always been happy ones. On the contrary, Catholic schools sometimes have been characterized as paternalistic and racist, and as having inflexible policies (Irvine & Foster, 1996). Furthermore, a recent analysis of the dramatic changes taking place in Catholic schools suggests that they are becoming more elite, educating an increasingly affluent and academically advantaged student body, and that the Catholic school advantage actually decreased at least 25% between the early 1980s and the 1990s (Baker & Riordan, 1998). Important lessons nevertheless can be learned about why Catholic schools have proven to be beneficial for students who might be considered uneducable by the public schools. For example, differences that generally are considered deficits in other settings, namely, the race, gender, and social class of students, are not thought of in the same ways in Catholic schools. In her review of the literature, Darlene York (1996) found that teachers held generally positive attitudes toward their African American students.

The research on the "Catholic school effect" holds great promise for public schools because it describes settings in which students are academically successful in spite of what in other settings might be considered insurmountable deficits and disadvantages. Most analysts agree that the favorable effects of Catholic schools on students of color can be explained by the interaction of a number of school-related variables: *a shared culture, a rigorous and untracked curriculum, high expectations for all students, the belief that the families of their students value learning, a climate characterized by order and discipline,* and *a caring and committed teaching staff* (Irvine & Foster, 1996). All of these conditions can be replicated by public schools. What is needed above all is the belief and attitude that all students are worth the effort.

## SUMMARY

Learning is a complicated matter. It is influenced by many factors: individual experiences and personal idiosyncrasies; biological differences; family motifs and identities; cultural values; ethnic, racial, and other identities with varying social status; school-based attitudes, behaviors, and practices; the relationships between students and their teachers; and societal ideologies, among others. To focus on just one or two of these is to miss the big picture. Understanding how learning can be influenced by the myriad of forces in society can help teachers and schools affect the learning of their students in a more positive direction.

In this chapter, we have considered a number of closely related and interdependent characteristics that can help define learning in a comprehensive way. It was my intention here to suggest that learning and achievement are not merely cognitive processes, but that learning needs to be understood in the broader context of the sociocultural and sociopolitical lives of students, teachers, and schools. An example of factors that lie outside individual students' capabilities and how these factors can become powerful indicators of students' success or failure in school will be considered in the next chapter.

# CHAPTER 2

# Learning and Inequality

Diversity without equality = oppression.
—Meyer Weinberg

THE SIMPLE SLOGAN "Celebrating Diversity" that is part of many multicultural education initiatives, although it may be well-meaning, glosses over severe structural inequalities that are replicated in schools every day through the combination of uneven access, unfair practices, and harmful beliefs. No amount of cultural festivals or ethnic celebrations can turn this situation around.

This chapter begins with the premise that inequality, lack of learning, and poor academic achievement are firmly linked. Although this statement is neither new nor earth-shattering, it bears repeating because there is a widespread assumption that students fail to learn primarily because they are unmotivated, their gene pool is inferior, their families do not care, or the cultural values of their particular ethnic group are not oriented toward education. This assumption leads to placing the blame for the failure to learn and achieve primarily on students and their families, communities, and cultures. The ideologies in which teachers and schools are immersed are commonly overlooked as contributing to the problem of academic failure.

The disproportionate failure of students of particular backgrounds in U.S. schools has been explained in numerous ways. As we saw earlier, the more mean-spirited among the explanations have focused on students' alleged low intelligence, cultural inferiority, lack of a value orientation to education, or uncaring parents (for a review, see Nieto, 1996). But even well-meaning explanations have tended to emphasize immutable or difficult-to-change characteristics. For example, factors identified as placing students "at risk" for failure have included minority group status, poverty, single-parent household, non-English-speaking background, and having a poorly educated mother (Pallas, Natriello, & McDill, 1989). In other words, students' very cultural and ethnic identity, among other characteristics, places them at risk without even taking into account the individual abilities or talents they may have.

It is not the purpose of this chapter, or of this book, to look for scapegoats for student failure; enough of that has already been done. Rather, I will suggest that in order to promote learning and achievement, we need to begin with a careful analysis of the societal and school conditions in which education takes place. In the United States, those conditions, as we shall see, have been consistently, systematically, and disproportionately unequal and unfair, and the major casualties have been those students who differ significantly in social class, gender, race, and ethnicity from what is considered the "mainstream." For instance, the fact that the United States has the highest rate of children living in poverty as well as the highest rate of prisoners per capita among industrialized nations (Hodgkinson, 1989) cannot be disconnected from the high rates of school failure, especially among poor children of color. Schools and society are inextricably linked, and these linkages can be seen in how inequalities are imbedded and perpetuated in schools. Inequality as manifested in schools is closely linked with racism and other forms of institutional and personal bias and discrimination. In this chapter, we will consider the roots of inequality and then analyze numerous ways in which inequality is created in our schools.

## THE ROOTS OF INEQUALITY:
## RACISM AND INSTITUTIONAL DISCRIMINATION

How racism and other forms of personal and institutional biases and discrimination are manifested in schools is at the root of the history of inequality in the United States in general, and in U.S. schools in particular. These biases are manifested, among other ways, in unequal funding, inadequate or stereotypical depictions of diversity in the curriculum, and low expectations of students who embody differences. However, the existence of racism and other biases is virtually ignored in most schools, and this happens for a number of reasons. For one, many teachers think that racism disappeared after the civil rights movement. In schools that promote a diverse curriculum, there is the belief that racism will evaporate automatically once the curriculum is in place. The ugly realities of racism and social class bias, among other forms of discrimination, and the ways in which these are manifested, are a taboo subject to discuss because they challenge the ideal that advancement and achievement are based on merit, not on social class status or racial privileges.

Racism creeps into schools in numerous ways, and it may pose nearly insurmountable obstacles to academic success. For instance, Patricia Gándara (1995) studied high-achieving Chicano professionals to find out what it was in their past that had helped them become academically successful in spite of the fact that they all had been raised in poor and working-class families in low-income neighborhoods. The study, although hopeful because of its focus on how Chicanos were able to achieve academically *despite* "risk factors" (in this case, their low-income and "minority" status), also demonstrated the pervasiveness of racism. Gándara found that factors that helped these particular Chicanos succeed would be difficult or impossible to replicate for most Chicanos: The majority of the high-achieving Chicanos she studied had light skin, had attended middle- or upper-class, primarily White schools even though they lived in poor and working-class neighborhoods, and had been tracked in high-ability classes. In most cases, persistent mothers or helpful teachers were the reason that these students were able to succeed. But these conditions are not equally available to all students. Chicanos who do not happen to have White skin, for example, sometimes are condemned before they even begin.

In one of my courses in multicultural education, I use the video *Ethnic Notions* (Riggs, 1987). The film considers the historical development of negative and destructive images of Blacks from the antebellum period to the present, including the mammy, Jim Crow, and Sambo. The extraordinarily vivid and dehumanizing images presented in the film make it difficult to watch. But I believe that all educators need to be aware of these images if they are to understand how racist images make their way into schools and other institutions. If we want to obliterate such images, we need to first recognize that they exist; to pretend that they do not is to whitewash history.

Below is the reaction to this video in the journal of Ann Scott, a doctoral student and teacher educator who viewed it in one of my courses. In her reaction, Ann provides a persuasive analysis of how racism and inequality are intimately connected. A similar case can be made for the roots of inequality and sexism, or social class discrimination, or anti-Semitism, or heterosexism/homophobia, or other biases.

## REACTION TO ETHNIC NOTIONS

*By Ann Scott*

Why was it so hard to watch? In part, I guess, because there were Black people in the room, and it made me ashamed to be White, to belong to the dominant culture that created the terrible images we were looking at, and promoted the images to serve such terrible ends. But it would have been almost as uncomfortable in a room full of Whites, because the material was innately disturbing. Images that caricature people in a cruel way, finding differences that may be slight or imagined and then emphasizing them to a grotesque degree, to what end? To make fools of people. To put them into an "other" category, to make them seem like another species. "They" are different, to be feared or mocked or patronized or controlled, reviled, or, at least, changed. "They will never be like us, they will never make it in our world" was the message during Reconstruction. And later, the men were portrayed as sexual predators, dangerous, violent, animal-like, to justify lynching. None of the images we looked at invited the viewer to empathize with, accept, love, admire, or respect the person being caricatured. . . .

How do these images function on an institutional level? Like propaganda, they are designed to uphold or create certain inaccuracies, to generate strong emotions in the dominant or ruling class (fear, contempt), to underestimate and disempower the people being labeled so that politicians and legislators can maintain the status quo. Whether it's the mammy or the violent Black male or the simpleminded Sambo or Jim Crow who is happy to be a slave and fit for nothing else, or the dandyish buffoon Zip Coon who would never make it in "White society," they give credence to the ideology being promoted; they keep the powerful in power and the rich rich.

This kind of imagery widens the divisions between races, and the wider and deeper the divisions, the easier people are to manipulate. If you remove the shades of gray, that is, the complexities and contradictions within all individuals, they become easy targets for propaganda. Race, though an artificial, man-made idea, is nevertheless an effective way of dividing people according to physical characteristics that are more or less obvious. What is not obvious, what is not even there, is invented in order to exaggerate difference. And people are often willing to see what they are told is there (an imaginary overlay is no less opaque than a real one). As divisions widen, communication between two sides gets more difficult to achieve. (9.22.93)

## CREATING INEQUALITY AMONG STUDENTS
## OF DIVERSE BACKGROUNDS

Failure to learn does not develop out of thin air; it is scrupulously created through policies, practices, attitudes, and beliefs. In a very concrete sense, the results of educational inequality explain by example what a society believes its young people are capable of achieving and what they deserve. For instance, offering only low-level courses in schools serving bicultural youngsters is a clear message that the students are not expected to achieve to high levels; in like manner, considering students to be "at risk" simply because of their ethnicity, native language, family characteristics, or social class is another unequivocal sign that some students have been defined by conventional wisdom as uneducable based simply on their identity.

Limited educational opportunities commonly result in poor achievement and lack of learning for *individual* students, but it is important to stress that unequal outcomes generally are based on students' membership in particular *groups* that are ranked according to the status of members' race, ethnicity, social class, and gender, among other differences. If this were not the case, and unless we subscribe to the theory of genetic inferiority, the consistent and disproportionate educational failure among American Indians, Latinos, African Americans, some Asian Americans, females, and poor and working-class students of all ethnic backgrounds would not be a recurring phenomenon.

### Educational Inequality in the United States

The history of public education in the United States is a complex and contradictory mosaic of unparalleled opportunities to learn for some, existing side by side with brutal deterrents to education for others. In the words of Linda Darling-Hammond (1995), "Institutionally sanctioned discrimination in access to educational resources is older than the American nation itself" (p. 465). In this way, education differs little from society in general, which regularly has distributed rewards and privileges along lines of race, class, gender, and other differences. A look at the living conditions of different groups is a telling example of inequality. For instance, a recent United Nations report ranked White Americans as having the highest standard of living in the world, with Black Americans in 31st place, and Latinos in thirty-fifth (as quoted in Sleeter, 1994).

Similar inequalities are found in schools, a small number of which are lavishly endowed, while many others are on the brink of financial and social disaster. Hence, schools are not an aberration of an otherwise just society characterized by fair play and equality. Although there are certainly exceptions to the rule, schools tend to reproduce fairly consistently the inequalities that exist in society. In spite of our nation's passionate ideology of equality, Deborah Meier (1995) has suggested cogently that "we are not predisposed to believe the startling proposition that we are all created equal" (p. 2).

The myth of meritocracy based on the creed of individual effort has upheld the notion that equality is accessible to all. What has made this ideal particularly impenetrable to criticism has been the seeming fairness of it all. That is, if one works hard enough, studies diligently, and lives according to the rules, one is certain to "make it." Legions of examples are provided in students' textbooks and in inspirational biographies of people who have become successful by following this simple recipe. "Not making it," by extension, means either that one has not followed these rules or that one is culturally or genetically deficient.

As a result of the entrenched ideology of meritocracy and individual effort, those who are not successful (in school, for example) are blamed for what are in fact primarily institutional problems. That is because in the official discourse of equality, there has been a deafening silence concerning the institutional barriers that make it almost impossible for some to "make it," while they virtually guarantee success for others. Little mention, for instance, is made of unearned privileges related to race, class, or gender that operate to solidify particular advantages in education, income, and professional advancement, among other things. Likewise ignored, in terms of education, is the fact that until 1954 only a small minority of White educational leaders ever openly confronted the inequalities and racism inherent in schools (Tyack, 1995). Alongside the doctrine of meritocracy exists the reality of oppression; in fact, oppression probably is fortified and maintained by the myth of meritocracy.

In a related vein, racist, classist, and sexist ideologies persist in society, although nowadays these are rarely acknowledged publicly. An exception to the public silence concerning the existence of discrimination was a survey in 1991 among Whites concerning their attitudes toward African Americans and Latinos. Fully 53% admitted that they believed African Americans were less intelligent than Whites, while 55% believed the same of Latinos (Fulwood, 1991, quoted in Welner & Oakes, 1996). It is inevitable that such ideas make their way into institutions such as schools. Given ingrained beliefs such as these, it is little wonder that exclusionary practices exist in schools.

There is no doubt that the United States has been a more open and equal society than many others. Until recently, it seemed to become more equal with the progress of time: The U.S. middle class, unmatched in sheer numbers or quality of life by any other society in the world, served as testimony to increased opportunities. This is no longer the case. The gains that were made in the past century are eroding dramatically, probably as a result of the massive structural changes taking place in the economy. According to a provocatively titled article by John Cassidy in *The New Yorker,* "Who Killed the Middle Class?"(1995), economic inequality has skyrocketed since the 1970s: While the income of most working- or middle-class families has stagnated, the top 5% of U.S. households receive 20% of the country's income, an increase of 29.1% since 1979. For the wealthiest 1%, the growth is even more spectacular: Between 1977 and 1989, *the average income of the wealthiest 1% of Americans rose by 78%.* In fact, middle-class income growth virtually stopped after 1973, making the very concept of the middle class questionable, although the myth of the United States as the land of unequaled opportunity dies hard.

Moreover, the equality that does exist did not happen by chance, nor was it ever simply handed over to those who are less fortunate. Rather, equality has always been hard won, and it has taken place essentially through the efforts of those who have suffered the greatest oppression. Paradoxically, the greatest victims of *inequality* traditionally have been the most ardent believers of the "American dream" of freedom, liberty, and equality; it is they who have been in the forefront of the struggles to make the ideals a reality for everyone (Banks, 1996). The abolition, suffrage, civil rights, and women's liberation movements are illustrations of this truth. In education, examples can be found in the fight for integrated schools and for such innovations as bilingual and multicultural education, community control, and open admissions at the university level. That is, the expressed ideology of our society has been actualized by those who have benefited least from it, and one of the major sites of this struggle for equality has been the public schools.

Rhetoric to the contrary notwithstanding, the journey to equality is far from over. Signs of persistent inequality are visible in many areas of society, including education. For instance, although it is generally acknowledged that the dropout rate for most groups is decreasing, the rate for Latino and African American students is increasing in many urban areas (*Digest,* 1995). In a related vein, Richard Fossey (1996) found that some urban school districts have experienced dramatic drops in the graduation rate. As one example, in New York City the graduation rate dropped from 60.3% in 1971 to 47.8% in 1988. In another conspicuous example, the gap between college attendance rates of the poor and the wealthy actually has *grown* since the 1970s (Levine & Ndiffer, 1996).

Education has always been recognized as a major gateway out of poverty, and it has served this function admirably for many. But for large

numbers of young people, particularly those who are culturally and racially different from the mainstream, and for females and low-income
students, academic success often has been elusive. There has never been
a perfect correspondence between the inequality that exists in society and
that found in schools, but by and large schools have reflected societal
inequalities quite faithfully through their policies and practices. In a comprehensive review of the research literature, Joel Spring (1995) demonstrated that tracking, counseling practices, disciplinary practices, participation in school activities, and instructional methods generally have
correlated with the social class and race of students. That is, school policies and practices have reflected accurately students' privileged or dominated status in society. Spring concluded that *inequality is a cultural value
of those who hold the power in a society, and this cultural value is embedded in
all societal institutions, including the public schools.* The result of enacting this
cultural value is the reproduction of existing inequalities.

The work of educational revisionists such as Spring has been fundamental in making the case that historically schools have tended to replicate the social order. In his groundbreaking analysis of how education
operates to reproduce inequality, Michael Katz (1971) described schools
as "universal, tax-supported, free, compulsory, bureaucratically arranged,
class-biased, and racist" (p. 106). In the same vein, Samuel Bowles and
Herbert Gintis (1976) found that schools have been quite consistent in
reproducing the social class of students' families. Although revisionist
theories have been criticized for being overly deterministic by giving little
credit to students and their communities for active resistance to inequality, still it is demonstrable that schools have always had a sorting function
as one of their primary roles (Oakes, 1985; Spring, 1989). The lofty and
democratic principles on which public education is grounded have existed
alongside undemocratic and oppressive elements that have worked, usually in contradictory and conflict-laden ways, to maintain the status quo.
Maxine Greene (1988) eloquently described how these oppressive elements have functioned and why so many people, particularly immigrants
and others from disenfranchised groups, have believed so desperately in
the covenant of the public schools:

> The Americanizing process, the process of induction itself, the lines of the
> school corridors, the tracking and grouping systems, the factory atmosphere,
> the racist, sexist, classist practices: All were justified on some level by a prom-
> ise of membership with the benefits that was supposed to entail. (p. 112)

Inequality has been practiced in public schools in numerous ways,
including through disparate funding, segregation, underrepresentation of

teachers of color, uneven access to high-level learning, biased counseling practices, and others. Some of these will be discussed below.

## Funding Inequality

That schools are financed unequally is no longer the dirty little secret that it was for so long, thanks to a groundbreaking and influential study by Jonathan Kozol (1991). In *Savage Inequalities,* Kozol demonstrated in graphic terms how school systems that are sometimes next door to one another provide radically different educational opportunities to the students they serve. These opportunities more often than not are based on the amount of funding the schools receive. Young people fortunate enough to live within a school district that spends enormous amounts on education are doubly fortunate because they have access to the goods and services that come along with those funds. Conversely, those who live across the river, or on the other side of the tracks, are not so lucky. The goods and services bought with increased funding include such privileges as smaller classes, in which children have been found to learn more than their peers who are in larger classes (Finn & Achilles, 1990; Mosteller, 1995). Increased funding also buys more experienced teachers. In her extensive review of related research, Linda Darling-Hammond (1996) found that money makes a difference in the quality of education children receive because it pays for more expert teachers, whose levels of preparation and skill in the classroom have been confirmed as the *single most important element* in determining students' achievement.

It is becoming increasingly evident that more money does indeed make a difference. One major study, for instance, found lower proficiency scores on the National Assessment of Educational Progress (NAEP) among children in those classrooms whose teachers reported a lack of adequate materials (Educational Testing Service, 1991). Although simply spending more money cannot in and of itself transform failure into success, if informed by purposeful and careful action as well as by a vision that all students are capable of high levels of learning, increased funding can and does make a dramatic difference in the education of children.

Rather than decreasing, funding disparities between rich and poor states and between rich and poor districts in the same state actually grew in the 1980s (Ascher & Burnett, 1993). Another study found that not only were per-pupil expenditures in large urban school systems lower than those in schools in wealthy suburbs, but they were in fact also lower than the national average (Council of Great City Schools, 1992). And international assessments have established that schools in the United States are among the *most unequal* in the industrialized world in terms of funding (Darling-Hammond, 1996). Funding inequalities are more than numbers and facts, however. They affect not only the day-to-day education but indeed the life chances of many youngsters. Thus, funding inequalities make a real difference in the lives of youngsters who are deprived of equality every day.

## Segregation

The physical separation of students from one another based on their race has been one of the most obvious signs of educational inequality in the United States. The segregation of African Americans is the best-known and most widely documented example. The harsh conditions in all-Black schools in the South provided evidence of the devastating effects of segregation (Weinberg, 1977). Despite the conventional wisdom that Black students in segregated settings lost out primarily because they did not have access to their White peers, segregation was harmful primarily because the schools Black children were forced to attend were inevitably inferior in funding, educational resources, and the quality of the training of the teachers.

But in spite of the appalling conditions of most segregated Black schools, some were successful at educating large numbers of African American youngsters, and this achievement was in no small part due to the presence of all-Black teaching staffs, ironically itself one of the products of segregation. Research by Emilie Walker (1993) about one such school suggested that its success was a result of the cultural synchrony between Black teachers and parents. She speculated that after integration, the profound cultural mismatch between White teachers and Black parents was a major cause of student underachievement and that this mismatch continues to negatively affect learning among African American students. Hence, even under grim conditions, some segregated schools were able to promote the learning of their students largely due to two conditions: the shared cultural values between teachers, children, and parents; and what bell hooks (1994) has described as Black teachers' counterhegemonic teaching practices that resisted White racist notions of inferiority.

Although the segregation of African Americans is the best known case, it is by no means the only one. For instance, the first example of successful litigation concerning segregation was among Mexican Americans fully 25 years before *Brown* v. *Board of Education of Topeka* (Donato, 1997; H. García, 1995). Segregation also has occurred with females and with Japanese and Chinese students (Sadker & Sadker, 1994; Spring, 1997; Weinberg, 1977), as well as with American Indians. In the case of

American Indians, segregation was accomplished by their forced removal to boarding schools, among other brutal strategies (Lomawaima, 1994). The legally sanctioned segregation of students based on race was effectively outlawed by the *Brown* decision in 1955, but de facto segregation has not disappeared as an educational practice, and some of its harshest manifestations have been in northern cities.

Although a substantial amount of desegregation occurred between 1965 and 1973 in the South, very little change was evident in the North during those same years (Schofield, 1991). Widespread segregation characterizes most urban schools in the United States today. Data collected until the early 1990s revealed that the amount of desegregation was remarkably similar to that achieved by 1972 (Schofield, 1991). Gary Orfield (1994) found that integration actually declined in the 1990s. Moreover, the negative effects of segregation are still disproportionately experienced by African American and Latino students. In fact, Latinos now are even more segregated than African Americans, and for both African American and Latino students, the gains made in desegregation as a result of *Brown v. Board of Education* are being undone (Orfield, Bachmeier, James, & Eitle, 1997). Because both African Americans and Latinos are much more likely than Whites to be concentrated in schools characterized by poverty, much of the educational damage of racial segregation grows out of its relationship with poverty (Orfield et al., 1997).

## Inequitable Access to Learning

The segregation of children according to race, ethnicity, and social class is still firmly entrenched in most places in the United States through what has been called *second-generation discrimination,* or practices such as fixed academic grouping and differential disciplinary practices (Meier, Stewart, & England, 1989). That is, segregation is not limited to the physical separation of students in different schools. It is also visible in the unequal access to learning evident in such practices as inflexible tracking and vastly differentiated curriculum and instruction experienced by students in distinct classrooms and schools. In this regard, Geneva Gay (1990) has suggested that *curriculum segregation* is a major indicator of inequality that takes place when assignments, pedagogical styles, and teaching materials differ according to the group of students with whom they are used. She maintains that the curriculum and instruction geared to middle-class males tend to have an academic focus, while those used with low-income students of color and female students emphasize low-status knowledge and skills. These differences in curriculum, according to Gay (1990), con-

vey "subtle—but powerful—messages about just how separate and unequal education is" (p. 56).

Almost a century ago, John Dewey (1916) cautioned against the evils
of unequal access to learning based on social class. In his vision of an
educational system for a truly democratic society, Dewey predated the
debate on ability grouping that was to erupt many decades later, by ex-
horting educators: "Democracy cannot flourish where the chief influences in selecting subject matter of instruction are utilitarian ends nar-
rowly conceived for the masses, and, for the higher education of the few,
the traditions of a specialized cultivated class" (p. 192). Yet ability group
tracking remains the most visible symptom of inequality of access to
knowledge. Legions of studies have followed Jeannie Oakes's (1985) now-
classic research on tracking and its detrimental effects, especially for economically and culturally dominated students, and most have reached
similar conclusions.

It has become increasingly clear that tracking is not simply a neutral
practice to make teaching more efficient or student learning more likely.
On the contrary, tracking decisions are a visible demonstration of the
deeply embedded cultural values that undergird societal and school-based
inequality. In effect, tracking decisions collude with class interests even
though these are articulated as if they were fair decisions based solely on
students' aptitudes. For example, a study by Amy Stuart Wells and Irene
Serna (1996) focusing on schools in the process of detracking found
strong evidence to suggest that students regularly were placed in particular tracks based more on their parents' privilege than on their own ability.
In a previous study, Oakes (1992) had found a strikingly similar pattern:
She discovered that White and Asian American students were placed by
their teachers and counselors in advanced classes, although comparably
scoring Latinos were not. Nor has tracking resulted in more equal outcomes. In one blatant example, the test scores of students placed in low-
ability classes actually *decreased significantly* after they had been in those
classes for just a year (Welner & Oakes, 1996).

Related to inequitable outcomes in achievement are inequitable
practices in tracked classrooms. One study, for instance, found that the
rate of participation and discussion in honors classes was higher than in
lower-tracked classes, leading to even more learning gaps between different groups (Gamoran, Nystrand, Berends, & LePre, 1995). Generally, the
result is that teaching varies according to the perceived ability of students.
Related to this, an intriguing study of a school district in the process of
detracking found that students of color benefited from their placement in
heterogeneous classes because they experienced an important change in
the quality of the interactions they had with their teachers (Villegas &

Watts, 1992). Such interactions, as we shall see later in this book, are a key ingredient in promoting student learning and achievement.

Tracking is at its most virulent in placement in gifted and talented programs and, at the other extreme, in special education programs. In her important research, Donna Ford (1996) found that gifted programs represented the *most segregated* of all programs in public schools, and that such programs are overwhelmingly bastions of White and middle-class students. In addition, decisions about who gets to be placed in programs for the gifted are made primarily by teachers and counselors, who may be less attuned to discovering talented students of color. As a result, racially and culturally diverse students are less likely than White students to be referred to programs for the gifted.

## Underrepresentation of Teachers of Color in Schools and Teacher Preparation Programs

How teachers of different backgrounds perceive and interact with their students brings us to another, closely related issue of inequality. It is by now a well-known fact that teachers of color are deplorably underrepresented in schools: of the 2.3 million teachers in the United States, about 10% are described as "minority," and this number has decreased recently and is expected to decline even further (U.S. Bureau of the Census, 1993). Moreover, preservice education programs are notorious for their homogeneity, using screening practices that discriminate against students of color in numerous ways (Zeichner & Hoeft, 1996). Because of their cultural uniformity, and unless there are conscious strategies to the contrary, preservice programs often serve as a mechanism for reproducing negative and racist attitudes and beliefs that later get translated into teaching approaches that continue to create inequitable education.

One example of preservice teachers' attitudes makes the point: In one study, preservice teachers' perspectives about students in inner-city schools, whom they most likely would be teaching in the near future, were unimaginably negative. For instance, except for one student, the general assumption among these preservice teachers was that the parents did not really care about their children or their children's education (Aaronsohn, Carter, & Howell, 1995). It is not surprising that these very same attitudes get reinforced daily in schools. But not only is the number of teachers of color in preservice education programs distressingly small, but there is also evidence that the perspectives and needs of these students are ignored, further alienating them from entering the profession (Zeichner & Hoeft, 1996). The underrepresentation of teachers of diverse backgrounds is therefore another way in which there is inequitable access to learning for students, particularly students of color.

What difference does representation make? First, because teachers of color often have themselves experienced inequality and alienation in their schooling, they frequently can relate to their students in ways that other teachers may not be able to. In fact, teachers of color often experience marginalization *as teachers* as well, sharing a bond with their marginalized students that other teachers may not understand (Montero-Sieburth & Pérez, 1987). Second, although White teachers by and large accept a "color-blind" stance as fair and impartial, teachers of diverse racial, cultural, and linguistic backgrounds generally reject this perspective as unfair and even racist (Olsen & Mullen, 1990). Not only do these teachers "see" their students' differences, but they also acknowledge the intrinsic worth of such differences and they use them as strengths and as a starting point in teaching.

Third, teachers of diverse backgrounds are usually familiar with the linguistic and cultural codes used by their students—codes that are often at odds with the official discourse (Gee, 1990) of schools. These teachers are frequently bicultural and/or bilingual themselves, and as a result they can act as a bridge for their students to the school culture (Olsen & Mullen, 1990). Fourth, teachers of color often know and share the hopes, dreams, and expectations of the families of the students they teach, and they tend to interpret these in more positive ways than other teachers, who often use a "deficit perspective" in trying to understand students and their families (Delgado-Gaitán, 1992; Flores, Cousin, & Díaz, 1991; Ladson-Billings, 1994; Lipman, 1997).

For bicultural students, then, there are often profound differences between the rules, expectations, and behaviors they encounter at home and at school. These differences may be ameliorated through the presence of teachers of their own background, whom students may perceive as advocates, mentors, supporters, and mediators. This is not to imply that teachers of color are invariably more sensitive, knowledgeable, and caring than their White counterparts, or that only teachers who share the race, culture, and language of their students can be successful with them. I have found that bicultural teachers also need to be educated about their students of other backgrounds, and even about students of their own background if they have had little experience with them (Nieto, 1998). Chances are, however, that if they are represented in the faculty, teachers of diverse backgrounds will lend important support to students of their own backgrounds while they enrich the perspectives of other students and of their fellow teachers.

The climate of classrooms and schools can change dramatically when the teachers and administrators are of diverse backgrounds. Mary Ginley, a teacher who worked for years in a low-income town with a large Puerto Rican community, described the major difference in her school after Dora Fuentes, the first Puerto Rican principal in the history of the town, was named.

## WHAT DIFFERENCE DOES DIFFERENCE MAKE?

*By Mary Ginley*

I remember when I was working at that school, I noticed that the conversations in the staff room weren't quite so negative; the things that were said at staff meetings were less outrageous, less "anti-kid" and most definitely not blatantly racist. I don't think that all the staff had had a remarkable change of heart within a year—Dora was an amazing woman but not quite that amazing. I think, though, that she made it very clear what was acceptable and what was unacceptable, in terms of how we talked about kids and their families and how we treated them. And so, no matter how a teacher thought or felt, kids were treated with respect and it was very rare that you heard a racist remark. Some might say it wasn't real, it didn't come from the heart. I say it doesn't matter; it was a first step and at least the kids were somewhat safe. (9.18.92)

### Pressures Toward Cultural and Linguistic Assimilation

Negative attitudes regarding languages and cultures that are different from officially sanctioned norms also can lead to educational inequality if such attitudes result in behaviors or in school policies and practices that restrict or discredit cultural and linguistic differences. That is, *the pressure that schools place on students to assimilate is itself an example of educational inequality.* Some might question the truth of this statement because although assimilation has been considered a positive, albeit initially painful, process, it has been viewed as a necessary passage and a prerequisite for success in school and society. Conventional wisdom is that by doing away with student differences, assimilation leads to *more* equality. There are two responses to this argument.

First, some students reach the schoolhouse door with the officially sanctioned language, culture, and background experiences and they are therefore more privileged from the very outset to succeed in the school setting. This is an inherently unfair situation: It is not that these particular conditions are innately better, but rather that they position some students to benefit more from school. Hence, it is not that the students who happen to have the valued characteristics have any particular talents or abilities due to the characteristics themselves, but rather that they have been fortunate enough to be born with the appropriate background or to have the kinds of experiences thought to be most suitable for schooling. Second, doing away with differences does not in itself guarantee an equal chance to learn. Assimilation can result in what Felix Boateng (1990) has called *deculturalization,* a process by which individuals are forcibly deprived of their culture. This does not mean the loss of a group's culture—something that usually takes several generations—but rather, it can result in the failure to acknowledge the important role that culture may have in students' values and behavior, and consequently in their learning.

In one of my graduate courses, I ask students to reflect on and write about the pressures they have felt to assimilate or conform, whether in school or other settings. The African American, Latino, Asian, and Indigenous students in my classes generally have little trouble listing, sometimes for pages, the many pressures they have faced, from processing (straightening) their hair, to being prohibited from speaking their native language in school, to feeling shame for the shape of their eyes or the color of their skin or the accents of their parents. Students of European American background generally have a much harder time of it, although working-class men and women, and women of all backgrounds, usually can come up with compelling examples as well. This in itself is a revealing exercise for the students, especially for those from European backgrounds, because it forces them to reflect on the price that some of their peers have had to pay for "fitting in." Ann Scott took the course a number of years ago and wrote about this in her journal.

### PRESSURES TO CONFORM

*By Ann Scott*

Discussion about pressure to conform in the class helped me to understand a little better and empathize with people not from the dominant culture. Some of the people who shared in class had had experiences that went beyond pressure to conform; they were expected to eradicate their own way of being. But what is offered to replace the self that must be erased?

My own experiences with pressures to conform can give me empathy, but I have never experienced the level of pressure that some of my classmates have. I've never been asked to give up my language, customs, to turn my back on my family, abandon my val-

ues, or change my name in order to become like the dominant culture because I'm already a member of the dominant culture. So my
own experiences, though painful, were of a different degree. I guess
I'm confused about all of this. Where I fit. What difference does the
level make? In order to really understand pressure like the Japanese woman in the class experienced, do I have to experience the
pressure to such a degree that it makes me feel shame about my primary identity? I have felt shame about my core identity in situations when I was made to feel less important, less legitimate than
someone who was from a wealthier class, someone much more educated than me, or someone in a powerful position who made it
clear that I was not worth bothering with. (9.22.93)

The need to adapt and accommodate to schools is not at issue here.
There is no question that all children regardless of linguistic background
need to learn English; likewise, the values and traditions of students from
all cultures cannot simply be reproduced in schools. In fact, this stance
implies a view of culture as static and inert, and the reality is that cultures
always change when they come in contact with one another. That is,
cultural change is inescapable in both the schools and society. Nonetheless, the coerced and one-way cultural change that is expected primarily
of students from dominated cultures is invariably negative and unequal
because it exerts pressure on some students, but not on all. Because assimilation can act as a disincentive to learning, alienation and marginalization may be the result. In fact, recent research has demonstrated that
academic achievement and learning may be fostered by encouraging the
*maintenance* and *affirmation* of students' cultures and languages, and that
assimilation is not necessarily a prerequisite for academic success (Gibson,
1991; Nieto, 1996; Zanger, 1993).

In the United States, the public schools have played a major role in
the assimilation process. In the case of American Indians and enslaved
Africans, education was denied or even outlawed (Weinberg, 1977), but
for European Americans, the school always served as the primary socializing and assimilating agent. The very creation of the common school during the nineteenth century was based in part on the perceived need to
assimilate immigrant and other students of widely diverse backgrounds
(Katz, 1971). Later, in the first decades of the twentieth century, the
country was faced with an unequaled number of Southern and Eastern
European immigrants, perceived to be not quite as "meltable" as previous
immigrants from Northern Europe. Of course, the reasons they were
thought to be "unmeltable" often had more to do with politics than with
culture. For example, the "foreign ideas" that they brought with them—

ideas such as socialism and anarchism—were perceived to be dangerous to the American way of life. As a result, the pressure to assimilate them was fierce, and this "Americanization movement" was most evident in the public schools (Appleton, 1983).

Although the "melting pot" metaphor has been claimed as the major symbol of pluralism in the United States, a rigid Anglo-conformity actually has been in place throughout much of our history. Public schools fulfilled their obligation to assimilate youngsters from diverse backgrounds by enforcing an Anglocentric curriculum and by punishing immigrant children for using their mother language. Schools assimilated students with practices that included flag ceremonies and other patriotic celebrations, the replacement of local heroes with national heroes in school curricula, and a focus on the history and traditions of the dominant White culture in the United States (Spring, 1997). In reality, few of these practices had to do with learning; their goal was to pressure students to become more like the idealized White, middle-class, English-speaking American.

Inequality in education also has been apparent in how students' languages and dialects are perceived and treated in the school. The most graphic example of the linguistic pressure to assimilate is when students are legally prohibited from using their native languages in the school, a situation that has occurred sporadically but repeatedly throughout U.S. history, even into the present (Crawford, 1992). Even in the absence of policies that legally prohibit the use of native languages, there are many subtle practices that discourage students from using their native languages in school. These practices convey the message to students that their native languages are not fit for communication or learning. Among such practices are failing to provide bilingual programs, humiliating students who use their native language to communicate among themselves, and even ridiculing students who have accents—a practice that students have reported not only among their fellow students, but even among their teachers (National Coalition of Advocates for Students, 1988; Olsen, 1988). The result of policies prohibiting the use of students' native language is probably incalculable in terms of emotional and psychic distress, not to mention the adverse effects on learning and academic achievement.

Why this kind of degradation takes place says a great deal about xenophobic tendencies in our society. The degradation of native languages has repercussions in the school setting, and it can be invalidating both for students' self-concept and for learning. Through interviews with immigrant parents of young children, Lily Wong Fillmore (1991) found that when preschool children are placed in English-only settings, they lose not only their first language but, more important, the ability to communicate effectively with their families. In the process, they also lose the academic advantage that fluency and literacy in a language would give them when they begin school. Quite early in their academic experience, these children also learn to feel ashamed of what their native language and culture represent. Similar findings have been reported with students who speak Black English. For example, in a review of relevant research by Donna Ford (1996), she found that teachers' negative attitudes may contribute to students' underachievement because students who speak Black English are more likely than other students to be seated farthest from the teacher, to be called on less often, to be given less time to respond to teachers' questions, and to receive negative criticism.

The continuing use of Black English is a reminder that some ethnic and racial groups, in fact, have maintained at least some of their cultural and linguistic traditions and practices in spite of decades, and even centuries, of pressure to assimilate. However, even among more newly arrived groups, it is important to point out that the project to assimilate immigrants did not end after the first decades of the twentieth century. With a huge new wave of immigrants since the 1980s—an immigration that numbered 10,139,300 from 1981 to 1992 (U.S. Department of Justice, 1993)—"Americanization" may be perceived to be "kinder and gentler," although it has the same painful results. In research by Virginia Vogel Zanger (1993), a student from the Dominican Republic expressed her feelings of alienation and exclusion by coining a verb that is eloquent in its simplicity: "They won't accept you if you're not like them. They want to *monoculture* [you]," she said (p. 172, emphasis added).

Adjusting to a new society is a remarkably complex process, one that usually includes learning a new language and different, sometimes confusing, cultural codes and behaviors. The process frequently is coupled with deep emotional loss and pain, even more evident in the case of immigrants who arrive in the United States as a result of war or profound economic devastation. Once they get here, they regularly are faced with a virulent racism that is difficult for them to understand or to reconcile with the images of the promised land they had expected to find. The pressure to assimilate also means that they are expected to discard their native languages and cultures *in favor of* instead of *in addition to* new ones, in the process abandoning their identity.

Considering the arduousness of the task before them, it is reasonable that young people take different amounts of time to adjust to their new settings. It can be a bewildering process. Cristina Igoa (1995), a teacher of immigrant children in California, has written about the price that her students, the newest immigrants, pay in the pressure to "be American."

In the words of Dung, a student from Vietnam: "It's hard—it's like fast-forward and you're in slow motion. Somebody was trying to fast-forward me" (p. 63).

## Other Manifestations of Educational Inequality

Educational inequality is manifested in other ways as well as those described above, and I will mention just a few of them here. For example, it is well known that counseling services assist young people in making consequential life choices, both about their secondary school options and about whether to pursue postsecondary education and, if so, how to go about it. Numerous testimonials attest to the fact that counselors often assume that bicultural students have fewer academic talents than culturally mainstream students. Stories abound of counselors who advise students to consider a vocational rather than academic track, who suggest that they are not "college material," or who simply have no time for students of color (Gándara, 1995; Nieto, 1996; Olsen, 1988; Poplin & Weeres, 1992). Yet, paradoxically, these are precisely the students who need counseling services most because their parents and families often are unable to help them make academic decisions due to their own lack of experience and familiarity with such issues.

In addition to personal testimonials, research confirms that students of different backgrounds have unequal access to appropriate counseling services. For instance, one study found that social class, ethnicity, and educational aspirations were all associated with access to counselors: Those students most in need of this access were the ones least likely to have it (Lee & Ekstrom, 1987). Furthermore, counseling is more than just information about course selection or college choices; although it may be unintentional, counseling also legitimates unequal access as if it were neutral and fair. One way in which this happens is through the silence concerning existing societal inequities that accompanies counseling (Fine, 1991; Hamovitch, 1996). That is, students often are made to feel that they are solely to blame for the ability tracks in which they are placed, or that if only they worked hard enough, they would have as good a chance of getting into elite universities as their more privileged peers. Yet neither of these assertions is completely true.

Another way in which educational inequality is visible is through the level of safety in different schools. According to the National Center for Education Statistics (1995), achievement can be positively or negatively affected by the climate of a school, including students' perceptions of their safety. Lack of safety is a disproportionately inequitable condition for Latino students, who are more likely than any others to report that disruptions by other students interfere with their learning, that fights among students of diverse ethnic backgrounds are frequent, and that, in general, they do not feel safe at school.

Retention, or holding students back in grade, although a common practice, has been shown to have few positive effects. Yet the practice persists, and in some cases it is being used more often because of strict promotion policies enacted in the wake of *A Nation at Risk,* among other factors (National Commission on Excellence in Education, 1983). For example, Melissa Roderick (1995) found that grade retention rates have risen by almost 40% over the past 2 decades. The proportion of students who are retained varies significantly by race and gender: More than half of African Americans and 48.5% of Latino males are below grade level, and consequently most have been held back at least once (Roderick, 1995). Because standardized test scores often are used to judge whether students should be held back or not, retention is doubly detrimental to students of color, for whom such tests have been shown to have negative effects (Darling-Hammond, 1995).

While it is certainly true that social promotion, that is, promoting students only by age rather than by ability, is a grave problem because it results in some students graduating from high school without minimum skills, an insistence on "higher standards" without the added resources and opportunities to meet those standards only ends up punishing further those students who need the most help. Proponents of retention claim that it persists because of the supposed benefits students will receive as a result, but the overall effect has not been to remediate students' academic deficiencies; on the contrary, retention often can lead to higher dropout rates. This link has been reported for many years (Bachman, Green, & Wirtanen, 1971; Margolis, 1968).

Disciplinary practices and policies also can lead to inequality in education. This is so because policies considered by teachers and schools to be neutral and objective are in fact often culturally loaded. A striking example is presented by Pauline Lipman (1997) in research that examined the influence of teachers' ideologies on the restructuring process in which their school was engaged. She cites the case of an African American student who was suspended for 10 days for wearing his overall straps unsnapped—a common African American style in that school—while White students who wore their pants with large holes cut out in the thighs—a common White style—were not disciplined at all. In her research, Rosa Hernández Sheets (1996) found that disciplinary practices affected students according to their ethnicity, with African American and Latino males most disproportionately and negatively affected.

As we have seen, inequality is not achieved just through conspicuous practices such as segregation or unequal funding. It also takes place through well-intentioned policies such as retention and ability group tracking, or because of conditions such as a lack of teachers of diverse backgrounds or the level of perceived safety in schools. Another important way in which inequality manifests itself is through pressure to assimilate to the cultural and linguistic mainstream.

## RESPONSES TO INEQUALITY

It is apparent from the previous discussion that inequality is no stranger to U.S. educational history. However, educational inequality is not a blanket that covers all groups equally. The manifestations of inequality may be different for different groups; consequently, redressing inequality will differ as well. While the goal of educational equality is shared by all groups, the means to reach that goal may be different. For instance, because of the brutal segregation they experienced, African Americans for many years focused their efforts on integration, believing this to be the surest way to participate in schooling on an equal basis. For Latinos, on the other hand, language policies that ignored or denied the prominence of native-language instruction in their learning became the most glaring illustration of inequality. Consequently, the struggle for bilingual education—a strategy whose outcome was often *more* rather than *less* segregation, at least for the short term—sometimes conflicted with the goal of integrated schooling of most African Americans (Báez, Fernández, Navarro, & Rice, 1986).

For American Indians, issues of sovereignty, the danger of extinction of numerous native languages, and bitter experiences in mission and boarding schools resulted in calls for self-determination in education (Deyhle & Swisher, 1997). In the case of females, it is increasingly clear that access to what have been considered nontraditional courses of study is one important way to obtain more equitable results (American Association of University Women Educational Foundation, 1992). As a result of differences such as these, strategies to attain equality in education among diverse groups sometimes have been diametrically opposed to one another. Responses to educational inequality vary among groups, and also among individuals.

### Group Responses

If we place the educational experiences of different social groups in their historical context, we can understand how their goals and strategies for equality have differed (AAUW, 1992; E. García, 1995; Lee & Slaughter-Defoe, 1995; Lomawaima, 1995; Nieto, 1995; Pang, 1995; Persell, 1997). Each case is unique, and even within similar groups there are many differences. Failure to understand these differences results in lumping all groups together as if they had experienced the same educational conditions. Moreover, educational inequality has not been evenly apportioned. That is, students have suffered the effects of inequality based on their relative standing in the society in general, and on their distance from the privileged position of middle-class or wealthy White males. Females of all backgrounds have faced some degree of inequality, but females of color have been even more vulnerable. Similarly, although poor and working-class students have not been treated equally, poor and working-class students of color have fared the worst. In effect, inequalities are multiplied by students' differences from the dominant culture, gender, and social class.

It is not only students' differences from the cultural norm that make a difference, however. In the case of people of color, the conditions under which they arrived in the United States and their political status have made a difference as well. John Ogbu (1987) has classified people of color into *voluntary minorities* (those who have been willing immigrants) and *involuntary minorities* (those whose cultures or countries have been conquered or subjugated by the United States). Accordingly, he characterizes American Indians, African Americans, Mexican Americans, and Puerto Ricans as *involuntary minorities* because they have been the victims of enslavement, internal colonialism, or conquest. As he points out, these are the groups that have faced the most severe level of educational failure in the United States, from poor academic achievement to high dropout rates.

Ogbu (1992) further explains that, given their dominated status and through a process that he calls *cultural inversion*, involuntary minorities tend to regard certain forms of behavior, events, meanings, and symbols as inappropriate for them because they consider those characteristics to be representative of White American culture. Students from involuntary minority immigrant groups thus create an *oppositional culture* to White culture because they fear that succumbing to a White cultural frame of reference—what he and Signithia Fordham have termed "the burden of acting White" (Fordham & Ogbu, 1986)—in effect means giving up their identities. Very often, however, this oppositional culture gets in the way of academic achievement in U.S. schools because it is contrary to the expected attitudes and behaviors of successful students.

*Voluntary minorities*, in contrast, have chosen to immigrate and generally see the United States as a land of unparalleled opportunity. Compared with the countries where many of them have come from and considering the harsh conditions in which they lived, the United States is indeed a haven for many of them. Examples of these voluntary minorities include West Indians, Central Americans, and Punjabis (Gibson & Ogbu, 1991). These groups historically have been far more successful in U.S. schools than have involuntary minorities. Their relative self-determination in terms of the decision to immigrate may be one reason for greater academic success; another may be a self-image that has not had the same long-term level of mistreatment and abuse as that of involuntary minorities.

Ogbu's theories concerning the persistent achievement gaps between voluntary and involuntary minorities have made an important contribution to our understanding of educational inequality. Although significant, however, his explanations are incomplete because they leave a number of questions unanswered. First, his ideas have been critiqued as overly deterministic and ahistorical because they fail to explain, for instance, the long struggle of the African American people for educational equality (Ladson-Billings, 1995b). Second, his explanation of *oppositional culture* has been criticized as being dangerously close to Oscar Lewis's (1965) concept of *the culture of poverty,* a theory roundly criticized for its racist and ethnocentric overtones (Foley, 1991; Rodríguez, 1995).

A more subtly nuanced explanation for oppositional culture has been developed by William Cross (1995). He differentiates between *Black defensive oppositional identity* and *Black alienated oppositional identity.* According to Cross, developing a defensive oppositional identity has a long history in the Black community, and until recently it was the normative protective strategy found among most Blacks. However, it is due to the sociopolitical context—specifically to the hyperconcentration of unemployed and undereducated Black adults since 1975—that young people have developed an alienated oppositional identity, "a strategy," according to Cross, "that achieves protection by rejecting involvement" (pp. 190–191). Cross suggests that what Fordham and Ogbu have called an oppositional identity is at odds not only with White culture, but with traditional Black culture as well.

Third, the role of teachers' attitudes and behaviors toward students of different backgrounds can be significant. For instance, Stacey Lee's (1996) study of Asian American students of different ethnic backgrounds found that teachers often expected them to excel simply based on their status as "model minority" students. When the students did not live up to this stereotype, they often were given passing grades even though they may not have deserved those grades. They were in effect rewarded for nonacademic attributes, specifically their polite behavior, and because teachers *perceived them to be successful* in spite of the academic problems they might have. Another criticism of Ogbu's work is that too many students simply do not fit the neat profile described by him. That is, the theories fail to explain the discrepancy in achievement among students who share similar backgrounds and experiences. For example, numerous African Americans have been academically successful, while many Asian American students have not been (Irvine & Foster, 1996; Lee, 1996). Finally, Ogbu's theories do not directly address how academic failure is created and replicated through school conditions of inequality.

## Individual Responses

Students are not simply the passive victims of inequality. Rather, they react to inequality in various ways, some more beneficial than others in terms of their long-range chances for academic success. One such reaction to teachers' and counselors' low expectations, for instance, has been to "prove them wrong" by developing a fierce determination to excel in school or go to college (Donaldson, 1996; Gándara, 1995). In this case, negative expectations can prove to be a motivating force to succeed. Other responses, although understandable, have been more negative in terms of their effects on students' learning and achievement. For example, a study by Rosa Hernández Sheets (1996) found that while all students felt unjustly treated *as individuals*, it was only students of color who felt that the disciplinary practices to which they were subjected were *also* disrespectful of their families, culture, and ethnicity.

Another reaction to inequality is what has been called *resistance* (Erickson, 1987; Giroux, 1983). According to this theory, students resist schooling in sundry ways, including vandalism, breaking school rules, and, in what is of interest in the present discussion, refusing to learn. In the words of Frederick Erickson (1987), "Learning what is deliberately taught can be seen as a form of political assent. Not learning can be seen as a form of political resistance" (p. 344). Resistance is related not only to ethnic cultural differences, but also to power differentials between students, their teachers, and the institution of school. Ray McDermott (1977), discussing the education of Black youth in the United States, provided one of the earliest explanations for this phenomenon:

> The bicultural child must acquire a sometimes mutually exclusive way of knowing how to act appropriately, one way for when Whites are present and another for when the interaction matrix is all Black. Where code shifting is most difficult is apparently in the bureaucratic setting in which the White code, in addition to being the only acceptable medium of information exchange, is also the medium for the expression of host group power and host

group access to the essential and even luxurious utilities of contemporary America. (p. 17)

Sometimes even capable students seem to refuse to take part in their learning. Ira Shor (Shor & Freire, 1987) calls this stance "'a performance strike' by students who refuse to study under current social conditions" (p. 5). Herbert Kohl (1994) has called it a strategy of *creative maladjustment* that can be expressed by the words, "I won't learn from you." Although it is sometimes taken for failure or inability to learn, Kohl asserts that this strategy is actually hard work and a sign of young people's healthy self-respect and integrity because *not learning* is a strategy to preserve one's identity and loyalty to family. Although it may prove to be harmful in the long run, this approach is logical given students' negative experiences in school, especially what they perceive as attacks on their identity. School policies and practices that pressure students to assimilate are one manifestation of this attack.

Research over the years, in fact, has discovered a curious and tragic connection between what students perceive as the pressure to succeed in school, and the need to abandon their families and their cultural values. For instance, an early study by John Scanzoni (1972) concluded that Black students who rejected their families had a greater chance for future success. Signithia Fordham's (1990) research on *racelessness* as a strategy to achieve academic success is a more recent case in point. That is, in order to succeed academically, some African American students believe that they need to take on a raceless identity. In spite of the fact that racelessness can help make African American students more academically resilient (Wang & Gordon, 1994) and therefore potentially successful, racelessness as a protective strategy also has great psychic costs. Some of these may be alienation from friends and family, a confused social identity, and cultural rootlessness.

Michelle Fine's (1991) study of dropouts in a New York City public high school makes this point eloquently. She found that while students who remained in school were considered "academic success stories"— and in a real sense, of course, they were—these students were often unquestioning of the social inequities around them, believing deeply in the myth of meritocracy even if they did not see it realized in their own families and communities. On the other hand, she found that the dropouts whom she studied had a much more critical perspective of their schooling and societal inequities. While not romanticizing the social or academic prospects of these young people, she maintained, "Dropouts failed in traditional academic terms. But perhaps, ironically, they retained some connection, even if problematic and temporary, to community, kin, peers, and racial/ethnic identity" (p. 135). In a more recent example, Bram Ha-movitch's (1996) study of an after-school program for "at-risk" youths concluded that its failure was due to the fact that "it allegorically asks [students] to dislike themselves and their own culture" (p. 302).

Given the overwhelming inequality in schools as we have seen in this chapter, school policies and practices may collude to create the per-ception among bicultural students that they cannot remain who they are and academically successful *at the same time*. A recent detracking study (Oakes, Well, Jones, & Datnow, 1997) made this point quite forcefully. The researchers found that because conventional explanations of intelli-gence are grounded in cultural manifestations or social deportment, many bicultural students felt that they needed to "act White" in order to be perceived as intelligent by their teachers. In exchange for academic success, students from culturally dominated groups often have been ex-pected to abandon part of themselves. One could reasonably conclude that this is not a fair exchange.

## SUMMARY

As we have seen in this chapter, educational inequality takes many guises and results in differential outcomes for students. More often than not, the outcomes correspond in many ways with students' racial, ethnic, gen-der, and social class characteristics. Whether inequality is an intended outcome or not does not really matter; the end result is what counts. The fact is that many school policies are based on the kindest of intentions but their outcomes are no less harmful than policies explicitly intended to be damaging. Yet much of the research also has indicated that academic failure is not inevitable. Despite the bleak picture outlined in this chapter, and regardless of appalling conditions of inequality, students can and in-deed have been academically successful in numerous situations. In truth, research concerning what works with bicultural students has found con-sistently that in general students respond positively to high expectations, educational environments characterized by caring and respect, positive and close relationships with their teachers, and interventions and educa-tional strategies that build on rather than demolish their native language and culture. All of these conditions are examples of providing educational equality; denying them is unjust for individual students and unhealthy for the general society.

Kofi Lomotey (1990) came to three conclusions about the educa-tional experiences of African American students, and he could just as well have been addressing the education of other students who suffer the effects of educational inequality:

> First, the underachievement of African-American students is persistent, pervasive, and disproportionate; the severity of the problem has been well documented. Second, the reasons that this situation persists are varied; there is no simple explanation. Third, there are clear examples of environments that have, over long periods of time, been successful in educating large numbers of African-American students. These models can be replicated; the situation is not hopeless. (p. 9)

An insidious undercurrent of power and privilege lies behind the immense differences in educational achievement among students of diverse backgrounds. That is, power and privilege rather than intelligence or ability are at the heart of inequality. At times, privilege is very visible, as in the case of vastly unequal funding for schools that serve different populations. Other times, privilege is more subtle. For example, stressing the culture and language of bicultural students—as in the case of bilingual programs or culturally relevant pedagogy—is a strategy that often is perceived as "special treatment," yet using the culture and language of dominant-group students is never thought of in the same way. But simply having a culture different from the mainstream does not by itself result in inequality; rather, inequality results because the characteristics of dominant-group students are consistently overvalued, while those of culturally dominated youngsters are undervalued.

Likewise, privilege often goes unnamed because to admit that it exists is to concede that the playing field is far from level. This is especially difficult to do in a society such as the United States, where there is a claim of equal opportunity for all. As we have seen in this chapter, although the ideal of equal educational opportunity is a worthy one to strive for, it is far from realized in practice.

CHAPTER 3

# Culture and Learning

[We] are not simply bearers of cultures, languages, and histories, with a
duty to reproduce them. We are the products of linguistic-cultural circumstances, actors with a capacity to resynthesize what we have been socialized into and to solve new and emerging problems of existence. We are not
duty-bound to conserve ancestral characteristics which are not structurally
useful. We are both socially determined and creators of human futures.
—Mary Kalantzis, Bill Cope, and Diana Slade, *Minority Languages*

THE TERM "CULTURE" can be problematic because it can mean different
things to different people in different contexts. For instance, culture is
sometimes used as if it pertained only to those with formal education and
privileged social status, implying activities such as attending the opera
once a month. In the present day, it generally is acknowledged that culture is not just what an elite group of people may do in their spare time,
but there are still various and conflicting ideas of what it actually means
in everyday life. Among many Whites in the United States, for instance,
culture is thought to be held exclusively by those different from them. As
a consequence, it is not unusual to hear people, especially those of European background, lament that they do not "have" culture in the same
way that African Americans, Asian Americans, Native Americans, or
other groups visibly different from the dominant group "have" it. In other
cases, culture is used interchangeably with ethnicity as if both simply
were passed down constant and eternal from one generation to the next.
At still other times, culture can mean the traditions one celebrates within
the family, in which case it is reduced to foods, dances, and holidays. Less
often is culture thought of as the values one holds dear, or the way one
looks at and interacts with the world.

In this chapter, I will explore the complex relationship between culture and learning. First, I will define culture through a number of interrelated characteristics that make it clear that culture is more than artifacts, rituals, and traditions. In fact, it is becoming increasingly indisputable that culture and cultural differences, including language, play a discernible although complicated role in learning. I will consider how culture and language influence learning by looking at some of the cultural discontinuities between school and home expectations of students from various backgrounds.

## DEFINING CULTURE

Elsewhere, I have defined culture as "the ever-changing values, traditions, social and political relationships, and worldview created, shared, and transformed by a group of people bound together by a combination of factors that can include a common history, geographic location, language, social class, and religion" (Nieto, forthcoming). As is clear from this definition, culture is complex and intricate; it includes content or product (the *what* of culture), process (*how* it is created and transformed), and the agents of culture (*who* is responsible for creating and changing it). Culture cannot be reduced to holidays, foods, or dances, although these are, of course, elements of culture. This definition also makes it clear that everyone has a culture because all people participate in the world through social and political relationships informed by history as well as by race, ethnicity, language, social class, gender, sexual orientation, and other circumstances related to identity and experience.

At least two issues need to be kept in mind if culture is to have any meaning for educators who want to understand how it is related to learning. First, culture needs to be thought of in an unsentimental way. Otherwise, it is sometimes little more than a yearning for a past that never existed, or an idealized, sanitized version of what exists in reality. The result may be an unadulterated, essentialized "culture on a pedestal" that bears little resemblance to the messy and contradictory culture of real life. The problem of viewing some aspects of culture as indispensable attributes that must be shared by all people within a particular group springs from a romanticized and uncritical understanding of culture. For instance, I have heard the argument that poetry cannot be considered Puerto Rican unless it is written in Spanish. Thus, the Spanish language becomes a *constitutive characteristic* of being Puerto Rican. While there is no argument that speaking Spanish is an important and even major aspect of Puerto Rican culture, it is by no means a prerequisite for Puerto Ricanness. There are hundreds of thousands of Puerto Ricans who identify themselves first and foremost as Puerto Rican but who do not speak Spanish due to the historical conditions in which they have lived.

The second consideration to be kept in mind is that the sociopolitical context of culture needs to be acknowledged. That is, cultures do not exist in a vacuum, but rather are situated in particular historical, social, political, and economic conditions, and therefore they are influenced by issues of power. The claim of Whites that they do not have a culture is a case in point. Whites frequently do not experience their culture *as a culture* because as the officially sanctioned and high-status culture, it "just is." Therefore, when Whites say that they do not "have" a culture, they in effect relegate culture to no more than quaint customs or colorful traditions. This stance is disingenuous at best because it fails to observe that Whites as a group participate disproportionately in a *culture of power* (Delpit, 1988) simply based on their race, although access to this power is not available to those who are not White (nor, it should be stressed, is it shared equally among Whites).

In what follows, I describe a set of attributes that are key to understanding how culture is implicated in learning, and how these notions of culture complicate a facile approach to multicultural education. These characteristics are complementary and interconnected, so much so that it is difficult to disentangle them from one another. I do so here only for purposes of clarity, not to suggest that they exist in isolation. The characteristics I review here include culture as *dynamic; multifaceted; embedded in context; influenced by social, economic, and political factors; created and socially constructed; learned;* and *dialectical.*

### Culture Is Dynamic

Culture does not exist outside of human beings. This means that cultures are not static relics, stagnant behaviors, or sterile values. Steven Arvizu's (1994) wonderful description of culture as a *verb* rather than a *noun* captures this essence of culture beautifully. That is, culture is dynamic, active, changing, always on the move. Even within their native contexts, cultures are always changing as a result of political, social, and other modifications in the immediate environment. When people with different backgrounds come in contact with one another, such change is to be expected even more.

But cultural change is not simply a one-way process. The popular conception of cultural change is that it is much like a transfusion: As one culture is emptied out of a person, a new one is poured in. In this conception, each culture is inert and permanent, and human beings do not influence the process to any significant degree. But the reality is that cultures are *always* hybrids, and that people select and reject particular elements of culture as suitable or not for particular contexts. Cultural values are not gotten rid of as easily as blood, nor are new ones simply infused. For instance, there is ample ethnographic evidence that in spite of the enormous political, social, and economic changes among American Indians in the past 100 years, their child-rearing practices, although they have, of course, changed, have also remained quite stable (Deyhle & Swisher, 1997). Likewise, among immigrants to the United States, there are indications that ethnic values and identities are preserved to some extent for many generations (Greenfield, 1994; McGoldrick, Pearce, & Giordano, 1982).

In some ways, we can think of culture as having both *surface* and *deep structure*, to borrow a concept from linguistics (Chomsky, 1965). For instance, in previous research (Nieto, 1996), when interviewing young people of diverse backgrounds I was initially surprised by the seeming homogeneity of the youth culture they manifested. That is, regardless of racial, ethnic, or linguistic background, or time in the United States—but usually intimately connected to a shared urban culture and social class—the youths often expressed strikingly similar tastes in music, food, clothes, television viewing habits, and so on. Yet, when I probed more deeply, I also found evidence of deeply held values from their ethnic heritage. For example, Marisol, a young Puerto Rican woman whom I interviewed, loved hip hop and rap music, pizza, and lasagna. She never mentioned Puerto Rican food, and Puerto Rican music to her was just the "old-fashioned" and boring music her parents listened to. Nonetheless, in her everyday interactions with her parents and siblings, and in the answers she gave to my interview questions, she reflected deep aspects of Puerto Rican culture such as respect for elders, a profound kinship with and devotion to family, and a desire to uphold important traditions such as staying with family rather than going out with friends on important holidays. Just as there is no such thing as a "pure race," there is likewise no "pure culture." That is, cultures influence *one another*, and even minority cultures and those with less status have an impact on majority cultures, sometimes in dramatic ways. Rap music, with its accompanying style of talk, dress, and movement, is a notable example among young people of diverse backgrounds in urban areas.

In terms of schooling, the problem with thinking of culture as static is that curriculum and pedagogy are designed as if culture indeed were unchanging. This issue was well expressed by Frederick Erickson (1990), who has argued that when culture is thought of as fixed, or simply as an aesthetic, the educational practice derived from it supports the status quo. This is because reality itself can then be perceived as inherently static.

Erickson goes on to say, "When we think of culture and social identity in more fluid terms, however, we can find a foundation for educational practice that is transformative" (p. 22). The view of culture as dynamic rather than fixed is unquestionably more befitting a conception of multicultural education as liberating pedagogy based on social justice.

## Culture Is Multifaceted

Closely related to the dynamic nature of culture is that cultural identifications are multiple, eclectic, mixed, and heterogeneous. This means, for one thing, that culture cannot be conflated with just ethnicity or race. As an example, Mexican or Mexican American culture may be familiar to us because it concerns an identity based primarily on ethnicity, the best-known site of culture. But one also can speak, for instance, of a lesbian culture because as a group, lesbians share a history and identity, along with particular social and political relationships. Thus, one can be culturally Mexican American and a lesbian at the same time. But having multiple cultural identities does not imply that each identity is claimed or manifested equally. A wealthy light-skinned Mexican American lesbian and a working-class Mexican American lesbian may have little in common other than their ethnic heritage and sexual orientation, and the oppression that comes along with these identities. People create their identities in different ways: While one Mexican American lesbian may identify herself first and foremost ethnically, another may identify herself as a lesbian, a third as both, and a fourth primarily as a member of the working class.

Because culture is not simply ethnicity, even among specific cultural groups there are many and often conflicting cultural identities. Skin color, time of arrival in the United States, language use, level of education, family dynamics, place of residence, and many other differences within groups may influence how one interprets or "lives" a culture. Further, the intersection of ethnicity and social class, or what Milton Gordon (1964) termed *ethclass,* is a key factor in defining culture. For instance, as a young girl I was surprised to meet middle-class Puerto Ricans when I spent a summer in Puerto Rico. Given my experiences until that time as a member of an urban U.S. Puerto Rican family that could best be described as working poor, I had thought that only Whites could be middle-class. Although I spoke Spanish fairly well and thought of myself as Puerto Rican, I discovered that in some ways I had more in common with my African American peers in my Brooklyn neighborhood and school than with the middle-class Puerto Ricans I met on the island. I began to see that my Puerto Rican culture was in fact quite different from Puerto Rican culture as defined on the island. Years later I understood that these differences had to do with location, experience, and social class.

Another important aspect of identity has to do with how interactions with people of other cultural groups may influence culture and identity. This is certainly the case in urban areas, where the identities of young people of many diverse ethnic and racial backgrounds defy easy categorization. Shirley Brice Heath (1995) has suggested that young urban dwellers in the United States are creating new cultural categories based on shared experiences because, according to her, these young people "think of themselves as a *who* and not a *what*" (p. 45). They engage not only in border crossings, but also in what Heath called "crossings and crisscrossings" (p. 48). Given the growing presence of people in the United States who claim a biracial, multiracial, or multiethnic identity, ethnicity alone is unable to fully define culture. The multiple identities of youths have important and far-reaching implications for the development and implementation of multicultural education: It is evident that simplistic and bounded conceptions that focus just on specific racial or ethnic groupings fail to capture the realities of many urban youths who live with complicated and heterogeneous realities.

**Culture Is Embedded in Context**

To say that culture is embedded in context is to say that it invariably is influenced by the environment in which it exists. The culture of Japanese students in Japan is of necessity different from that of Japanese immigrant students in the United States or of Japanese immigrant students in Peru or Brazil. When culture is presented to students as if it were context-free, they learn to think of it as quite separate from the lives that people lead every day. It is what Frederick Erickson (1990) has described as the fragmenting of people's lives "as we freeze them outside time, outside a world of struggle in concrete history" (p. 34). Culture is commonly decontextualized. In the United States, decontextualization typically occurs in the school curriculum and in media images outside of school. A notable case is that of American Indians, who customarily have been removed from their cultural and historical rootedness through images that eternalize them as either noble heroes or uncivilized savages, and typically as a combination of both (Churchill, 1992). On the other hand, the history of oppression, dehumanization, resistance, and struggle of the many Indigenous Nations rarely is studied in schools. If there is any doubt about the image of American Indians held by most non-Indian children in the United States, ask even 6-year-olds and they will provide in precise detail the most stereotypical and ahistorical portrait of Indians, as Erickson (1990) noted, "outside time" (p. 34). If these children happen to live in a geographic region where there are no reservations or large concentrations of Indians, they often are shocked to learn that Indians are still around today and that they are teachers, or truck drivers, or artists. Even when American Indians are included in the curriculum as existing in the present, the idyllic images of them tend to reinforce common stereotypes. For instance, while we may be happy to show students pictures of powwows, we are less likely to discuss how reservations have been used as toxic dumping sites.

A further example of how culture is influenced by context will suffice. Puerto Ricans generally eat a great deal of rice in many different manifestations. Rice is a primary Puerto Rican staple. There is even a saying that demonstrates how common it is: "Puertorriqueños somos como el arroz blanco: Estamos por todas partes" (Puerto Ricans are like white rice: We are everywhere), an adage that says as much about rice as it does about the diaspora of the Puerto Rican people, almost half of whom live outside the island. As a rule, Puerto Ricans eat short-grained rice, but I prefer long-grained rice, and other Puerto Ricans often made me feel practically like a cultural traitor when I admitted it. I remember my amazement when a fellow academic, a renowned Puerto Rican historian, explained the real reason behind the preference for short-grained rice. This preference did not grow out of the blue, nor does any particular quality of the rice make it inherently better. On the contrary, the predilection for short-grained rice was influenced by the historical context of Puerto Ricans as a colonized people.

It seems that near the beginning of the twentieth century when Puerto Rico was first taken over by the United States as spoils of the Spanish-American War, there was a surplus of short-grained rice in the United States. Colonies frequently have been the destination for unwanted or surplus goods from the metropolis, so Puerto Rico became the dumping ground for short-grained rice, which had lower status than long-grained rice in the United States. After this, of course, the preference for short-grained rice became part of the culture. As is true of all cultural values, however, this particular taste was influenced by history, economics, and power, which will be further elaborated in what follows.

## Culture Is Influenced by Social, Economic, and Political Factors

As is evident from the above, intimately related to the fact that culture is bound to a particular context, is that it is greatly influenced by the political, historical, and economic conditions in which it is found. It exists not in isolation but through concrete relationships characterized by differential access to power. As a result, dominant social groups in a society often determine what counts as culture. This is why, for example, a dominant cultural group unabashedly can designate itself as "the norm" and others as "culturally deprived" (Lewis, 1965; Reissman, 1962). Those who are so designated may not necessarily see themselves in this way, but naming by others takes on great power; eventually many of those who are designated as "culturally deprived" may learn to believe it. Yet "culturally deprived" actually means simply that the group in question does not share in the culture—and consequently in the power—of the dominant group. The paradox of this stance is that while Whites see themselves as culturally neutral or "cultureless," at the same time they insist, through constant messages in the dominant ideology, that theirs is the valued and valuable culture.

The theories of sociologist Pierre Bourdieu (1986) are significant here. According to him, it is not simply money, or *economic capital*, that determines one's standing in the social structure; equally important are what he has termed *social capital* and *cultural capital*. Social capital is made up of social obligations and networks that are convertible into economic capital. These will be considered further in Chapter 4. Cultural capital, which is more immediately important to us here, can be defined as the acquired tastes, values, languages, and dialects, or the educational qualifications, that mark a person as belonging to a privileged social and cultural class. Just as in the case of learning one's native culture and language, cultural capital is acquired in the absence of any deliberate or explicit teaching; it is therefore unconsciously learned. The initial accumulation of cultural capital, in the words of Bourdieu (1986), is "the best hidden form of hereditary transmission of capital" (p. 246).

In essence, then, culture is deeply entangled with economic and political privilege. That is, the tastes, values, languages, and dialects that have the greatest status are associated with the dominant social class *not because these tastes, values, languages, or dialects are inherently better but because they have higher social prestige as determined by the group with the greatest power.* As a case in point, for many years linguists have proposed that Black English is a rich and creative variety of English, as logical and appropriate as standard English for purposes of communication (Labov, 1972; Smitherman, 1977). Yet the conventional wisdom still common among teachers is that Black English is simply "bad English." Thus, rather than building on students' native discourse—what has been termed *additive bilingualism* (Lambert, 1975)—most teachers simply attempt to eradicate Black English and replace it with standard English, a *subtractive* form of bilingualism. On the other hand, when expressions from Black English make their way into standard English because they are used by middle-class Whites, they immediately take on a higher social status and thus become acceptable.

The example of Black English underscores the impact that culture may have on learning and academic achievement. Most schools are organized to reflect and support the cultural capital of privileged social and cultural groups; in the United States, that group is middle-class or upper-class, English-speaking Whites. As a result of their identity and upbringing, some children arrive at the schoolhouse door with a built-in privilege because they have learned this cultural capital primarily in the same way as they have learned to walk, that is, unconsciously and effortlessly. Their culture, in this case, the variety of English that they speak, seems both natural and correct. Yet as suggested by Carol Lee and Diana Slaughter-Defoe (1995), because of the low prestige of Black English, "the influences of language on learning for African Americans are both complex and problematic" (p. 357).

This example also places in bold relief the arbitrary nature of cultural capital. Paulo Freire (Shor & Freire, 1987) captured the frivolous essence of such designations when he asked, "When did a certain form of grammar become 'correct'? Who named the language of the elite as 'correct,' as the standard?" He answered his own question by stating, "They did, of course. But, why not call it 'upper-class dominating English' instead of 'Standard English.' That authentic naming would reveal, instead of obscure, the politics of power and language in society" (p. 45). Further on, in discussing the same topic, he added, "This so-called 'standard' is a deeply *ideological* concept, but it is necessary to teach correct usage while also criticizing its political implications" (p. 71).

One could envision another, quite different, scenario. If, for instance, through some extraordinary turn of events, working-class African Americans were to become the esteemed social group in the United States, Black English probably would become the new standard. In turn, schools would make certain that the curriculum, texts, and other materials would reflect this new form of cultural capital; in addition, only those teachers who were intimately familiar with Black English and who considered it an innately superior variety of English would be hired. Accordingly, the children of working-class African American homes would enter school with a built-in advantage compared with other children, who would be considered "culturally deprived" because they did not have the cultural capital of Black English. As far-fetched as this scenario is, given current economic and political realities in the United States, it serves as a graphic example of the capricious nature of determining whose culture becomes highly valued.

## Culture Is Created and Socially Constructed

As discussed previously, culture often is thought of as a product-in-place, and as something handed down that must be kept the way it is. Not only does this result in a static view of culture, but it also implies that culture is already finished. As we have seen, culture is constantly evolving, and the reason that it evolves is because *human beings change it.* The action of people on culture takes place in big ways and small, by everyday people and by those who have power. When Jonathan Kozol (1978) went to Cuba to research the successful massive literacy campaign that had just taken place, he spoke with young people in schools, many of whom had been the teachers of the peasants who learned to read. He was awed by the young people's responses when he asked them what was meant by *history.* He recounted that when he had asked that same question of students in Schenectady, New York, the answers had been fairly uniform: "History is everything that happened in the past and is now over. . . . History is what is done by serious and important people" (p. 176). In contrast, when he asked young people in Cuba the same question, their answers were starkly different: "It is the past, but there are things that we do now which will be part of history someday" (p. 176). These young people saw that history was not just what was written in history books, or the actions of "important people" in conquest, war, or politics. What they had done in the literacy campaign was also history.

In the same way, culture is what we do every day. Cultures change as a result of the decisions that we, as cultural agents, make about our traditions, attitudes, behaviors, and values. Were it not so, we would forever be mere pawns or victims of the actions of others. Sometimes, of course, cultural values develop as a result of victimization. The previous example of short-grained rice is a case in point. But even here, people took what they were given and made it a positive value. Without such valuing, short-grained rice would not have become part of the culture. The cuisine of poor people throughout the world is another illustration of how culture is created. Poor people often get nothing but leftovers, the parts of animals or plants that nobody else wants. What they have done with these remains has sometimes been nothing short of extraordinary. This is cultural creation in action. Put another way, in the words of Frederick Erickson (1997): "Culture can be thought of as a construction—it constructs us and we construct it" (p. 39). Culture, then, is not a passive legacy, but an active operation that takes place through contact and interactions with others. Culture is a social construction because it cannot exist outside of social contact and collaboration.

## Culture Is Learned

Closely related to the fact that culture is created and socially constructed is the fact that it is *learned.* That is, culture is not handed down through our genes, nor is it inherited. This is very clear to see, for example, when children from a particular ethnic group (for instance, Korean) are adopted by families from another ethnic group (usually European American). Although the children may still be considered ethnically and racially Korean, they will in all likelihood be *culturally* European American, unless their parents made a conscious and determined effort to teach them the culture and history of their heritage while raising them, or the children themselves later decide to do so.

Culture, especially ethnic and religious culture, is learned through interactions with families and communities. It usually is not consciously taught, or consciously learned. That is why it seems so natural and effortless. Although this process does not hold true of all cultures—for example, deaf or gay culture—we predictably learn culture while sitting on our mothers' or grandmothers' laps, standing by our fathers, listening to the conversations of family members around us, and modeling our behavior on theirs. In fact, most people do not even think about their culture unless it is in a subordinate position to another culture or—if they belong to a majority culture—when they leave the confines of home and are no longer part of the cultural norm.

That culture is learned is also apparent in the very concept of *biculturalism*. Bilingual education, for instance, very often is called *bilingual/bicultural education* because it is based on the principle that one can learn two languages and two cultural systems in order to function and even to succeed in different linguistic and cultural contexts. This point was made in research by Gloria Ladson-Billings (1994). Of the eight teachers she identified as successful with African American youths, three were White, and of them, one had a White culture of reference, another a bicultural culture of reference, and the third an African American culture of reference. However, becoming bicultural is not as simple as discarding one set of clothes for another. Because culture is complex, "learning" a culture that is not one's native culture is an exceedingly difficult task, one accomplished only through direct, sustained, and profound involvement with it. Because most teachers in the United States have not been through this process, it can be difficult for them to understand how excruciating the process is for their students. Furthermore, it is difficult to become bicultural in an untroubled sense because it means internalizing two cultural systems whose inherent values may be diametrically opposed.

In the United States, it is generally only students from dominated cultures who need to become bicultural as a requirement for academic and societal success. That they do so is a testament to great strength and resiliency. The fact that these newcomers, in spite of being young, feeling isolated, and facing what can be terrifying situations in unfamiliar environments, nonetheless can incorporate the cultural motifs of disparate values and behaviors says a great deal about human tenacity. What they accomplish might best be thought of as *critical biculturalism*, a biculturalism that is neither facile nor uncomplicated, but full of inconsistencies and challenges.

## Culture Is Dialectical

Culture often is thought of as a seamless web of interrelated and mutually supportive values and behaviors, yet nothing could be further from the truth. Because they are complex systems that are created by people and influenced by social, economic, and political factors, cultures are also dialectical, conflicted, and full of inherent tensions. A culture is neither "good" nor "bad" in general, but rather embodies values that have grown out of historical and social conditions and necessities. As individuals, we may find elements of our own or others' cultures uplifting or repugnant. That culture is dialectical does not mean that we need to embrace all of its contradictory manifestations in order to be "authentic" members of the culture.

Young people whose cultures are disparaged by society sometimes feel that they have to accept either one culture or the other wholly and uncritically. This was found to be the case, for instance, among Romani (Gypsy) youth in research carried out in Hungary (Forray & Hegedüs, 1989). Prevalent gender expectations of Romani boys and girls tend to be fairly fixed and stereotypical. Yet because the family is often the only place where culturally dominated young people can positively strengthen their self-image, Romani girls may correctly perceive that breaking free of even limited expectations of their future life options also results in giving up their ethnic identity and abandoning their families. Through questionnaires collected from elementary school teachers of Romani children, it became clear that teachers' negative attitudes and behaviors concerning the fixed gender roles in the Romani culture were at least partly responsible for strengthening the expected gender-based behavior among girls in school. Had teachers been able to develop a more culturally balanced and sensitive approach, it is conceivable that the Romani girls might have felt safe to explore other options without feeling that they were cultural traitors.

That culture is dialectical also leads to an awareness that there is no special virtue in preserving particular elements of culture as if they existed outside of social, political, and historical spaces. Mary Kalantzis and her colleagues (1989) have described this contradiction eloquently:

Preserving "communities" is not a good for its own sake, as if peoples should be preserved as museum pieces, so that they are not lost to posterity. "Communities" are always mixed, contradictory, conflict-ridden and by no means socially isolated entities. Active cultural re-creation, if people so wish, might involve consciously dropping one language in preference for another or abandoning some cultural tradition or other—such as sexism. (p. 12)

The work of the Puerto Rican sociologist Rafael Ramírez (1974) is particularly relevant here. Ramírez has suggested that we can think of every culture as a coin that has two contradictory faces or subsystems. He calls these the *culture of survival* and the *culture of liberation*, and each is important in defining the complexity of culture. The culture of survival embodies those attitudes, values, traditions, and behaviors that are developed in response to political, economic, or social forces, some of which may be interpreted as a threat to the survival of the culture in some way. They can either limit (e.g., the unequal treatment of women) or expand (i.e., mutual cooperation) people's perspectives within a particular culture. In the case of the role of women, values and behaviors of both males and females grew out of the necessity to view women, because of their unique biology, as primary caregivers. The need to survive is thus manifested in many cultures in perfectly understandable, although not always ethical or equitable ways, given the history of the species. According to Ramírez:

> The culture of survival is characterized mainly by the contradiction that it sustains, affirms, and provides certain power but, at the same time, does not confront or alter the oppressive elements and institutions nor affect the structure of political and economic power that controls the system. (p. 86)

Ramírez has defined the culture of liberation as the values, attitudes, traditions, and behaviors that embody liberatory aspects of culture. This face of culture, according to Ramírez, is part of the process of decolonization, and of questioning unjust structures and values, and it "comprises those elements that promote a new social order in which the democratization of the sociopolitical institutions, economic equality and cooperation and solidarity in interpersonal relations predominate" (p. 88). In this way, Ramírez says, authoritarianism is contrasted with democracy, racism with consciousness of racial and ethnic identity, and sexism with gender equality. Human rights that are generally accepted by most societies can be included in the framework of the culture of liberation. As we shall see later, understanding the contradictory nature of culture is important if students and teachers are to develop a critical, instead of a romantic, perspective of their own and other people's cultures.


## LANGUAGE AS CULTURE

As we have seen in several examples above, language is deeply implicated with culture and an important part of it. That is, the language, language variety, or dialect one speaks is culture made manifest, although it is not, of course, all there is to culture. This explains why, for instance, so many assimilationist movements both inside and outside of schools—from the forced removal of American Indian children to boarding schools beginning in the nineteenth century, to the recent English-Only Movement—have had native-language devaluation and elimination as major themes. In a very real sense, language is power, and this truth has been at the core of such movements. In the words of Richard Ruiz (1991), "A major dimension of the power of language is the power to define, to decide the nature of lived experience" (p. 218). Doing away with a language, or prohibiting its use, tears away at the soul of a people. Consequently, it is not surprising that language often has served as a powerful symbol and organizing tool for language-minority groups. For instance, using the example of four Indigenous minority cultures (Navajo, Huala Pai, Maori, and Hawaiian), Carlos Ovando and Karen Gourd (1996) have shown how language maintenance and revitalization movements have been used by marginalized groups as major vehicles to attain power within society, to create a sense of peoplehood, and to challenge officially sanctioned structures and languages.

In the United States, attitudes about languages and language varieties other than the mainstream language have oscillated between grudging acceptance and outright hostility. These attitudes have been rationalized as necessary for political and social cohesion and for academic success (Crawford, 1992). Laws as well as school policies have reflected for the most part negative attitudes about native-language maintenance: Examples include the virtual disappearance of native-language instruction between the two world wars, recent court cases involving workers who dared to speak their native language among themselves, and even mothers who, in the privacy of their own homes, speak with their children in their own language, the language that reflects their nurture and love. This was the case of a young mother chastised by a judge for speaking Spanish to her child (cited in Cummins, 1996). Marta Laureano, who was involved in a child custody case in Texas, was admonished by Judge Samuel Kiser that she was relegating her daughter to a future as a housemaid if she continued speaking Spanish to her. He also charged that speaking Spanish to her was "bordering on abuse" and ordered her to speak only English at home (Cummins, 1996, p. 21).

If research were to prove that maintaining native-language use was a detriment to learning, there might be some reason to consider assimilation as a positive process. This has not proven to be the case, however. David Dolson's (1985) research on the home language use and academic performance of Latino students, for instance, found that those from *additive* bilingual home contexts—that is, homes where Spanish continued to be used even after children learned English—significantly outperformed their peers from *subtractive* homes—where the Spanish was replaced by English. Moreover, he discovered that more Spanish at home usually resulted in better *English* skills as well, supporting the idea that Spanish-language use in the home fosters improved academic performance. Lourdes Díaz Soto's (1993) research among 30 Hispanic families of young children with low and high academic achievement found that parents of the higher-achieving children inevitably favored a native-language environment to a greater extent than those of lower-achieving youngsters. Her findings, rather than suggesting the suppression or elimination of native-language use at home and school—an attitude that is all too common in schools—support just the opposite.

Similar conclusions have been reached by researchers using the case of Black English or Black dialect. In one study, for example, dialect-speaking 4-year-olds enrolled in a Head Start program were able to recall more details with greater accuracy when they retold stories in their cultural dialect rather than in standard English (Hall, Reder, & Cole, 1979). A more recent research study by Geneva Smitherman (1994) concerning the impact of Black English Vernacular (BEV) on the writing of African American students echoed this finding among older students. Using essays written by African American students for the National Assessment of Educational Progress (NAEP), Smitherman demonstrated that the use of African American discourse style correlated positively with higher scores.

There is even some evidence to support the hypothesis that speaking only English may act as a *barrier* to academic success for bicultural students. Research by David Adams and his colleagues (Adams, Astone, Nuñez-Wormack, & Smodlaka, 1994) examining the predictive value of English proficiency, Spanish proficiency, and the use of each at home relative to the academic achievement of Latino students in five cities, found that recent immigrants who were *more* fluent in Spanish performed better than did second- or third-generation Latinos. They also found a small but negative influence of English-language proficiency on the academic performance of the Mexican American students in the sample; that is, better English proficiency meant lower academic performance among Mexican American youths. How to analyze this finding? The researchers conjectured that there might be what they called a "counterforce" against the traditional relationship between English proficiency and academic performance. They continued, "This counterforce may very well be the peer pressure students experience which works against school achievement, in spite of the students' English-language proficiency" (Adams et al., 1994, pp. 11–12).

This research confirms that simply speaking English is no guarantee that academic success will follow. There seem to be several reasons for this. First, when children are able to keep up with their native language at home, they develop *metalinguistic awareness*, that is, a greater understanding of how language itself works, and of how to use language for further learning. Based on her extensive research concerning second language acquisition, Virginia Collier (1995) has suggested that practicing English at home among students who are more proficient in another language actually can slow down cognitive development because it is only when parents and their children speak the language they know best that they are working at their "level of cognitive maturity" (p. 14). Furthermore, given the negative attitudes that we have seen among teachers about languages and language varieties other than standard English, and especially about languages they consider to have a low status, children who speak these languages may become further alienated from school and what it represents. In essence, students may disidentify with school. For example, the research by Adams and his colleagues (1994) supports the hypothesis that the identification of second- and third-generation Americans with school and academic achievement is weak owing to the repeated and consistent school failure among some groups (Ogbu, 1987). Knowing English may not be sufficient to defy the weak identification with schooling.

## LINKS AMONG CULTURE, LANGUAGE, AND LEARNING

Given the preceding discussion, it is indisputable that culture, language, and learning are connected. In what follows, some of the links will be made more explicit, beginning with a discussion of child-rearing practices.

## Child-Rearing Practices and Learning

Child-rearing is above all a teaching and learning process, making the home the first context for learning. The earliest and most significant socialization of children takes place within their families and communities. Just as they learn to walk and talk, children also learn *how to learn* as defined within their particular cultural contexts. Children's interactions with parents or other caregivers thus pave the way for how they will fare in school. That is, where students' cultural values and behaviors "fit" with school policies and practices, learning can take place in a fairly straightforward manner; where they clash, learning may be experienced in a negative way.

Early research on child-rearing practices often focused on maladaptive responses to school and helped explain the relative lack of success of children from nonmainstream families. A more positive approach was proposed by Manuel Ramirez and Alfredo Castañeda (1974). While granting that families of different cultural groups employ different child-rearing practices and that these practices influence children's learning in school, Ramirez and Castañeda suggested that, rather than expect families to do all the changing, schools too needed to change by responding to the different ways of learning that children bring to school. The child-rearing styles of caregivers from diverse cultures, according to these researchers, resulted in different *learning styles*, or diverse ways of receiving and processing information. They concluded that the only appropriate response of schools in a pluralistic and democratic society was to develop learning environments that were, in their words, "culturally democratic," that is, environments that reflect the learning styles of all students within them. This perspective was radically different from the usual expectation that all children arrive at school with the same ways of learning. Given the notion reviewed in Chapter 2 that schools create and perpetuate inequality through policies and practices, including the pressure to assimilate, the perspective suggested by Ramirez and Castañeda makes a good deal of sense.

Ramirez and Castañeda were among the first researchers to suggest that all learning styles, not just the analytic style generally favored by majority-group students and practiced in most schools, are suitable for academic work. They built on the theories of Herman Witkin (1962) that people have either a *field independent* learning style (usually defined as preferring to learn in an analytic matter with materials devoid of social context) or a *field dependent* learning style (understood as favoring highly social and contextualized settings). Based on their research with children of various cultural backgrounds, they concluded that European American children tend to be field independent, and Mexican American, American Indian, and African American children tend to be field *sensitive,* the term they substituted for the more negatively charged *dependent.* They suggested that students need to be provided environments where they can learn according to their preferred style, while also becoming *bicognitive,* that is, comfortable and proficient in both styles.

The proposition that students from diverse backgrounds use various approaches to learning and that schools need to make accommodations for them represented a considerable advance in both the theory and practice of education. Nevertheless, much of the learning style research can be criticized on a number of grounds. First, there is no agreement on the number or range of learning styles that actually exist. Second, this research has inclined toward overdetermination, basing students' learning styles almost exclusively on their culture when in fact we know that learning is a much more complex matter. Third, some assessment and instructional strategies and adaptations developed as a result of the learning style research have been overly mechanical and technical, although they might never have been intended to be used as such. For instance, one of the few reviews that looked seriously at the outcomes of adapting instruction to the visual learning style presumably favored by American Indian children concluded that there was virtually no evidence that such adaptations resulted in greater learning (Kleinfeld & Nelson, 1991).

An example of how this kind of research has been poorly used can be found in professional development workshops or education texts that provide lists of "attributes" of students of particular cultural backgrounds based on the learning styles they are reputed to have ("Vietnamese children are . . . " or "African American children learn best when . . . "). All too often, the effect of such categorizations is that the existing stereotypes of children from particular backgrounds become even more rigid. Moreover, categorizing students' learning styles based on race or ethnicity can veer dangerously close to the racist implications drawn from distinctions on IQ tests (Herrnstein & Murray, 1994; Jensen, 1969). For instance, Asa Hilliard (1989) has voiced grave reservations about the use of the term *learning style* as an excuse for low expectations on the part of teachers, and on poor instruction based on these expectations. In this case, the remedy can be worse than the illness itself.

In spite of the theoretical and implementation problems with learning style research, Donna Deyhle and Karen Swisher (1997) suggest that ethnographic studies can prove to be insightful in providing evidence concerning the significance of child-rearing values on learning styles. In these studies, students' learning styles are gleaned from many hours of observation and analysis. Deyhle and Swisher believe that becoming aware of students' preferred ways of learning can be useful, although it is by no means sufficient to guarantee that appropriate environments are created for student learning. Their reasonable conclusion is: "Knowledge of group tendencies presents a framework through which to observe and understand individual behaviors" (p. 151). As we reviewed in Chapter 1, cross-cultural psychologists have developed a more conceptually sophisticated explanation for how families of diverse cultural backgrounds influence learning and the cognitive development of their children through their child-rearing practices and interactions, and based on the kind of ecological system in which they live (Greenfield, 1994; Greenfield & Cocking, 1994).

Although research in learning styles has brought the issue of culture and its possible impact on learning to the forefront, the field is fraught with conflict due to criticisms such as those mentioned above, among others (for an analysis of these, see Irvine & York, 1995). One way to ameliorate what can be the overly deterministic tone of this research is to speak of *learning preferences* instead of *styles*. In this case, the implication is that numerous factors influence how people learn, and that in fact all individuals differ in some ways from one another in how they learn. In any event, learning styles or preferences by themselves, although providing an important piece of the puzzle for understanding student learning, do not adequately explain the vastly different outcomes of student achievement. Others have suggested a shift in focus from *learning style* to *cultural style* or *teaching style* (Hilliard, 1989/90; Ladson-Billings, 1992).

## Cultural, Linguistic, and Communication Discontinuities Between Home and School

The discontinuities experienced by students whose cultures and/or languages differ substantially from the mainstream, and how these might interfere with learning, are questions that have gained enormous significance in the past 2 decades, especially by educators using an anthropological perspective. One such theory, the *communication process explanation* (Erickson, 1993), is based on the fact that although students may be socialized to learn in particular ways at home, these cultural and communication patterns may be missing in the school setting. The research undergirding this argument has generally been ethnographic in nature, and it has been based on months, and sometimes years, of extensive fieldwork and analysis.

Two significant early studies were groundbreaking in the field and serve as examples of this theory. Susan Philips's (1982) ethnographic research among American Indian schoolchildren on the Warm Springs Reservation in Oregon concluded that the core values with which the children were raised—including harmony, internal locus of control, shared authority, voluntary participation, and cooperation—often were violated in the school setting. For instance, she found that the children did poorly in classroom contexts that demanded individualized performance and emphasized competition. However, they became motivated learners when the context did not require them to perform in public and when cooperation was valued over competition, as in student-directed group projects. Given the assessment practices of most schools, these students were at a disadvantage because their learning was not always demonstrated in the kinds of behaviors expected of them, such as individual performance and recitation.

Philips's insights were a powerful challenge to previous deficit-based conclusions that American Indian children were "slow," "inarticulate," or "culturally deprived," and that they were therefore incapable of learning. Her research provided an alternative, culturally based explanation for the apparent discontinuities between home and school. In a similar vein, Shirley Brice Heath's (1983) research in a working-class African American community she called "Trackton" is a compelling example of cultural and communication discontinuities. In her research, she discovered that the questioning rituals in which parents and other adults in the community engaged with children were not preparing them adequately for the kinds of activities they would face in schools. Furthermore, when Heath observed White middle-class teachers in their own homes, she found that their questions, both to their own children and to their students, differed a great deal from the kinds of questions that the parents of children in Trackton asked. Teachers' questions invariably pulled attributes such as size, shape, or color out of context and asked children to name them. Hugh Mehan (1991) has called these questions "mini-lessons" that prepare children from middle-class homes for the kinds of questions they will hear in school.

On the other hand, the parents of the children from Trackton asked them questions about whole events or objects, and about their uses, causes, and effects. Parents often asked their children questions that were linguistically complex and that required analogical comparisons and complex metaphors rather than "correct" answers out of context. The result of these differences was a lack of communication among teachers and students in the school. Students who at home would be talkative and expressive would become silent and unresponsive in school because of the nature of the questions that teachers asked; this behavior led teachers to conclude that the children were slow to learn or deficient in language skills. It was only through their fieldwork as ethnographers of their own classrooms that the teachers became aware of the differences in questioning rituals and of the kinds of questions that their students' families and other adults in the community asked. Teachers were then able to change some of their questioning procedures to take advantage of the skills that the children already had, building on these skills to then ask more traditional "school" questions. The results were striking, as students became responsive and enthusiastic learners, a dramatic departure from their previous behavior.

A. Wade Boykin (1994) also has reviewed the implications of cultural discontinuities for African American students. According to him, in general Black students in the United States practice a cultural style that he calls *Afrocultural expression*. This style emphasizes spirituality, harmony, movement, verve, communalism, oral tradition, and expressive individualism, elements that are either missing, downplayed, or disparaged in most mainstream classrooms. As a result, there are often incompatibilities between Black students' cultural styles and the learning environment in most schools, and Black students may end up losing out. The problem is not that their styles are incompatible with learning, but rather that these styles are not valued in most classrooms as legitimate conduits for learning.

These examples provide evidence that home cultures and native languages sometimes get in the way of student learning *not because of the nature of the home cultures or native languages themselves, but rather because they do not conform to the way that schools define learning.* On the other hand, this cultural mismatch is not inevitable: There are numerous examples of research in the past 2 decades that has concluded that culture and language can work in a mutual and collaborative manner to promote learning rather than obstruct it. Teachers and schools, not only students, need to accommodate to cultural and linguistic differences. According to Margaret Gibson (1991), schooling itself may contribute unintentionally to the educational problems of bicultural students by pressuring them to assimilate against their wishes. Maintaining their language and culture is a far healthier response on the part of young people than adopting an oppositional identity that may effectively limit the possibility of academic achievement.

Other research has confirmed the benefits of maintaining a cultural identification. For instance, in her research among Navajo students, Donna Deyhle (1992) found that those who came from the most traditional Navajo homes, spoke their native language, and participated in traditional religious and social activities were among the most academically successful students in school. Similar findings have been reported for students from other cultural groups as well. A study of Cambodian refugee children by the Metropolitan Indochinese Children and Adolescent Service found that the more they adapted their behavior to fit in with mainstream U.S. culture, the more their emotional adjustment suffered (National Coalition, 1988). Another study of Southeast Asian students found a significant connection between grades and culture; that is, higher grade point averages correlated with the maintenance of traditional values, ethnic pride, and close social and cultural ties with members of the same ethnic group (Rumbaut & Ima, 1987). Likewise, based on her extensive research with adolescent students of color of diverse ethnic backgrounds, Jean Phinney (1993) determined that adolescents who have explored their ethnicity and are clear about its importance in their lives are more likely to be better adjusted than those who have not.

### Responses to Cultural Discontinuities

Because many children from diverse cultural backgrounds experience school failure, we need to address how cultural discontinuities between students' homes and their schools affect learning. There have been a number of attempts to adapt learning environments to more closely match the native cultures of students. Responding to cultural discontinuities takes many forms and can mean anything from developing specific instructional strategies to providing environments that are totally culturally responsive.

Culturally responsive education, an approach based on using students' cultures as an important source of their education, can go a long way in improving the education of students whose cultures and backgrounds have been maligned or omitted in schools. This approach offers crucial insights for understanding the lack of achievement of students from culturally subordinated groups. One of the best known of these is KEEP (the Kamehameha Elementary Education Program) in Hawaii (Au, 1980). KEEP was established because cultural discontinuities in instruction were identified as a major problem in the poor academic achievement of Native Hawaiian children. Educational modifications in KEEP included changing from a purely phonics approach to one emphasizing comprehension, from individual work desks to work centers with heterogeneous groups, and from high praise to more culturally appropriate practices, including indirect and group praise. The KEEP culturally compatible K-3 language arts approach has met with great success in student learning and achievement. Similar positive conclusions have been reached when the cultures of students of diverse backgrounds have been used as a bridge to the dominant culture (Abi-Nader, 1993; Hollins, King, & Hayman, 1994; Irvine, 1997; Ladson-Billings, 1994).

In spite of the promising approaches highlighted by this research, a number of serious problems remain. For one, culturally responsive pedagogy sometimes is based on a static view of culture that may even verge on the stereotypical. Students of particular backgrounds may be thought of as walking embodiments of specific cultural values and behaviors, with no individual personalities and perspectives of their own. An unavoidable result is that entire cultures are identified by a rigid set of characteristics. Culturally congruent approaches, applied uncritically and mechanistically, fall into the same trap as monocultural education; that is, they may be based on an essentialist notion of culture that assumes that all students from the same cultural background learn in the same way. If this is the case, pedagogy and curriculum become, in the words of Erickson (1990), "cosmetically relevant" rather than "genuinely transformative" (p. 23).

A result of essentialist notions is that the diversity of individual students' experiences and identities may be overlooked, and their culture may be used to homogenize all students of the same group. This happens, for instance, when teachers make comments such as, "Korean children prefer to work on their own," because such statements deny the individual idiosyncrasies, preferences, and outlooks of particular students and their families. All cultures operate in synergy, creating new and different forms that borrow from and lend substance to one another. In other words, the multifaceted, contested, and complex nature of culture sometimes is not taken into consideration in culturally responsive pedagogy. Because cultures never exist in a pristine state, untouched by their context, any approach to meaningful and effective pedagogy needs to take into account how students' languages, cultures, and other differences exist within, and are influenced by, mainstream U.S. culture as well as by other subcultures with which they come into contact.

A culturally responsive stance sometimes considers those of nonmajority backgrounds to exist in complete contrast to the majority population, but this is rarely true. I recall, for example, the reaction of a young African American student after he visited an American Indian community in the Northeast: "They have VCRs!" he exclaimed in surprise tinged with disappointment. This young man attended a progressive alternative school with a multicultural curriculum with which I was associated many years ago. The school was a wonderful place in many ways, and the curriculum emphasized positive and liberatory aspects of the histories and cultures of people of color. Nevertheless, we were not immune from falling victim to developing our own static, albeit more positive, romanticized vision of what people of diverse cultures were like. In this case, in preparing students for the trip, we somehow had managed to remove all vestiges of materialistic contemporary life from Indigenous people, and the result was that the children developed an unrealistic and partial view of an entire group of people.

These caveats concerning cultural discontinuities also were explored in research with a Mexicano community by Olga Vasquez, Lucinda Pease-Alvarez, and Sheila Shannon (1994). In a number of case studies of children from this community, they found that a great deal of *convergence* existed between the children's home and school language interaction patterns. Although these researchers did not question that cultural discontinuities exist, they rejected the suggestion that home–school discontinuity can predict the success or failure of an entire cultural group. Instead, based on research in which they saw firsthand the students' multiple linguistic and cultural skills, they urged educators to consider "the complexity of their students' experiences in a multilayered network of cultures and reference groups" (p. 187).

Finally, a focus on cultural discontinuities alone may hide the structural inequalities described in Chapter 2 with which so many students, especially those who live in poverty, contend on a daily basis. It is therefore necessary to look beyond cultural responsiveness alone to help explain student academic success.

## CONCLUSION: IMPLICATIONS

What are the implications for teachers and schools concerning the links among language, culture, and learning? I would suggest that at least three issues need to be emphasized.

1. *Students' identification with, and maintenance of, their native culture and language can have a positive influence on learning.* The judgment that cultural identification and maintenance are important for academic achievement is not new, but it bears repeating because it is still far from accepted in most schools and classrooms. Research in the past 2 decades consistently has found that students who are allowed and encouraged to identify with their native languages and cultures in their schools and communities can improve their learning. This finding is also a direct and aggressive challenge to the assimilationist perspective that learning can take place only after one has left behind the language and culture of one's birth. Research in this area has made it clear that students' cultures are important to them and their families. However, maintaining them is also problematic because the identities of bicultural students generally are disparaged or dismissed by schools.

2. *The role of the teacher as cultural accommodator and mediator is fundamental in promoting student learning.* In much of the research reviewed, it

has become apparent that teachers have a great deal to do with whether and how students learn. Consequently, teachers' role as cultural mediators in their students' learning becomes even more urgent. In many cases, teachers need to teach children how to "do school" in order to be academically successful. This kind of mediation may not be necessary for the children of middle-class and culturally mainstream families, but very often it is required for students whose families do not have the high-status cultural capital required for academic success. Teachers need to support this kind of learning while at the same time affirming the cultures and languages that children bring to school as viable and valuable resources for learning.

3. *A focus on cultural differences in isolation from the broader school and societal context will likely not lead to increased learning or empowerment.* Personal and institutional accommodations to student differences need to be in place in order for students to become successful learners. Obviously, these accommodations require drastic shifts in teachers' beliefs and attitudes, and in schools' policies and practices: Instead of simply tinkering with a few cultural additions to the curriculum or adopting a new teaching strategy, a wholesale transformation of schools is in order if we are serious about affording all students an equal chance to learn.

# 4

# Who Does the Accommodating?
# Institutional Transformation
# to Promote Learning

> Hegemonic practices are not only ramified throughout the general society
> and in the local community outside the school; they are also alive and well
> inside the classroom. They permeate and frame the school experience of
> students who are members of stigmatized social groups.
> —Frederick Erickson, "Transformation and School Success"

THIS CHAPTER BEGINS with the question, "Who does the accommodating?"
because it seeks to challenge the prevailing assumption that it is only
students from marginalized groups and their families—those who are
ethnically, racially, linguistically, socioeconomically, and in other ways
different from what is considered the "mainstream"—who should always
conform in order to be successful in school. I propose an alternative perspective: that in order to advance student learning, teachers and schools
also need to change in substantive and significant ways.

In this chapter, I suggest that schools need to undergo an *institutional*
transformation because their policies and practices, as we saw in Chapter 2, consistently have favored some students over others. That is,
schools have never really provided the "level playing field" that they have
claimed. In subsequent chapters, I will consider how multicultural education can provide the basis for teachers to undergo an equally profound
*personal* transformation. The distinction between personal and institutional change is often arbitrary. It is in the *interplay* between personal and
institutional change that substantive transformation occurs. For instance,

teachers' attitudes and beliefs about their students' families can influence a school's policies on parent involvement either positively or negatively. Likewise, an institutional commitment to do away with tracking can have a profound impact on teachers' attitudes about the nature of intelligence, again in either a positive or a negative way. In both cases, the goals or intentions behind specific changes, and the processes in which they unfold, are paramount in determining the impact they can have. For the sake of clarity, I have separated personal from institutional transformation, but I urge readers to understand these processes as interdependent and as quite a bit more untidy than I indicate here.

In what follows, I will first revisit the concept of "accommodation" as it applies to bicultural students. Next, I will discuss curriculum and pedagogy as beliefs and values rather than as specific content or strategies. I will review a number of classroom-based and institutional accommodations that can promote the learning of bicultural students. Throughout the chapter, I incorporate numerous excerpts from teachers' journals to highlight the issues discussed.

## REVISITING "ACCOMMODATION"

The question, "Who does the accommodating," springs from the notion, developed in important research by Margaret Gibson (1987), that culturally marginalized groups who are successful in school have found a way to achieve "accommodation without acculturation." Specifically, Gibson analyzed the case of Punjabi Indian students in the United States, and she found that as a group they were academically successful in spite of barriers related to social class, lack of parental education, nonexistent English language skills when they began their education, racism on the part of peers and even teachers, and a culture that makes them very different from dominant-group students. Punjabi students are urged by their parents to maintain their native language and their cultural values and practices; that is, to "accommodate without acculturating" to the dominant culture. According to Gibson, Punjabi students as a group are academically successful because they are willing to "play the school game" by the rules of the dominant group in order to get a good education. In effect, they view their academic success as an additional set of skills, rather than as a replacement for their traditional culture.

The notion that students could accommodate to the culture of the school without buckling under the pressure to completely acculturate represented a significant move forward from the conventional wisdom that total assimilation was needed in order to succeed in school. Indeed, this research presented a new and more humane model of academic success than previously had been in place, that is, that students needed to deny their families and cultures in order to succeed in school. But in spite of the progress that this thinking signaled in the education of bicultural students, I will push this concept of "accommodation without assimilation" further by submitting that *accommodation cannot be a one-way process.* That is, although those whom John Ogbu (1987) has called "voluntary minorities" (such as the Punjabi students in Margaret Gibson's research above) may be able to accommodate to the culture of U.S. schools, the same may not be true, for both historical and sociopolitical reasons, of involuntary minorities such as African Americans, American Indians, Mexican Americans, and Puerto Ricans. I would argue that having to undergo a unilateral accommodation places an undue burden on some bicultural students and their families.

A one-way accommodation results in at least two outcomes of dubious merit: First, it sets up some bicultural students as impossible models of success for others to follow, effectively exacerbating hostility and competition (this is especially the case with Asians, often identified as "model minorities" [see Lee, 1996]); and second, it allows teachers and schools to avoid considering their own practices as conspiring to create failure. Rather than continue to tolerate dismal academic failure of some students generation after generation, we need to advance a strategy that contests asymmetrical accommodation.

But what does it mean for teachers and schools to accommodate to the lives of children? In one of my courses, I ask the participants, many of them teachers, to write about what they do, if anything, to make their classrooms more welcoming for all students. Mary Ginley, who took the course with me in 1992, wrote about accommodation in her work with young children. Mary is a gifted teacher; in fact, she was "Massachusetts Teacher of the Year" in 1997. She taught in a working-class and overwhelmingly Puerto Rican school for many years and now teaches in a largely privileged European American suburb.

At the same time that I asked participants to write about accommodation, I also posed a problem on which I asked them to reflect and write: A new student from India comes to your school and on her first day in the cafeteria, she begins eating rice with her hands. Several of the children make fun of her. You are her teacher and you happen to be in the lunchroom when this happens. What do you do? In the following excerpt, Mary responded to both of these questions. Interestingly, she did not connect these issues until the end.

## START FROM WHERE KIDS ARE AT

*By Mary Ginley*

The issue of accommodation has been one I've been looking at for years. As a kindergarten teacher with 20 or more young children in my care year after year, it was very clear to me early on that I couldn't expect 5-year-olds to do all the accommodating. My philosophy has always been—start from where they are and go together to someplace else. Still, when more and more Puerto Rican children entered my classroom, I had trouble starting from where they were, because I didn't *know* where they were and it was hard for them to tell me. We talked, we shared, we learned some Spanish, and we sang some songs. But essentially, very little changed in my classroom. I wanted every child to feel safe, to feel comfortable and valued—but I'm not sure it really happened. I think I said many of the right words, but I don't think that was enough.

O.K. A child from India begins to eat rice with her hands in the lunchroom. Terrific—now what happens? For a while, I'd encourage her to eat according to her custom and encourage the children to accept her and begin to learn that we all don't eat the same way. However, when in Rome . . . Of course I would teach her how we eat in American lunchrooms. And then I would explore with the class the concept of good manners—What are they? Are they the same all over the world? Depending on the age of the children, either I would ask each child to choose a country and do a research project on the manners, behaviors, and customs of that country or, with younger children, I would look at different customs and ways of eating through children's books or films. (9.14.92)

After we talked about the situation concerning the Indian girl during the following week's class, Mary revisited the question:

The rice issue—the lesson learned: Always ask myself, Who does the accommodating? In my notes, this question is IMMEDIATELY before the story of the child with the rice and I still missed it! It's amazing how middle-class and narrow I can be—even when I'm trying to be sensitive to the needs of others. I suppose I'm one of those well-meaning teachers who devalues children without even realizing it. I have a lot to learn.

The kind of self-reflection in which Mary engaged is a model for other teachers. The surprise and disappointment she felt when she realized that she had failed to connect two very related issues is what allowed her to go back, rethink, and ultimately grow in her awareness that accommodating to differences is not always comfortable or easy to do.

Before proceeding, I want to make it clear that I am not proposing a simplistic reversal of the equation; that is, I am not suggesting that schools and teachers need to do *all* the accommodating to students and their families. To suggest this would be both fanciful and unrealistic. It is not the purpose of schools to preserve students' home cultures and languages as if they were pristine and unchanging artifacts, or as if they existed in isolation from our highly complex, industrialized, technological, and culturally pluralistic society. There is no question, for example, that all students in the United States need to learn English, that they need to be instructed in the culture of schools, or that they can benefit from developing a critical bicultural identity as a strategy of accommodation. There is also no question that accommodations such as these can be personally painful and difficult, although at the same time expansive and liberating. Nevertheless, there is no reason why cultural, linguistic, and other accommodations need to be made *at the expense of losing their identities*. As we have seen in previous chapters, this is too high a price to pay for academic success.

What I am proposing is an *additive* or multicultural form of identity, much as Lambert (1975) suggested *additive bilingualism* in terms of language. It seems to me that this approach is in the long run a far healthier and more effective strategy for learning than is a *subtractive* bilingualism or multiculturalism. Hence, following the lead of Jim Cummins (1996), I prefer to think of teaching and learning not as an accommodation— which inevitably implies loss rather than gain—but rather as a *negotiation* among students and their families, and teachers and schools. It must be, however, a negotiation that is mutually defined, constructed, and achieved.

## CURRICULUM AND PEDAGOGY AS BELIEFS AND VALUES

As we have been reminded time and again, the pedagogy in most U.S. classrooms has remained substantially unchanged for over a century. John Goodlad (1984), in extensive research in secondary schools, found that textbooks were often a substitute for pedagogy, that teaching methods tended to be mechanistic and unengaging, and that memorization and rote learning were favored consistently over creativity and critical thinking. In like manner, Larry Cuban's (1993) exhaustive study of how teachers have taught over the past century concluded that teacher-centered instruction has persevered by and large as the basic strategy of instruction in spite of progressive educational movements to promote student-centered teaching.

Teachers are not the sole generators and advocates of uninspired pedagogy; often they are the victims of school policies and practices that restrict their freedom of choice by allowing few innovations, or of societal contexts that are difficult to change. As a consequence, the context in which teachers work, through the ideologies that are reproduced in schools and society, is also responsible for the pedagogies practiced in classrooms. A recent case in point has been the hysteria over whole language versus phonics, where very often educators are the last to be consulted concerning what makes pedagogical sense in the classroom. Everyone from linguists to politicians have joined the fray, resulting in the press and politicians in California and elsewhere declaring whole language a failure, as well as the astonishing attempt on the part of state legislatures to pass laws prohibiting the use of whole language in both teacher preparation programs and public school classrooms (Berliner, 1997). To say that this climate does not place a chill on the choices that teachers make in their classrooms is to be disingenuous. It is clear, then, that rigid ideologies inside and outside of schools work hand in hand to create pedagogical stagnation.

There is also a tendency for teachers and teacher educators alike to think of curriculum as a product-in-place and as an unchanging truth that must be passed on unquestioningly. But as Michael Apple (1993) reminds us, "The curriculum is never simply a neutral assemblage of knowledge, somehow appearing in the texts and classrooms of a nation" (p. 222). Rather, curriculum is always selective, partial, and, therefore, ultimately biased. Because the knowledge selected for inclusion in the curriculum as a rule reflects the perspectives, tastes, and world views of powerful groups in society, the lives and concerns of the groups that are most marginalized are for the most part missing from the curriculum. But the process of curriculum selection is not linear, simple, or automatic, but convoluted, complex, and contested. That curriculum has been contested hotly in the recent past is apparent in the "canon debates" and other broad-based challenges to established knowledge all the way from pre-schools through university settings. These debates confirm the fact that developing, selecting, adapting, and implementing curriculum are inherently *political* processes, although they commonly are thought of as devoid of any particular political intention. In referring to the literary canon, Henry Louis Gates, Jr., (1992) has captured perfectly the irony of this situation:

> That people can maintain a straight face while they protest the irruption of politics into something that has always been political from the beginning— well, it says something about how remarkably successful official literary histories have been in presenting themselves as natural and neutral objects, untainted by worldly interests. (p. 33)

Many students are subjected to stale teaching and irrelevant curricula, but it is especially children of color, those who live in poverty, speak a native language other than English, or attend poorly financed schools who are affected disproportionately and negatively by pedagogy and curriculum. This is true for several reasons. First, frequently these students are tracked into low-level ability groups (Oakes, 1990) and very often they are thought by their teachers to need "basic skills" before moving on to more interesting knowledge and creative tasks (Haberman, 1991). Second, teachers in poorly funded schools tend to be the least experienced and therefore they usually have scant knowledge of alternative pedagogical strategies or current curriculum thinking (Darling-Hammond, 1995). Finally, in the case of students with limited English proficiency, the singular focus on their learning English results in overshadowing all other considerations of curriculum and pedagogy.

Although I hold to the conviction that there are no "special" pedagogies or curricula for bicultural students, I nonetheless believe that there *are* particular values, beliefs, or attitudes that need to undergird pedagogy and curriculum. This is particularly important for those students who have been subjected to what Martin Haberman (1991) has termed "a pedagogy of poverty," or a basic urban style based on memorization, rote learning, and little faith in their abilities. Yet as Jerome Bruner (1996) reminds us, "a choice of pedagogy inevitably communicates a conception of the learning process and the learner. Pedagogy is never innocent. It is a medium that carries its own message" (p. 63). Given this reality, then, it might make more sense to have teacher education courses labeled "Attitudes About . . . ," "Beliefs in . . . ," "Values Concerning . . . ," and "Ideological Frameworks" rather than the current crop labeled "Methods in . . . ," "Curriculum for . . . ," and "Instructional Frameworks."

I am not claiming that specific strategies or techniques should not be taught. But methods and materials have held an inordinately important role in teacher preparation and inservice education, resulting in an almost obsessive preoccupation with the idea that mastering particular methods or techniques will in and of itself result in better teaching or learning. Methods and techniques should, of course, be learned, but they are useless unless practiced within a framework of education for social justice.

## Teaching as a Journey

Teachers' reflections about their pedagogy can help us understand how attitudes and values frame classroom practice. They also demonstrate how teaching can be viewed as a journey. Mary Ginley, for instance, began her teaching career in the turbulent political climate of the 1960s, and as a nun serving in a convent for 9 years, she was profoundly affected by the questions and the resistance that characterized that period in our history. She wrote the following journal entry after another participant in our course did a presentation about her own transformation as a teacher.

### MY JOURNEY

*By Mary Ginley*

Arlene's presentation made me reflect on my own journey: When did I start changing? Or did I ever not change? I was always asking questions, from the very beginning. For a child brought up in a small city in western Massachusetts in the 1950s, daughter of a GE executive who negotiated the sale of missiles to the government, sometimes I wonder how I ever came to where I am. I know my parents can't imagine where I came from. My sisters aren't like this. My brother isn't either. Maybe it was the convent. I wasn't a very good nun but in some ways it was an interesting place to be in the late 1960s, where, along with a few other not very good nuns, I could ask questions and get used to the fact that there aren't a lot of very easy answers to the most important questions.

So I guess I never felt I had any answers, just a lot of questions. And because of that, teaching has never been easy. I never have felt comfortable, never had much of a stockpile of never-fail lesson plans or specific activities for curriculum. I rarely saved anything, mainly because I wasn't organized but also because I always figured next year's group would be different and have different needs. I guess from the very beginning I took my cues from the kids. It made life interesting but it wasn't a very efficient way to go about it. If I had been more organized and systematic I'd have some good lessons and activities stored away, a bag of tricks I could pull out from year to year instead of constantly reinventing the wheel every

year and killing myself every week coming up with meaningful activities to go with particular units. It definitely has its benefits: My
life is never boring and I've learned a lot along the way. But I know
I could be a bit more structured. It really is a bit extreme to throw
away planbooks at the end of the year. There actually might be
some good material in them. I think maybe I threw everything
away because nothing seemed good enough to save. So all I have
for my over 20 years of teaching is a thousand children's books and
a few ideas in my head about how to use them and a lot of questions about what do I really want kids to learn and how do I go
about it.

Mary's reflections on her teaching practices say little about specific curricula or strategies, but volumes about her values, beliefs, and concerns
about children, and about the need for teachers to accommodate to
their students.

## A Critical Stance Concerning Pedagogy and Curriculum

Lilia Bartolomé (1994) has criticized what she terms "the methods fetish"
in most teacher preparation programs and schools. She emphasizes that
the issue of teaching should not focus on particular methodologies as
much as on the question of why culturally and politically subordinated
students in our society by and large do not succeed academically. Bartolomé argues that it is more important for teachers to know the historical
role that schools and the society in general have played in legitimating
academic failure and denying bicultural students any sense of humanity
than it is to be an expert at a particular strategy. Consequently, she asserts
that "the teacher's politically clear educational philosophy" (p. 179) is far
more important than specific methods. Jim Cummins (1996) echoes this
view when he states, "The interactions that take place between students
and teachers and among students are more central to student success
than any method for teaching literacy, or science, or math" (p. 1).
     Of course, particular instructional strategies and a humanizing peda-
gogy should not be thought of as dichotomies. A humanizing pedagogy
can successfully make use of innovative and creative methods. But there
is no set "bag of tricks" or single approach to help all students learn. What
matters most are the intentions and goals behind the pedagogy. For example, according to Jacqueline Jordan Irvine (1992), gifted teachers often
ignore and sometimes even violate what commonly may be thought of
as "principles of effective teaching." That is to say, for skilled teachers, no
strategy is sacrosanct because any strategy used in a mindless or uncritical
way will not necessarily result in increased learning. Moreover, if such

strategies fail, they may further solidify teachers' attitudes that some students are simply incapable of learning.

The very act of teaching carries with it a social and political commitment to students and to uncovering a fuller and more complicated truth. Marilyn Cochran-Smith (1991) has used the phrase "teaching against the grain" to suggest that effective teaching is not a generic skill that simply can be learned at the university and then applied to classrooms. She argues that "teaching against the grain" means looking at education critically and placing it within its historical context. Instead of a simple strategy, "teaching against the grain" challenges the idea that education is a neutral activity or a technical endeavor. To teach with this attitude takes great courage and vision because it dares to challenge official knowledge and prevailing truths about "what works."

Mary Ginley recounted an experience with her second graders in which this attitude was evident. In her classroom, Mary uses what she calls "morning questions" to initiate dialogue with students about matters both big and small. These "morning questions"—sometimes just a query about what the kids did on the weekend and at other times more critical issues—are a good example of what it means to teach against the grain.

## MORNING QUESTIONS

### By Mary Ginley

I caught the tail end of a discussion the librarian was having with my class at the end of their library period. I stood outside waiting for them to be dismissed and listened to them tell him very patiently that the Pilgrims robbed the Wampanoags' graves for food and although the Pilgrims signed treaties with them, the peace didn't last for long . . . that there was war less than 50 years after the first Thanksgiving . . . that Native Americans were driven from their homes and forced to resettle as more English came to Massachusetts. He looked a bit sick when he dismissed the kids—but he didn't say anything to me.

One of the morning questions that day was, "If you were a Wampanoag, would you have helped the Pilgrims that first winter?" We had some nos—I wasn't among them (I didn't think I could let people starve). My principal said no—you don't help your enemy when you know they will ultimately destroy you. (11.18.92)

As is clear from Mary's example, there is no one right way to answer most questions, no "politically correct" response. This scenario demonstrates that when real learning takes place, there is room for dialogue, disagreement, and the illumination of students, teachers, and others.

Another aspect of the critical stance concerning curriculum and pedagogy has been well articulated by Lisa Delpit (1988). In her work, Delpit has insisted that even progressive pedagogical strategies and approaches that at their core may be potentially empowering may nonetheless at times be inappropriate for some students. Focusing her critique in particular on whole language, Delpit has found that many teachers, especially White middle-class teachers who are unfamiliar with the culture of students of other backgrounds, tend to make assumptions about what those students need, based on limited knowledge and experience. African American teachers and other teachers who are themselves bicultural are often frustrated by the wholesale implementation of approaches such as whole language. In turn, these teachers, because of their tendency to use more traditional methods, sometimes are considered unenlightened or old-fashioned by teachers who are proponents of whole language.

María de la Luz Reyes (1992) also has criticized approaches such as whole language and process writing. She points out that, given students' differential levels of privilege and access to cultural capital, not all will necessarily benefit equally from these approaches. In the case of language-minority children, for instance, Reyes presents examples of how students' cultural and linguistic strengths sometimes are ignored when teachers implement process strategies uncritically. Yet she maintains that there is a widespread belief among proponents of such approaches that a "one-size-fits-all" pedagogy is good for all students. Although Reyes does not call for abandoning process approaches—a philosophy that she basically approves of when it is implemented more critically—she does assert that they need to be modified to increase the likelihood of success with learners of diverse backgrounds. Anne Dyson (1992) goes a step further, suggesting that although advocates of process approaches are dismayed by the rigid practices of some teachers who use them, such an outcome may be inevitable because of the theoretical and instructional distance these approaches have from the intimate realities of the lives of particular children.

In the above critiques, the question of accommodation becomes clear: That is, should students be accommodated to fit the approach, or should the approach accommodate student differences? Lizette Román, a bilingual teacher of primarily working-class and poor Latino students in a largely middle-class town, also has been frustrated with pedagogical strategies that are seen as "magical cures." In one of the courses she took with me, Lizette wrote in her journal about teaching styles that sometimes are uncritically mandated.

## PEDAGOGICAL STRATEGIES AS MAGICAL CURES

By Lizette Román

I cannot help thinking of the many approaches or teaching styles that are in vogue every so often. They are offered, and many times enforced, as if they were the magical and generic cures for all failures that happen in school, with teachers never stopping to realize that teaching is not merely a group of strategies, but a combination of ingredients. On many occasions, these "cures" do function with a particular group of children. Probably they work because they respond to the particular needs and learning styles of a particular group. I believe that more often than not these "successes" have to do with a combination of factors such as students' learning style, teachers' knowledge, and specific teaching approaches rather than the method itself. Examples of many of these techniques are cooperative learning, whole language, or phonics. These methods will always have supporters or detractors if nobody takes the time to explain that nothing works for everybody. These strategies can and should be introduced to teachers, but always keeping in mind that not all children, even those from the same cultural background, necessarily respond to one cultural learning style. Students are individuals within their group.

On many occasions, teachers who have found ways to promote and enrich their teaching feel ostracized by their school community if they dare to share that what is working for their students is not exactly the new "hit" on the market. These teachers may be culturally sensitive to the needs of their students, but they find themselves in a situation where new ideas are enforced rather than proposed or offered as just another alternative. (11.30.96)

Another critical stance regarding teaching and learning pertains to how the large purposes of education are viewed. Rather than a focus on a specific program of study or approach, progressive teachers engage in a broad-ranging emancipatory pedagogy. For instance, bell hooks (1994) recalls that in order to resist White racist ideology, Black teachers in the segregated South often viewed their teaching as a counterhegemonic act. Although they did not use this language to describe their work, their actions made it clear that they were dedicated to creating conditions in school that would empower Black students to become cultural workers and intellectuals in spite of the endless societal messages that this was an impossible task. Their work was, in essence, a political commitment.

A present-day example of teaching as liberation is found in Gloria Ladson-Billings's (1994) research on effective teachers of African American students. In reviewing the major tenets of the literacy programs of the eight teachers in her study, Ladson-Billings found that they acknowledged their role as political beings and they viewed their work with students essentially as a collective struggle against the status quo. Ladson-Billings called these teachers "culturally relevant teachers," but she resisted limiting this term to simply cultural practices. She concluded: "Culturally relevant teaching is about questioning (and preparing students to question) the structural inequality, the racism, and the injustice that exist in society" (Ladson-Billings, 1994, p. 18).

How does multicultural education fit into this project? Because all education is embedded in a particular sociopolitical context, multicultural education cannot consist simply of lesson plans that differ in content from traditional curriculum, nor can it be just new or innovative pedagogical strategies with no connection to the lives of the students with whom they are used. Multicultural education needs to be placed within a framework of empowering attitudes and beliefs rather than viewed as just pedagogy or curriculum. Without this framework, concerns about student learning can get lost. Having said this, however, it is also true that particular curricular, pedagogical, and program accommodations can make a dramatic difference in promoting the learning of students who previously have not experienced academic success. Some of these will be discussed below.

## PRINCIPLES UNDERLYING BELIEFS AND VALUES THAT HELP CREATE POSITIVE LEARNING COMMUNITIES

I agree with John Dewey's (1916) idea that learning occurs essentially in community with others. That is, the notion of *community* is at the center of learning. In spite of all the policy changes that might be made at the state level, or in a school district, or even in a single school, the education of students will change very little unless each classroom becomes a learning community. Whether we consciously create them or not, classrooms are communities and, like all communities, some are more or less effective than others. Similarly, each classroom develops a particular culture with its own values, rituals, and symbols that either welcome or reject its members. The culture that undergirds each classroom provides potent messages to students and teachers about their roles and responsibilities, talents and limitations, and future prospects.

Creating a classroom climate in which all students feel that they have good ideas, that they have a right to learn, and that they are important and worthwhile is not an easy task. In this section, we will consider some fundamental principles for building a classroom climate that promotes the learning of all students. These principles build on the strengths of students and their families, and they help create rigorous, caring, and democratic spaces for learning.

## All Students Have Talents and Strengths

There is ample evidence that some educators believe that bicultural students have few experiential or cultural strengths that can benefit their education. Teachers consider them to be "walking sets of deficiencies" (Nieto, 1994), or "culturally deprived" just because they speak a language other than English as their native language, or because they have just one parent, or because of their social class, race, gender, or ethnicity. Rather than begin with this deficit view of students, it makes sense to begin with a more positive and, in the end, more complete view of students and their families, and to accommodate school policies and practices to reflect these positive beliefs.

There is no question that many students cope on a daily basis with complex and difficult problems. Unfortunately, these problems sometimes are used as a rationalization by schools and teachers to have low expectations of what students are capable of learning. Just the opposite should be the case: Because schools in our society have been expected historically to provide an equal and equitable education for all students— not just those who have no problems in their lives or who fit the image of successful students due to the privileged position of their race, social class, gender, or native language—schools remain the last hope for youngsters from nonmainstream backgrounds.

Mary Ginley wrote in her journal about the limitations of teachers who do not know how to build on the strengths of their students, especially when the students' families ordinarily are not held in high regard in schools and society.

### BEING NICE IS NOT ENOUGH

*By Mary Ginley*

Every child needs to feel welcome, to feel comfortable. School is a foreign land to most kids (where else in the world would you spend time circling answers and filling in the blanks?), but the more dis-

tant a child's culture and language are from the culture and language of school, the more at risk that child is. A warm, friendly,
helpful teacher is nice but it isn't enough. We have plenty of warm
friendly teachers who tell the kids nicely to forget their Spanish and
ask mommy and daddy to speak to them in English at home; who
give them easier tasks so they won't feel badly when the work becomes difficult; who never learn about what life is like at home or
what they eat or what music they like or what stories they have
been told or what their history is. Instead, we smile and give them
a hug and tell them to eat our food and listen to our stories and
dance to our music. We teach them to read with our words and
wonder why it's so hard for them. We ask them to sit quietly and
we'll tell them what's important and what they must know to "get
ready for the next grade." And we never ask them who they are
and where they want to go. (10.7.92)

One way to find out who they are and where they want to go is by
using students' native discourse in school policies and practices. Discourse
here refers not only to different languages, but to any communication
system that does not conform with a society's dominant and high-status
communication system. It can refer to African American students who
speak Black English or who use a narrative style different from the mainstream, as well as to Appalachian students with a rich oral tradition that is
unacknowledged in school settings (Bennett, 1991; Smitherman, 1994).
When students reach the schoolhouse door and their native discourse is
dismissed as inappropriate for further learning, they learn to perceive the
school and home as irreconcilable environments. In what follows, I will
focus specifically on native-language instruction as a case study of a policy
that reflects an alternative to this kind of thinking.

Because it challenges the historical assimilative goal of schooling in
the United States, native-language instruction has been contested hotly
since it reappeared on the educational scene in 1968 (Arias & Casanova,
1993; Crawford, 1992; Ovando & Collier, 1998). Despite its proven effectiveness in promoting student learning, bilingual education has been accused of everything from serving as a jobs program for Latino and other
language-minority professionals, to posing a terrorist threat to our survival as a nation (see Crawford, 1992, for a comprehensive history). The
very thought that children in schools in the United States could be using
a language other than English to learn has enraged some citizens and
politicians, as we have seen in recent attempts to impose "English Only"
and to do away with bilingual education programs. The positive effect of
bilingual education on student achievement has been largely overshad-

owed by these reactions. The opposition to bilingual education gets in the way of promoting student learning because it springs from a political climate in which the very knowledge of languages other than English is suspect. According to Luis Moll (1992):

> This is also a context where the obsession of speaking English reigns supreme—as if the children were somehow incapable of learning that language well, or if the parents and teachers were unaware of the importance of English in U.S. society—and usually at the expense of other educational or academic matters. (pp. 20–21)

When the focus on learning English is disconnected from learning in general, the result is that the strengths and talents of students that could be used in the service of their education are wasted. These strengths, in the case of language-minority students, include the knowledge and use of their native languages. But in a climate where languages other than English are viewed as problems, strengths are converted into deficits. Monolingual speakers of languages other than English are then thought of as deficient in English, rather than as fluent in another language. And because deficits need to be "fixed," the remedy often becomes the immediate replacement of the student's native language with English. Because of the negative status of the native language, the bilingual program itself is developed as a compensatory program that is not quite as good as the "mainstream" program. As a consequence, bilingual teachers often feel alienated from the rest of the staff, as if they were less competent than other teachers. Little wonder, then, that mainstream teachers as well as parents learn to see the bilingual program as a way station until "real learning" can begin. Lizette Román wrote in her journal about this.

## PERCEPTIONS OF THE BILINGUAL PROGRAM
### By Lizette Román

Unfortunately, most bilingual programs exist because they are mandated by law, not because they are perceived as a necessity by many school systems. The main problem that we bilingual teachers face every day is the misconception that mainstream teachers, principals, and even entire school systems have about bilingual education. These misconceptions affect even the purchasing of school materials in Spanish, since the program is not seen as a priority. As a consequence, in many school districts bilingual education is doubly disadvantaged, first because it is seen as remedial and, second, because little attention is paid to it.

Many mainstream teachers and administrators see bilingual education as a remediation program and do not validate what bilingual teachers do in their classrooms even when what they are teaching is part of the same curriculum. They perceive the knowledge of another language as a "learning problem" or as a handicap toward mainstreaming students. The majority think that there must be something wrong with these children who cannot perform well in English. As soon as the children transfer out of the bilingual program, these teachers believe that *this* is the moment when the learning of these children starts. The perception of the majority distorts the importance and the purpose of bilingual education. It extends to bilingual children and their parents. Bilingual children and their parents sense that their language places them in a program where they are perceived to be inferior to the rest of the children. What isolates children in the bilingual program is not the way the program is conducted, but the perceptions the majority has about people who speak a language different from the mainstream. (10.9.96)

What happens when teachers and schools build on, rather than tear down, the native discourses of their students? In an extensive review of related literature, Eugene García (1993) reached these conclusions based on the research concerning the use of children's native language in teaching:

- Time spent on learning the native language has not been found to be "time lost" in developing English.
- There is no cognitive cost to developing multilingualism.
- Particularly for children who may be at risk for reading failure, reading should be taught in the native language because it can be readily transferred to English.

More recently, in their extensive research on 42,000 language-minority children participating in various models of bilingual education throughout the United States, Wayne Thomas and Virginia Collier (1997) concluded that developmental bilingual programs, that is, programs in which the native language of students was used most extensively, were far and away the most successful in terms of promoting student achievement in all subject areas, including English; the least effective were ESL pullout programs.

A particularly effective way to use students' native-language skills, as well as to promote bilingualism as a value among monolingual children, is what has been called "two-way" bilingual education (Christian, 1994). In these programs, monolingual English speakers and students who speak a language other than English as their native language learn together in both languages. After a comprehensive review of this and other bilingual programs, David Dolson and Jan Mayer (1992) suggested that two-way programs represent a positive way to promote the learning of language-minority students while also promoting the ideals of a culturally and linguistically pluralistic society:

> Perhaps, by implementing such programs on a wider scale, we can alter, in a positive direction, the pernicious cycle of underachievement among language-minority youth. Bilingual immersion offers educators an alternative to other school programs which neglect the invaluable multilingual and crosscultural resources brought to our schools by immigrant and other language-minority pupils. (p. 152)

Two-way programs are a reminder that sometimes conditions in students' lives that might be considered barriers to learning, such as speaking a language other than English or being a member of a culturally dominated group, are not by themselves problems or roadblocks. These conditions may in fact enrich the learning of students, but often they are perceived as handicaps by an assimilationist society bent on encouraging cultural and linguistic homogeneity.

## All Students Are Capable of High Levels of Learning

If all students have important talents and strengths that can be used in the service of their learning, then it follows that all students are capable of reaching high levels of learning. But too often society's low expectations of students, based on their life situations, pose even greater barriers to success than the difficult situations themselves. For example, if students do not speak English, an assumption may be made that they are incapable of learning anything (Flores, Cousin, & Díaz, 1991); or if they do not have consistent experiences with or access to libraries, museums, or other cultural institutions considered key for preparing students for school, the assumption is that they are not "ready to learn" (Haberman, 1991).

The belief that "all students can learn," although an admirable statement, has become little more than a slogan in much of the educational reform movement. Pauline Lipman (1997) found this to be the case in a study of a school undergoing restructuring using site-based management as the major focus of change. She discovered that newfound power within the building among the primarily White teaching staff did not affect to any great degree the deficit beliefs teachers held about their African American students. Even in their restructuring motto, "Success for All," she found that teachers constructed success differently for diverse populations: For their White students, the teachers thought of success as academic excellence, whereas for their African American students, especially those perceived to be discipline problems, success was defined as "feeling good about school, adjusting to rules and expectations, having positive interactions with adults, and attaining a sense of belonging" (p. 24). This example is not given to suggest that site-based management is a bad idea, or that teachers should not have more control over schools. But reforms such as site-based management, although they may be a positive step in creating a vital teaching environment for teachers, will not likely make a notable difference unless they are accompanied by powerful and positive beliefs and values concerning students.

In my classes, I ask participants to read a range of articles about the influence of students' social class and other differences on teachers' perceptions and classroom practices (see, for instance, Anyon, 1981; Erickson, 1987; Flores et al., 1991). Lizette Román, who taught in an impoverished city and currently teaches in a largely middle-class White town, thinks about these issues a great deal. In this journal entry, she reflected on the outcome that teachers' negative perceptions can have on students such as hers.

### SOCIAL CLASS, LANGUAGE, AND LEARNING

By Lizette Román

Many of the teachers who work in working-class schools do not belong to the same social class as their students. If the teacher is not understanding and respectful toward the needs of students from different social classes, his or her social class values can interfere or clash with those of their students. Prejudgments and misconceptions about students can get in the way, consequently influencing the teacher's expectations. If there is no empathy between teachers and students, there will be no connection and no effective learning will take place.

By no means do I intend to generalize that all teachers from backgrounds different from their students will have lower expectations of them. Ultimately, a teacher who takes pride in her work will have high expectations of herself and her students regardless of the students' social class. Unfortunately, as a number of studies point out, school knowledge is affected by social class. For a teacher who cares, it is an enormous and stressful job, especially if she teaches in a lower social class community because the low expectations of a whole school permeate through the self-esteem of these children. That teacher could spend a whole year trying to heighten expectations and working to raise the students' self-esteem. Gradually, if lucky, she will see an improvement in the students. Next year, she will be crossing her fingers that the new teacher will care as much as she did for her students. Depending on the "damage" inflicted by other teachers, or by the environment in which students learned during the previous year and the amount of confidence and high expectations they gained in her classroom, students will survive the following year. (10.23.96)

If we are serious about giving all students more options for their lives, particularly students from communities that have been denied the necessary resources with which to access these options, we need to begin with the assumption that they are indeed capable, both individually and as a group. Too many students have been dismissed simply because they were not born with the material resources or family conditions that are considered important for learning.

There have been numerous examples of dramatic success when school policies and practices are changed to reflect powerful ideas about students' abilities. Consider, for example, the case of Central Park East Elementary School in East Harlem, New York, a school with a student body of overwhelmingly Latino and African American students. Deborah Meier (1995), the principal of the school, has written a stirring account of academic success among youngsters often thought incapable of such success in other settings. The school, which accepts students from the neighborhood and not from "elite" or favored groups, has documented astonishing success: An in-depth study of the first seven graduating classes of the school found that 90% earned high school diplomas, and two-thirds went on to college, nearly double the rate for the city as a whole.

Two particular policies associated with the belief that all students can learn have been found consistently to promote high levels of learning: the availability of advanced courses to populations that usually have limited access to such courses, especially bicultural and female students; and the detracking of schools (AAUW, 1992; Wheelock, 1992). In an inspiring example of the positive effects of detracking, Rosa Sheets (1995) wrote of her experience with Spanish-speaking high school students who had failed a Spanish course because the traditional textbook-driven and grammatical approach to language learning placed them at a disadvantage. Sheets decided to recruit these students into an advanced class that emphasized their roles as resources in the Spanish-language classroom. Changing from a remedial to an enrichment approach was a creative and effective strategy: Within a semester, all the original students had taken and passed the AP Spanish-language exam, earning college credit while just sophomores and juniors in high school; a year later, they passed the far more rigorous AP Spanish literature exam. Over the course of 3 years, Latinos who previously had been labeled as "at risk" in Spanish were performing no differently from students labeled as "gifted and talented" (Sheets, 1995).

Another example of how raising the expectations for more students can improve learning is EQUITY 2000, originally started in 1990 and sponsored by the College Board as a pilot program to improve the participation and learning of all students, but especially students of color, in high-status mathematics and science classes (see Gay, 1996, for a more extensive discussion). Currently operating in about 700 schools, the program now involves nearly half a million students. One of the positive results of this project has been that the number of students of all backgrounds enrolled in algebra and geometry has increased significantly. Likewise, the number of students enrolled in AP classes and taking AP exams has increased for all students, from an increase of 26% for European American students to an extraordinary increase of 371% for Puerto Rican students.

Detracking, or the elimination of rigid ability grouping, also has been found to be constructive in promoting learning by a greater number of students (see Wheelock, 1992, for numerous cases of schools that have detracked). Another outstanding example is found in a study by Hugh Mehan and his associates (1992). Based on research on San Diego's AVID (Advancement via Individual Determination), this program is an alternative to compensatory and remedial tracking for underachieving high school students, particularly those from ethnic and linguistic minority backgrounds. Not only were low-level tracks eliminated, but low- and high-achieving students were placed together in a rigorous academic program. They also were provided with strong social and academic support. The result has been that formerly low-achieving students have begun enrolling in unprecedented numbers in colleges and universities (Mehan et al., 1992). This program has built on the learning that occurs when students of diverse backgrounds work together (whether diversity is defined in terms of "ability," ethnicity, race, social class, or other differences).

## Students' Families and Communities Are Meaningful Partners in Promoting Learning

Beginning with the premise that children and their families have important talents that can promote learning has important implications for accommodating school policies and practices to the lives of students. This premise implies that teachers need to learn culturally responsive ways of teaching all of their students. For example, as Mary Ginley mentioned earlier, it is common practice in schools to try to convince parents whose native language is other than English that they should speak only English with their children. This recommendation makes little sense for at least three reasons: First, these parents often speak little English themselves and their children are thus provided with a less than adequate model of oral English; second, this practice often results in cutting off, rather than stimulating, communication between parents and children, and the result is that children's language abilities are thwarted; and third, if young people are encouraged to learn English at the expense of their native language, rather than in conjunction with it, they may lose important connections that help maintain close and loving relations with family members. In this regard, a nationwide survey of over 1,000 families for whom English was a second language found evidence of serious disruptions of family relations when young children learned English in school and lost their native language (NABE no-cost study, 1991).

A far more reasonable recommendation, and one that honors the contributions that parents can make to their children's education, is to *encourage* them to speak their native language with their children, to speak it often, and to use it consistently. In school, this means that students not only would *not* be punished for speaking their native languages, but they would be encouraged to do so in the service of their learning. A rich communicative legacy, both in school and at home, would be the result.

Luis Moll's (1992) research on incorporating "funds of knowledge" in the curriculum, that is, using the experiences and skills of all families to encourage student learning, is a more hopeful and productive way of approaching families than is the viewpoint that students have only deficits that must be repaired. One way to do this is by building on "family motifs" (Nieto & Rolón, 1997) because the significance of "family" in the education of children often is overlooked by schools. Building on family motifs, that is, on the values, traditions, and talents at the heart of a family, can be used in the service of education. Although many families of all backgrounds face tremendous challenges and negative situations, positive virtues can be found in almost all families, and using them can make the classroom an environment in which all children feel a sense of belonging. Failing to do so perpetuates the message that not everybody belongs there.

## Students Learn Best When They Are Engaged, Active, and Working in Collaboration with Others

Collaborative learning is based on several related principles, and two are especially central to our discussion here: that creating a more equal status among students of different levels of achievement can result in higher achievement for all; and that working on common problems enhances interethnic understanding and solidarity. Moreover, as Jerome Bruner (1996) has suggested, when students work together in community, they scaffold one another's learning. Although sometimes used uncritically, the benefits of collaborative learning among students of diverse backgrounds are well known (Cohen, 1994; Cohen & Lotan, 1997). Particularly effective teachers of learners of diverse backgrounds typically have developed learning communities that are collaborative rather than individualistic (Olsen & Mullen, 1990). For such teachers, learning occurs most effectively in community.

Research also highlights the benefits of small teams in promoting learning. An exceptional example is found in Philip Uri Treisman's (1992) work at UC–Berkeley. Because Treisman was concerned with the poor achievement of numerous African American students in calculus courses, he surveyed the faculty to help him figure out what was wrong. Almost without exception, the faculty sought explanations in the students themselves, ranging from their poor motivation, to lack of parental support, to poor preparation, thus exonerating faculty from any responsibility. But when he reviewed the students' backgrounds, Treisman found that their family income actually was negatively correlated with their grades in calculus; in addition, their previous math scores were also higher than their achievement in calculus would indicate. So, their backgrounds did not really explain why they should not be doing well.

When Treisman investigated more closely, he found that many African American students had few peers they could relate to at the college and, as a consequence, they studied alone. Hence, he redesigned the remedial calculus courses as an "honors workshop" open to all students; for students who were not doing well, it was a required collaboration that Treisman told them would help because their previous math scores indicated that they were ready to tackle calculus. This workshop provided students with rigorous work, often surpassing the level of the courses in which they were enrolled. Not only were all students treated as talented individuals, but they were all expected to work as a group to enhance their collective achievement. A key point is that the academic content of the course was *not* watered down; rather, it was enriched. The pedagogy, however, was improved. The result of this "honors workshop" was that African American students who took part in it eventually outperformed their White peers; in addition, only 4% of those who participated ended up getting a D or an F in the course, compared with 60% previously.

The idea of working in teams has been extended to other settings as well. For instance, Paul George and Kathy Shewey (1993), in an extensive survey of effective middle schools, found that most of them shared a number of practices, including interdisciplinary "teams." Shirley Brice Heath and Milbrey McLaughlin's (1993) research regarding youth-based organizations serving youngsters in urban areas also found that the most successful of the organizations were those that developed small, cohesive groups that engaged in "intensive, demanding, goal-focused, and rewarding work" (p. 220). The fact that students were able to relate in a more comfortable way to a "home" or "team" in both of these examples is a telling comment on how accommodations can have a direct, positive, and dramatic influence on students.

Similarly, engaging in dialogue is an important way for students to become actively engaged in school. Learning based on dialogue is most often associated with Paulo Freire, and Freire has defined dialogic education as a process in which "the object to be known is put on the table *between* the two subjects of knowing. They meet around it and through it for mutual inquiry" (Shor & Freire, 1987, p. 99). Freire continues:

> What is dialogue in this way of knowing? Precisely this connection, this epistemological relation. The object to be known in one place links the two cognitive subjects, leading them to reflect together on the object. Dialogue is the sealing together of the teacher and the students in the joint act of knowing and re-knowing the object of study. (p. 100)

Lamentably, in some situations dialogue can become little more than a technique or, worse yet, a dogma. In these cases, the assumption is made that *nothing* can be known if it is not known through dialogue, or that *everybody* must participate in order to learn. If based on the insistence that everyone must "share" in exactly the same way in order to learn, dialogue actually might prove to be counterproductive for some students—for reasons ranging from individual learning preferences to social class socialization to cultural values.

## Student Learning Is Promoted When There Is a Strong Connection to Teachers, Schools, and Learning

Growing evidence is pointing to the importance of student identification with teachers and schools in promoting learning. For instance, as reported in a survey of African American young men in four cities (Harris & Associates, 1994), a close relationship with teachers is an essential ingredient in helping students stay in school. Specifically, the young men who stayed in school reported that their teachers gave them hope for the future, while those who dropped out of school said they had much weaker personal relationships with their teachers. A study by Hollins and Spencer (1990) found similar results: High school-age African American students identified as their favorite teachers those who had positive interactions with them and who acknowledged aspects of their lives outside of the classroom.

Forging strong identification with teachers and schools is a fundamental ingredient in student learning because it helps students define schools as places that can give them an academic identity with which they can relate. The conclusion reached by Signithia Fordham and John Ogbu (1986) in their research among African American youths in a Washington, DC, high school, that academic success meant "acting White," is a reminder that a positive connection between their backgrounds and school learning had not been made. Given that academic success often is defined in ways that are alienating to bicultural students, Deborah Meier (1995) has suggested that "many kids don't want to be 'well-educated' because they can't even imagine what it is that could be 'wantable'" (p. 163). According to Claude Steele (1992), this attitude is a logical response to the presumption on the part of many U.S. educators that Black and other nonmajority-group students have background deficits that must be remediated through special programs. This attitude automatically identifies these students with substandard intellectual ability. As a result,

> For too many black students school is simply the place where, more concertedly, persistently, and authoritatively than anywhere else in society, they learn how little valued they are. (p. 78)

The role of teachers and schools is crucial in reversing this situation, and it includes several elements. Primary among them is the need for teachers to forge deep and meaningful relationships with their students. But a number of conditions make developing these relationships difficult. For one, the student body in the United States is becoming more diverse than ever, while the teacher population is becoming less so. Teachers of

European American background have had very little experience with bicultural students, and they may in fact harbor negative or stereotypical ideas about them. Further, many teacher education programs have a poor record of educating teachers for diversity (Dilworth, 1992; Ladson-Billings, 1995a; Zeichner & Hoeft, 1996). In order to develop meaningful relationships with their students, teachers first need to transform their own attitudes and beliefs about the value and worthiness of nonmajority-group students.

Nowhere is the need more evident for teachers to begin their own transformation before they can begin to help young people identify with schools. This is because teachers and schools need to make academic success what Meier called a "wantable" identity, while at the same time not disparaging or dismissing the identities with which students come to school. Part of making academic success "wantable" means teaching students to appropriate "other Discourses" (Gee, 1990). That is, to be successful, people need to learn, feel comfortable in, and claim as their own the discourses of the environments in which they function. For students, that includes the discourse of academic learning.

Also needed, according to Ricardo Stanton-Salazar (1997), are the kinds of social networks that traditionally have functioned for mainstream students as routes to privilege and power but that for the most part have been withheld from bicultural students. This process requires what he calls *institutional agents*, that is, individuals who help young people negotiate institutional resources and opportunities, including information about academic programs, career decision making and college admissions, role modeling, and emotional and moral support. It is only through these institutional agents that bicultural students, who generally do not have such resources at their disposition in their homes or communities, are able to develop the *social capital* (Bourdieu, 1986) needed for academic success. In the end, according to Stanton-Salazar, teachers who become institutional agents for their bicultural students, in effect, make a political decision: They reconceptualize their role as one that disrupts the established social order that rewards some students for simply showing up at school with a particular social capital, while punishing others who have had no such social capital given to them. These teachers challenge the status quo by actively serving as agents of support for bicultural students.

After reading an article by Jim Cummins (1986) that had a tremendous impact on her, Lizette Román reflected on the urgency for teachers to connect with their students. At the same time, she considered the limits of such connections if they were not attentive to the wider sociopolitical context.

## CONNECTING WITH STUDENTS

*By Lizette Román*

As an educator, on many occasions I have asked myself why some students seem to do better than others, especially when I am sure they are capable. Perhaps I have taken for granted that being from the same culture gives me an advantage over teachers who do not belong to the same cultural background as my students. Only after years of experience, both good and bad, have I come to realize that just because I am similar to them in many aspects—we have the same language and come from the same culture—I do not have the same experiences. Most of my students were born here. This reading of Jim Cummins helped me to clarify why many of our children are wrongly diagnosed, and why they frequently perform at lower grade levels. These are usually the same students who were born here, or came to live here when they were very young. Knowledge and understanding of students' culture by itself does not guarantee success. It is a combination of elements. The problem is that when we start working in school systems, the decisions of what is appropriate for these students are made and enforced by those who do not understand the implications of their own assumptions. The children go from one expensive project to another, usually projects that are compensatory or "banking" in nature; we could say we are gambling on the future of these students.

I clearly remember a principal in one of the school districts in which I worked expressing surprise about why my students were so loyal to me and so difficult with other teachers. It was because my students and I had a *connection*. I respected and validated them, but still many of them were referred for special education, many of them were failing, many refused to transition to mainstream classes even if they were ready. What I read in Cummins's article made sense to me: It is important to teach them in their language, but also it is vital that their education be based on meaning, that they write constantly on what is important to them, and that they make connections from their learning. (12.4.96)

Lizette's reflections remind us that it is necessary to look beyond students' so-called "risk factors" because an overreliance on these may lead educators to despair that anything can be done to reverse the situation. It is more important to investigate the protective networks that help students define themselves as intellectually capable. There has been a recent surge of interest in "resilience" among students who ordinarily might be expected to fail in school because of such "risk factors" (Wang & Gordon, 1994). This focus is crucial because it underscores the fact that educators can learn what school factors help some students succeed academically, and these can be replicated for other students. For instance, a study of Mexican American tenth graders from similar social class backgrounds sought to determine why some of them were successful academically while others were not (Alva, 1991). A major finding of the study was that a supportive network of teachers and friends was linked to the academic success of students.

Research by Sharon Nelson-Barber and Elise Trumbull Estrin (1995) connects this issue to science and mathematics achievement among American Indian students. The authors maintain that a majority of teachers recognize neither these students' existing knowledge nor the learning strategies that could help them achieve in these areas, and they suggest using ethnoscience and ethnomathematics as a way to connect with students' home and community experiences. Even here, however, they make it clear that this approach is insufficient if it is not connected to developing a strong identification with students:

> Using math and science content from students' lives will not compensate for lack of a real relationship between teacher and student. Reliance on method or content alone is an inadequate strategy. If teachers respect and value students, that stance will be communicated and likely have important positive consequences—whether the curriculum and methodology parallel students' experience or not. (Nelson-Barber & Estrin, 1995, p. 182)

The positive influence of a strong identification between students and teachers is further explored in research by Jeannette Abi-Nader (1993) that analyzed the success of the Program in Learning According to Needs (PLAN), a program that gave students an opportunity to forge alliances with their teachers and therefore to see themselves as academically capable. In this program for Hispanic high school students, most of whom were the children of single mothers living on welfare, the 65% success rate for graduating from high school and going on to college was nothing short of phenomenal. Through her extensive observations and interviews with program participants, Abi-Nader found that the concept of *familia* was consciously incorporated into the program as inspiration for the students to achieve. In fact, the students in the program attributed their decisions to complete high school and go on to college to the effective integration of their cultural values into the program's operating principles. These principles included providing a feeling of belonging for all members and creating a sense of mutual responsibility within the group. Actual strategies included peer tutoring, mentoring, and modeling academic behaviors. In addition, family values of caring and support were evident in all aspects of the program, and achieving for others (especially for their mothers) was often invoked to motivate students.

As is clear from these examples, the personal relationships that developed between teachers and students, and among students, are an indication to students that they are valuable members of the learning community. Creating a community of learners also implies, then, that students are cared for and about by their teachers. The climate for learning, that is, cannot be separated from a climate in which care, concern, and love are central. By "love" I do not mean a mawkish or sentimental demonstration of concern for students. Rather, I am suggesting that love is at the core of good teaching because it is predicated on high standards, rigorous demands, and respect for students, their identities, and their families.

Mary Ginley spoke in class about the absolute necessity to love all her students; without love, she maintained, she couldn't really teach them. Some, she confessed, were harder to love than others, but in all of her years of teaching, she had never failed to love any of her students. In what follows, Mary wrote about what it means to love her students.

### TEACHING AS LOVE

*By Mary Ginley*

I read in a book on writing process that the first thing a teacher has to do is fall in love with her students . . . and she cannot do that until she knows them. I have always spent time at the beginning of the year getting to know the children: talking to them, listening to them as they play, as they talk to their friends, as they try to tell me who they are. But this year, I took it very seriously. In addition to my usual ways to find out who was sitting in front of me, I asked the parents to tell me who their children were: what they loved, what they hated, what they were afraid of, what made them angry . . . and what the parents wanted for them, what their goals were, their hopes, their concerns. Some wrote long letters, others called me on the phone, others came and talked before and after school. So I'm getting to know them—and love them—a lot more quickly than other years. I should have done this years ago.

### CONCLUSION: TRANSFORMING SCHOOL POLICIES AND PRACTICES

It is my contention that *all* school policies and practices, not simply pedagogy and curriculum, need to change if student learning is to be fostered.

Accordingly, the very climate of schools needs to undergo a critical transformation in order to make it clear that students of diverse backgrounds are expected and encouraged to learn. More than just rely on specific strategies, schools need to *create the conditions for learning*. This means that focusing on one or two interventions as the answer to a school's problems is simplistic because while such changes may give the appearance of structural transformation, little will happen if the changes are based on the same old attitudes and beliefs as before.

As revealed in a recent study (Louis, Marks, & Kruse, 1996), structural elements in school reform have received an inordinate amount of attention, while concerns about improving the culture, climate, and interpersonal relationships in schools have received a low priority. In their study of restructuring schools, the researchers found that *respect* for students and teachers needs to be at the core of a positive school culture before structural changes can result in improvement in student learning. An example of systemic, school-wide change is found in an exploratory study of six high schools in largely Latino communities by Tamara Lucas, Rosemary Henze, and Rubén Donato (1990). The researchers found that these successful schools underwent dramatic changes in their policies and practices to promote school learning, including the following:

- Spanish classes specifically geared for Spanish-speaking students
- Policies that encouraged students to speak their native language in school
- College information and advising for all students
- Rigorous high-level courses for all students
- Spanish classes for teachers and other staff members
- Hiring, retention, and promotion of a diverse staff
- Staff development that focused on issues of second-language development, effective instruction, cross-cultural counseling, and ethnic and cultural information
- Salary bonuses for teachers who received a bilingual or ESL credential

In analyzing why these particular schools were successful in promoting the academic achievement of Latino language-minority students, the researchers found a constellation of features that were responsible. These included a high value on students' language and cultures; high expectations of language-minority students that were expressed in concrete ways; the priority given by school leaders to the education of language-minority students; and staff development that was specifically designed to help staff serve these students more effectively (Lucas et al., 1990). As we can see from this groundbreaking study, changing schools' policies and practices worked hand in hand with changing the *perceptions* of educators concerning the value and identity of their students.

The question posed at the beginning of this chapter—"Who does the accommodating?"—can have only one answer in a democratic society that claims to provide equal educational opportunity for all students: Accommodation needs to be shared by everyone. Until recently, it was overwhelmingly bicultural students and their families who were expected to accommodate to schools, and accommodation generally meant that they had to lose their very identities in the process. Increasingly, however, the cost of one-way accommodation is recognized as too high a price to pay. That is, if accommodation results in a widening gulf of achievement among students of different backgrounds, increasing dropout rates, low rates of academic achievement, and the loss of the tremendous cultural and linguistic resources that bicultural students possess, then it must be challenged.

# CHAPTER 5

# Critical Pedagogy, Empowerment, and Learning

> [I]ncorporating student experiences as a way of giving primacy to students'
> voices changes the relationships of power and collaboration in the class-
> room.
> —María E. Torres-Guzmán, "Stories of Hope in the Midst of Despair"

MOST PROPONENTS OF multicultural education would agree that one of its major goals is to assist students to develop decision-making and social action skills (Banks, 1997; Bennett, 1995; Ramsey, 1998; Sleeter & Grant, 1993). These skills need to be developed in harmony with meaningful learning about the world so that both the academic achievement and the personal and social growth of students are promoted. That being the case, critical pedagogy and empowerment are at the very heart of learning. To understand the link between learning and empowerment, I will begin by exploring the links between critical pedagogy and multicultural education. We saw in Chapter 4 how changing school policies and practices to accommodate to the lives of students might affect learning in a positive direction. The personal transformation of students will be the subject of this chapter, and it will conclude with an exploration of how students can help transform schools to become sites of democratic and liberating learning. A number of teachers' reflections are included as well.

## DEFINING CRITICAL PEDAGOGY AND EMPOWERMENT

Critical pedagogy is an approach through which students and teachers engage in learning as a mutual encounter with the world. Critical pedagogy also implies *praxis*, that is, developing the important social action predispositions and attitudes that are the backbone of a democratic society, and learning to use them to help alter patterns of domination and oppression. But critical pedagogy does not imply a linear process from *knowledge* to *reflection* to *action*. It is not a mechanistic strategy or a technical process, but a way of thinking more openly and critically about learning. Critical pedagogy is not a standard set of practices, but rather a particular stance vis-à-vis knowledge, the process of learning and teaching, and the educational environment in which these take place (Leistyna, Woodrum, & Sherblom, 1996; Walsh, 1991).

According to Paulo Freire (1970b), the opposite of a critical or empowering approach is "banking education" or "domesticating education," where students learn to regurgitate and passively accept the knowledge they are handed. A critical education, on the other hand, expects students to engage in learning with others, to be curious, to question, and to become problem solvers. Because a critical pedagogy is founded on the belief that problems and issues can be viewed from a variety of perspectives, there is rarely just one right answer to most problems. When students have the opportunity to view situations and events from a number of viewpoints, and when they begin to analyze and question what they are learning, critical thinking, reflection, and action are promoted.

Most students usually do not have access to a wide range of viewpoints, but this is essential if they are to develop the important critical judgment and decision-making skills they will need to become productive members of a democratic society. Critical pedagogy begins where students are at; it is based on using students' present reality as a foundation for further learning rather than doing away with or belittling what they know and who they are. Critical pedagogy acknowledges cultural, linguistic, social class, and other forms of knowledge based on student diversity. It encourages students to use their experiences to extend their learning, and it insists on student voice as a primary element in curriculum and classroom pedagogy. At the same time, critical pedagogy does not simply privilege individual and personal experience as the source of all knowledge; experience becomes another way, but by no means the only one, in which to confront and analyze knowledge.

Ira Shor's (1992) analysis of critical pedagogy begins with the assumption that because no curriculum can be truly neutral, it is the responsibility of schools to present students with a broad range of information they will need to learn not only to read and write, but to read and write *critically* and in the service of social change. Moreover, critical pedagogy does not operate on the principle of substituting one canon for another; instead, students and teachers are invited to reflect on multiple and contradictory perspectives to understand reality more fully. Without a critical perspective, reality frequently is presented to students as a given, and underlying conflicts and problems are barely mentioned.

As a case in point, textbooks in all subject areas are guilty of omissions and distortions; they generally exclude information about unpopular perspectives, or they give short shrift to the perspectives of disempowered groups in society. Few of the books to which students have access present the viewpoints of those who have been the backbone of our society, from enslaved Africans to immigrant labor, to other working-class people (Apple & Christian-Smith, 1991; J. García, 1993; Loewen, 1995; Zinn, 1980). Likewise, the immigrant experience shared by many groups in U.S. history is treated, if at all, as a romantic and successful odyssey instead of as a more complicated process that has been also a wrenching experience of pain and loss. When the immigrant experience is taught, the model presented is generally the European immigrant in the late nineteenth and early twentieth centuries. But the historical context, racial climate, and economic structures experienced by American Indians, enslaved Africans, conquered Mexicans, and colonized Puerto Ricans, or of more recent immigrants from Latin America and Asia, are far different than was true for the vast majority of Europeans who arrived a century ago.

Where does *empowerment* fit into critical pedagogy? Empowerment is both the *purpose* and the *outcome* of critical pedagogy, and empowerment is the other side of the coin of domination. That is, while *power* is implicated in both, in domination it is used to control, and in empowerment it is used to liberate. As described by Seth Kreisberg (1992), domination is characterized by *power over* and implicated with violence, selfishness, hierarchy, and victimization. On the other hand, empowerment is characterized by *power with,* and it challenges those patterns of domination. According to Kreisberg, empowerment is manifest in *relationships of co-agency.* That is, it is not simply the development of individual consciousness, but a social engagement. In education, empowerment suggests a redefinition of relationships between and among teachers and students, parents, and administrators.

Given this more complex understanding of empowerment, a number of questions arise. Can empowerment ever be just individual advancement, or is it always a social and collective act? Richard Ruiz (1991) has asked the penetrating question, "Would empowered students become critical, or merely successful?" (p. 222). Although becoming successful is certainly a marked improvement over being unsuccessful, Ruiz poses an intriguing question. Banks and Banks (1995a) express the dilemma rightly when they challenge pedagogies that prepare students merely to fit into an unjust society rather than to challenge the injustices that undergird that society. The question then becomes, is empowerment simply a replication of business as usual, or does it propose a different paradigm by challenging the model of success as just individual advancement? Paulo Freire (Shor & Freire, 1987) insisted that liberation is a *social act;* nevertheless, although he rejected the idea of empowerment as self-liberation, he also wrote, "While individual empowerment or the empowerment of some students, the feeling of being changed, is not enough concerning the transformation of the whole society, it is *absolutely necessary* for the process of social transformation" (p. 110).

I would add that, given the dreadful state of affairs of the education of bicultural students in the United States, becoming successful students is a necessary and essential component of empowerment, although it is an insufficient one. While it is safe to say that empowerment is a collective and social process, being academically successful as individuals and developing a critical stance toward the world are not necessarily in conflict. In truth, being successful and critical can go hand in hand. Lilia Bartolomé (1994) suggested as much when she proposed that teachers can support positive social change through their pedagogical strategies, including heterogeneous groups and democratic learning environments. How can strategies such as these lead to empowerment rather than simply to individual achievement? She explained that students, "once accustomed to the rights and responsibilities of full citizenship in the classroom, will come to expect respectful treatment and authentic estimation in other contexts" (p. 179).

Multicultural education as practiced in many schools has little to do with critical pedagogy and empowerment; in many cases, it is reduced to only a celebratory approach. But if it is to make a real difference in student learning, multicultural education needs to be situated within a more critical perspective.

## MULTICULTURAL EDUCATION AS CRITICAL PEDAGOGY

The connection between critical pedagogy and multicultural education is receiving growing attention in the educational literature, and it is a promising avenue for expanding and informing both of these philosophical frameworks (Gay, 1995b; May, 1999; McLaren, 1995; Nieto, 1996; Shor, 1992; Sleeter & McLaren, 1995). Multicultural education has played an important role in opening up pedagogical and curricular spaces. Approaches such as interdisciplinary studies, peer tutoring, cooperative learning, action research, and team teaching, among others, have been instituted or resurrected as a result of the multicultural education movement. Likewise, curriculum focusing on previously buried knowledge has been made more available through the efforts of educators with a multicultural perspective. But simply having an expanded repertoire of teaching methods and skills, or augmenting the established canon, will not necessarily affect student learning in any fundamental way unless these are placed within a broader sociopolitical framework.

The fact that multicultural education frequently is detached from its more progressive and critical components was made very clear in a long-term research study of a professional development course by Christine Sleeter (1992). In this study, she found that teachers were quite eager to institute changes in pedagogy but less willing to make more substantive changes in their overall teaching philosophy or their perspectives concerning the nature of difference, privilege, and power. Accordingly, some teachers began interpreting multicultural education primarily as cooperative learning, a safe way of "doing" multicultural education without having to make more wide-ranging philosophical adjustments in their thinking and behavior. Although cooperative education in and of itself is a positive step that can bring about other important changes in classrooms, it will not necessarily lead to developing a critical multicultural perspective. Instituting cooperative groups is far less risky than confronting privilege and racism in the curriculum and other school and classroom practices.

The chasm between multicultural education defined as critical pedagogy by scholars and actual school practices defined as multicultural by teachers in schools is wide indeed. Why does this happen? For one reason, as ideological spaces, schools usually allow teachers and students little control and autonomy. Given their relative lack of power in the school setting, teachers are often reluctant to challenge school policies and practices. For another, dominant ideologies are expressed at numerous sites in schools—the curriculum, pedagogies, tracking systems, and hierarchies and relationships among administrators, teachers, students, and parents—and it is difficult to challenge them all in the absence of a systemic transformation. It is much easier to make superficial, nonthreatening changes that fit in with the status quo than it is to propose more substantive changes that "make waves." Yet multicultural education and critical pedagogy are natural allies because both concern ethical and political issues that engage the world critically and challenge power relations (Sleeter & McLaren, 1995).

UNIVERSITY COLLEGE WINCHESTER
LIBRARY

Multicultural education has a greater possibility of positively affecting student learning when it is approached through the lens of critical pedagogy. When one views specific strategies critically, for instance, it is harder to fall into the trap of using them as panaceas. When certain strategies or approaches are seized as if they were the antidote to the crisis of learning, and then they do not produce the desired results, the problem is aggravated. That is, teachers may blame students as the source of failure instead of acknowledging that the problem may lie in how the particular strategy was used. For example, although small-group work is sometimes presented as a solution to student failure to learn, its inherently problematic features often are overlooked: that some students become even more passive as a result of these strategies; that procedural problems take precedence over learning; and that learning in cooperative groups too often focuses on drill and the mastering of disunited bits of knowledge (McCaslin & Good, 1992). The result can be to diminish the impact of a wonderful strategy with tremendous potential.

Viewing multicultural education critically complicates the question of pedagogy and curriculum; it encourages teachers who are interested in transformative education to rethink what and how they teach, and to constantly question their decisions. The major issue is not to make particular strategies, approaches, or even content prescriptive, but rather to *examine critically the environment in which those strategies and curriculum are played out.* Cooperative learning, for example, can take place in the most uncooperative and oppressive of settings, while extraordinary and high-level learning can happen in traditional-looking classrooms with nailed-down seats in rigid rows. In like manner, Shakespeare can be taught in an empowering way, while content about ancient African civilizations can be taught quite uncritically. It all depends on the attitudes and beliefs undergirding the practices and curriculum in question. Adopting potentially transformative content or strategies such as whole language or process approaches *as strategies* rather than as *a philosophy* trivializes their potential.

The above should not be read as an indictment of any particular approach or curriculum. I believe that progressive educators always look for instructional strategies and curriculum that are empowering and that help more students learn. My reluctance to espouse specific strategies or content is based on the belief that these do not exist in a vacuum but within the larger sociopolitical context of schools and society. Accordingly, there is no one right way to teach, and no singular way works for all students all the time. What is fundamental is to use students' experiences and talents in the curriculum and pedagogy, and to have a firm political commitment to students. In what follows, I will describe what I mean by using students' identities and prior experiences in their learning.

## Building on Students' Strengths

The first and most important lesson I learned as a novice teacher was this: *build on what your students know.* In spite of its very simplicity and exquisite common sense, this idea is radical because it is based on the judgment that intelligence is not the sole province of students from specific groups but of all students regardless of their identity and status. Unfortunately, however, bicultural students very often are thought not to have *any* strengths upon which to build. Even speaking another language—a condition that in most parts of the world would classify as an asset—is a liability for bicultural students in the United States.

The oft-repeated phrase, "All students can learn," is a worthy ideal, but it has become more a slogan than a belief. Rather than repeat it endlessly, teachers need to develop the attitude that all students have talents and strengths upon which to build their learning. A valuable example of building on students' talents can be found in an analysis by Peter Kiang (1995) of what Southeast Asian American students bring to their learning. He identified at least a dozen vital sources of strength, among them the students' homeland reference points, critical thinking skills, well-tested survival strategies, resilience, bilingual and bicultural skills, and dynamic views of identity and changing gender roles. Teachers generally do not consider these strengths to be high-status cultural capital, and consequently they may ignore them as resources for learning. But teachers who are successful with bicultural students regularly begin with the premise that students have valuable insights and skills that can be used in the service of their learning. This was certainly the case with the effective teachers of students of diverse backgrounds in California identified in research by Laurie Olsen and Nina Mullen (1990). The curriculum approach used by the teachers they profiled usually shared a number of features: It was based on the specific experiences of students; it was developed in a climate of high expectations and positive affirmation of students' intellectual abilities; it validated and built on students' cultures while also broadening their perspectives; it reflected excitement about diversity; and it emphasized students learning from one another as well as from the teacher.

Building on students' strengths means, first, acknowledging that students have significant experiences, insights, and talents to bring to their learning, and, second, finding ways to use them in the classroom. If teachers begin with the supposition that students bring nothing, they interpret their role as simply needing to fill students with knowledge. On the other hand, if teachers begin with an awareness that all students have useful experiences that can become the foundation of their learning, their role becomes a radically different one: to research what their students' strengths might be, and then to co-construct learning experiences to build on those strengths. In his comprehensive review of the characteristics of effective teachers of linguistically and culturally diverse students, Eugene García (1994) concluded that these teachers incorporated into the curriculum attributes of the local cultures, used instructional strategies that were student-centered and collaborative, and, most significantly, cared deeply about their students.

Maria Botelho, a former early childhood teacher and librarian who returned to graduate school to complete her doctorate, vividly remembers what it was like to begin school as a young immigrant student in Cambridge, Massachusetts. After viewing a short video on bilingual education (*Quality Bilingual Education,* available from the Massachusetts Association for Bilingual Education) in one of my classes, she felt almost as if she had stepped back in time. The video highlights a number of students, one of them Carla, a young Portuguese student in a bilingual class in Cambridge. Maria reflected on her reactions to the video in her journal.

### LEAVING MY WORLD OUTSIDE

#### By Maria Botelho

I viewed the video *Quality Bilingual Education* twice. I wept both times. The Portuguese-speaking girl, Carla, attended kindergarten in a school that is less than a block from where my parents live in Cambridge; it was too close to home, so to speak. Like Carla, I entered the Cambridge Public Schools speaking only Portuguese. Unlike Carla, I was placed in a mainstream first-grade class. I still remember my teacher bringing over a piece of paper with some writing on it (a worksheet) and crayons. I fell asleep. There I learned quietly about her world, and my world was left with my coat, outside the classroom door. (10.25.95)

A week later, Maria returned to the same theme in her journal. Now, however, she wrote as a teacher, with some advice for that first-grade teacher.

## LETTER TO MS. CURRY

*By Maria Botelho*

A first grader sits with her three classmates in an austere classroom ready to "read" a book called *Nat the Rat*. The teacher begins small-group instruction by asking the four children to open their books. The group reads chorally: "This is Nat. Nat is a rat. Nat the rat sits on a mat. Nat sees a cat. . . ."

The class in which these children sit is devoid of environmental print and no real-life samples of literacy can be found here. The cultures represented in this small reading group are nowhere reflected in the school reading program. One is reminded of the pedagogical constraints placed on the creative possibilities for literacy and the absence of the purpose and meaning of literacy in real-life situations. One also is reminded of the teacher's misconceptions about learning. In other words, the teacher does not see the correlation between the strategies used in literacy learning and language learning. The children perform patiently.

I am the first grader in this classroom. School literacy for me was meaningless, not connected to my home and community life. It did not build on what I already knew about language (oral and written): I was proficient in Portuguese; I could read in Portuguese; I knew what books were about, having experimented with my older siblings' college books; I loved to tell stories; and I knew many stories and songs. There was no attempt to build on my language knowledge. It was assumed that I was a blank slate and the job of the teacher, in this case, Ms. Curry, was to write on me.

If I had the chance to go back in time, I would discuss critical literacy practices with Ms. Curry. As a teacher, and as that student, I would tell her:

1. Use your students to inform your curriculum; consider community literature through dialogic pedagogy.
2. Try to locate generative themes among your students, such as exploring the immigrant experience.
3. Let's have an apprenticeship in thinking; show us what it means to be a masterful reader and writer.
4. Let us create our own meanings that are direct responses to the needs and values within each of our families and communities.
5. Don't be afraid to make political connections among school, community, and our society.

6. Let us explore the continuum of literacy experience so that we can see the multiplicity of literacy contexts as extant in real life.

7. Stock your shelves with real children's literature; let us get to know book language, not "basalese."

8. Make use of the diversity of literacy resources in our homes and communities so that we and our families can be teachers as well as learners in the classroom.

9. Share school literacies with our families so that we can perform what we know at home.

10. Reconcile your role as teacher so that you are both teacher and learner.

11. Introduce us to the genres of democracy; if you're inexperienced with them, let's learn about them together.

12. Being literate can be a noisy process; let us think loudly about the processes of language learning.

13. Education is life itself; please let our world into the classroom so that we can see the real, functional, and meaningful uses of literacy.

14. Please support our parents in their efforts for us to maintain our home language and culture.

15. And, finally, read the article by Robert Peterson ["Teaching How to Read the World and Change It: Critical Pedagogy in the Intermediate Grades," 1991); it provides concrete examples of how one teacher applied the essence of Paulo Freire's approach in his classroom so that the teacher and the children used language to read the world.

This is a long list, Ms. Curry, but please consider the fact that your pedagogy of literacy was dysfunctional. It was stripped of context, meaning, and function. I was lucky in that my family provided me with a backup education. I saw my family use written language in real, meaningful, and purposeful ways as they went about their daily routines and rituals. (11.1.95)

In the following section, I will explore how teachers can go about accommodating the perspectives and experiences of their students and their students' families in curriculum and pedagogy.

## Bridging Cultures, Bridging Lives

Early in the semester when I teach my introductory graduate course in multicultural education, I ask the students, many of whom are teachers, to research and write about their family roots. I suggest that they telephone family members if they can, and that they write in their journals about what they have found. In addition, I ask them to discuss their identity, what it means to them, and what it meant to go through the process of writing down their family stories. In the following session, we take a good deal of time to listen to their stories and to the family folklore they have uncovered. These sessions tend to be fascinating; many of the stories have been poignant and inspiring. Over the years, a number of course participants have made discoveries about their families or their background that have changed their lives.

One example is the story of Elizabeth Capifali. A veteran teacher of 16 years in Harlem, Elizabeth just recently had begun her doctoral studies when she started delving more deeply into her cultural background as a result of a course she took in multicultural education. Elizabeth had been brought up in the Bronx, the daughter of a Puerto Rican father and Filipino mother. As a young child, she had felt compelled to identify more with her Filipino heritage because at that time in New York City it was a more "acceptable" culture. Although she was fluent in Spanish and had been an excellent teacher who had loved and been devoted to her students, exploring her cultural background had a profound impact on how she viewed herself and her responsibilities as a future teacher educator. Below is a poem that she wrote after the first class meeting.

## LOOKING FROM THE EDGE

### By Elizabeth Capifali

As I stand on the periphery of life around me
I ask myself, do I not deserve to partake of the sweetness of this
    land?
I've asked myself this question ever since I was a child,
But, a HAND always kept me at a safe distance.
"DO NOT TRESPASS" always seemed to be the message.
I have leaped into the enveloping arms of life waiting for me and I
    am Living!
Still, hands try to hold me back, but I am stronger now,
I push them aside and say, "Let me in." (10.12.94)

A year later, at the time she took a course on the Puerto Rican experience, she had given the subject of her background considerable thought and she contemplated how her experience of rediscovering her roots had affected her. Here we see too how a teacher's explorations can serve as a bridge to students who have known similar feelings of alienation.

## A BOOST OF ADRENALINE

*By Elizabeth Capifali*

It is almost embarrassing to realize how limited my knowledge is of Puerto Ricans. Learning about one's culture is like a boost of adrenaline being introduced into your system (I have asthma so I know how welcoming it is to have adrenaline running through my veins!). I think it is essential to be aware of what we don't know so that we can make an effort to begin to acquire that knowledge. I don't feel the intimacy that I would like to when reading about the history of my people. I realize that this lack of belonging is due to the fact that I have never been exposed in a formal or informal way to the facts, and I feel somewhat betrayed. This is part of American history, and it has been completely ignored! Reaching back to my past and making that connection is a process that I began last year when I was introduced to some of the great women and men who went to New York City before the depression. It was an empowering experience for me, and I have a very strong desire to continue along that path of discovery. (9.12.95)

Although the "family roots" activity is always informative and engaging, its purpose is not to delve voyeuristically into the private lives of course participants. Rather, it is to use this experience of uncovering and revealing their own identities to think about how their students' identities are constructed, negotiated, and reflected, or not, in schools. This activity also leads us to ponder that the kinds of differences revealed in these stories are usually not allowed in school talk. Difference, in many schools, becomes a topic to avoid, or at least to diminish. Ann Scott's journal entry about her search for her roots focused on the fact that her natural inclination had always been to build on similarities rather than focus on differences.

## DIFFERENCES MATTER

*By Ann Scott*

One of the things I learned from the family roots exercise we did in class is that it required us to pay attention to the differences in each other. As a White person and a member of the dominant culture, I have often felt I should begin relating to people from other ethnic backgrounds by ignoring the difference in us: by looking for, focusing on what we have in common. As a way of attaining community, compassion, of bonding. But it doesn't work. What happens is a kind of negation, a denial, of the differences. And of course the differences matter, because our ethnicity shapes our destiny, it shapes our present, and it shaped our history before us. So the differences sit there, ignored, looming bigger and bigger as time goes on, shrouded in misunderstanding and neglect, more of a barrier to communication than if we had named them, acknowledged them, celebrated them, and then tried to get on with things. (9.17.93)

Ann is suggesting that teachers need to first acknowledge these differences and then act as a bridge between their students' differences and the culture of the dominant society. Especially for dominant-group teachers, this means recognizing their privilege.

The metaphor of a bridge is appropriate for teachers who want to be effective with students of diverse backgrounds. This is a lesson I learned from Diane Sweet, a former student of mine who had been an engineer until she fell in love with teaching and decided to change careers (needless to say, at considerable loss of prestige and money). Diane was well aware of the benefits of bridges, and she applied the metaphor to teaching: A bridge provides access to a different shore without closing off the possibility of returning home; a bridge is built on solid ground but soars toward the heavens; a bridge connects two places that otherwise might never be able to meet. The best thing about bridges is that they do not need to be burned once they are used; on the contrary, they become more valuable with use because they help visitors from *both* sides become adjusted to different contexts. Unfortunately, however, this is a far cry from how diverse languages and cultures tend to be viewed in schools: The conventional wisdom is that if native languages and cultures are used at all, it should be only until one learns the *important* language and culture, and then they should be discarded or burned. It is definitely a one-way street with no turning back. The metaphor of the bridge suggests a different stance: You can have two homes, and the bridge can help you cross the difficult and conflict-laden spaces between them.

Teachers who take seriously their responsibility for working with students of diverse backgrounds become bridges, or what Esteban Díaz and his colleagues (1992) called *sociocultural mediators.* According to these researchers, when teachers view their role as sociocultural mediators, they communicate to their students a deep respect for their particular cultural knowledge. An example of teacher as sociocultural mediator is found in earlier research by Esteban Díaz, Luis Moll, and Hugh Mehan (1986). They studied reading and writing in bilingual settings and found that effective teachers used students' social and linguistic resources in the classroom, in the process helping students succeed academically. For instance, rather than focus on whether English or Spanish was used in instruction, these teachers highlighted comprehension as the primary goal. The result was a 3-year increase in English reading, with similar results reported in writing. The researchers concluded that classroom interactions on the part of both teachers and students need to be modified in the direction of a common goal: academic success with cultural integrity.

Another example of teacher as bridge can be found in a classroom ethnographic study reported by Martha Montero-Sieburth and Marla Pérez (1987). The teacher, Marla, used her intimate knowledge of the community, culture, and lives of her students as a bridge to help them become critical learners. Rather than the general impression that many bicultural students get that school and home can never be connected, the students in this classroom found that school was a place where their daily lives could be connected with their academic learning. For example, the teacher's role became a highly varied one, and she came to see herself as a "teacher, friend, mentor, social worker, translator, counselor, advocate, prosecutor, group therapist, hygienist, and monitor" (p. 183). She made it clear that she cared about and for her students, and she made her class-room a place where students could reflect and talk about their lives and experiences in a way that was not allowed in other classrooms. In the process, she turned her classroom into "problem-posing forums" in which the issues that were important to students became the focus of the curric-ulum. At the same time, she consciously taught the students the norms of mainstream school and society to facilitate their identity as successful students (Montero-Sieburth & Pérez, 1987).

In an example closer to home, my husband Ángel, who was a high school social studies bilingual teacher at the time, experienced firsthand how students can become inspired when the curriculum connects with their lives in a direct way, and, conversely, how some teachers and schools can feel so threatened by this kind of learning. This is how it came about: I had been asked to give a talk at a dinner to celebrate the achievements of Puerto Ricans and other Latinos, and it happened to take place in the community where he taught. The day after the talk, the local newspaper had a front-page article about the event, and within a week I received a letter that can only be described as venomous. With no return address but with a local postmark, the letter was addressed to me at my office—the newspaper had identified my university affiliation—and it was typed on a plain sheet of paper. I reproduce it below exactly as it came to me, with all the original errors (but I have omitted the names of the individuals and towns used by the writer).

## LETTER FROM "A PROUD, CLEAN AMERICAN CITIZEN"

*February 12, 1985*

*Dear Miss Nieto,*

*After reading your statements in the [local newspaper] Monday evening on your view that "latinos" are "making own way", i would like to offer my personal opinion. This opinion is shared by countless other AMERI-CANS also.*

*First of all, your people must become civilized in AMERICA before they can become socially accepted into any community outside of their own. Look at the way the PR's have made shambles out of public housing. COOKING CHICKENS in their bathtubs is not the norm in AMERICA. Civilized people usually use a grill or an oven. PR's are lazy, dirty and have absolutely no motivation in our AMERICAN society. Motovation, in my opinion, is simply not banging on bongo drums in the middle of a hot summers night.*

*Crime is up because of the spics in our cities. look, for instance at the shooting death of state trooper J. H. last year by a group of spics when Officer H. stopped their car. Look, for instance in [another town] yesterday when 82 spics were arrested for cock fights set up in a social club, while drinking and taking drugs. Look for instance at yesterdays murder of D.J. in [another town] after a spic E.J. stabbed him to death while Mr. J. was in his automobile. I could go on and on.*

*SURE their are crimes committed by other factions in AMERICAN society, but not on the magnitude of the spics. Your people live like pigs, don't know our customs, our language, deface our country like the cockroaches they like to live with.*

*If you like your customs so much, why don't all of you get on the next banana boat back to pr and stay there. Our cities will be much cleaner and our crime rate would drop at least 20%. On a closing note, two years ago my next door neighbor an old woman of 92, was robbed of $6.51. Our AMERICAN POLICE apprehended three teenage pr's from [a nearby town] (8 miles away), and promptly charged and arrested them.*

*Go back to pr where you belong, MOST AMERICANS don't like you or admire your lackluster accomplishments in this society.*

*A PROUD, CLEAN AMERICAN CITIZEN*

*P.S. There are no cockroaches in our beautiful home.*

Needless to say, the letter was deeply disturbing to me, as it was a vicious reminder that hatred of this kind is not a thing of the past and that racism and ethnocentrism are never far from the surface when difference and power are concerned. In spite of the ludicrous nature of the characterizations (cooking chickens in bathtubs?), I was both enraged and terrorized by it. Ángel asked me if he could take the letter to school and use it in his social studies class, and I agreed. He often had broached issues that connected his students' lives with the academic content they were learning because he wanted them to understand that their experiences also could be an important source of the curriculum. He wanted them to see that the U.S. Constitution, the struggle for freedom, the story of the industrial revolution, and every other part of the history they studied was relevant to their lives.

Ángel's students, all of whom were Puerto Rican, were riveted by the letter. It became the catalyst for their curriculum for a number of days as students talked about their direct and painful experiences with racism and hatred. They also read about and discussed the history of discrimination faced by other groups in the United States, and the importance of citizenship and social and political action. The students saw that these concerns were directly related to school and learning, and they immersed themselves in study. This was a school system where Puerto Ricans made up well over half of the student body and where their dropout rate was over 60%. Many of them did not believe that they belonged, and they felt alienated and marginalized from school.

Rather than welcoming the students' enthusiasm and excitement about learning, one of Ángel's colleagues chastised him for using the letter. "How could you bring that hateful letter into this school?" she asked, deeply offended. It was not that she was unaware of these issues; it was simply that she felt that school was not the place to bring them up. School should be, in her view, a "safe" place, a haven where students should not be exposed to "this sort of thing." The irony, of course, was that students were exposed to these experiences every day, but they usually did not have the opportunity to discuss them openly in school; as a result, the school was not a safe place for these discussions. The letter was a tool for bridging a part of students' everyday lives with the curriculum. The point of this anecdote is not to imply that curriculum should become nothing more than a hate-filled chronicle of abuses. On the contrary, I believe that the curriculum can become a beacon of hope and joy, but only if it is presented in an honest, direct, and comprehensive way, and if it acknowledges the lives of the very students to whom it is directed.

We have seen numerous examples of how negative attitudes about language and culture find their way into schools and teachers' thinking. Turning this situation around is not a matter of instituting a particular strategy, but rather a matter of incorporating students' and families' perspectives and experiences into schools. An ethnographic study by Concha

Delgado-Gaitán and Henry Trueba (1991) of first-generation Latino children found that the children's home environments often provided rich linguistic and cultural resources. The researchers concluded that, from an educational point of view, the children were ready to learn when they reached school. Unfortunately, however, the schools were not ready to take advantage of what the children brought with them. Delgado-Gaitán and Trueba concluded that "children's language and opportunities for development of higher cognitive skills were much richer in their homes and communities than in the classroom" (p. 140).

In another example of how negative views of language and culture can negatively influence student engagement with school, Margaret Gibson (1995) investigated the factors that promoted or impeded success among Mexican-descent students in a California high school. She found that students and their parents generally viewed acculturation in an additive way, that is, as adding another culture and language instead of eliminating their native ones. Nevertheless, the school environment consistently reinforced a subtractive acculturation. Moreover, although parents perceived language maintenance for their children as absolutely essential, almost half of the teachers believed that *monolingualism was the best avenue for success*. As incredible as this belief may seem to be, it had a decided impact on teachers' behaviors and attitudes concerning their students who spoke Spanish. Gibson found that the negative attitudes teachers had about the Spanish language influenced how students felt about school, about their teachers, and even about their own identity and culture. Specifically, she found that those students who expressed the greatest unease with the devaluation of their language and culture were also those at the greatest risk of dropping out: These students felt the pressure to either reject their identities and become successful students, or accept their identities and reject academic success.

In order to make genuine cultural learning a part of the classroom environment, Frederick Erickson (1997) has suggested that students and teachers be used as primary resources in the curriculum. Specifically, Erickson recommends using *critical autobiography* both as curriculum and as the basis for action research. This strategy entails making particular student and family cultures the object of study by all students. What makes this approach *critical* is that culture is approached not as a fixed or static state of being, but rather as socially constructed and changing; the goal is not to encase cultures in protective wrappings but instead to deconstruct the meanings behind them. In this way, students and teachers can develop a critical stance about their own and other people's cultures and histories. This process also relieves students of having to be "cultural experts," a prime danger in classrooms where teachers assume that students' cultural membership automatically makes them capable of teaching others about their culture, a questionable assumption at best.

## EMPOWERMENT AND LEARNING

When a critical perspective is used, students can become instruments of their own learning and use what they learn in productive and critical ways; their knowledge can be used to explore the reasons for certain conditions in their lives and to design strategies for changing them. Moreover, critical pedagogy helps to expand teachers' perspectives regarding their students' knowledge and intellectual capabilities. A critical, empowering pedagogy can have a powerful influence on learning because when students approach their education as active agents, they begin to understand that they have a role to play in the world.

Students frequently have been overlooked as central players in school restructuring and reform efforts. If included at all, it is most often as recipients of particular policies and practices. Yet just as the redefinition of the role of teachers is crucial in developing a critical pedagogy (Cummins, 1996), so too is the redefinition of students' roles. According to Dick Corbett and Bruce Wilson (1995), this role redefinition is a "linchpin between adult reform behavior and student success" (p. 12). Some examples of the positive influence that critical pedagogy can have on student learning follow.

### Embracing "Dangerous Discourses"

In their case study of teachers' responses to multicultural texts, Ellen Bigler and James Collins (1995) found that merely opening up the possibility of using a multicultural approach in schools and classrooms can pose a threat because it has the potential to unearth the deep "silences" (Fine, 1991) that exist in schools concerning issues such as race and class. While they found that teachers in the school they studied were by and large happy to "celebrate diversity" if it did not go too far, most of them became uneasy when the talk turned to racism or inequality. In their research, they defined "dangerous discourses" as any discussion that challenged the accepted literary canon or that questioned underlying social ideologies. These discussions were avoided studiously by most teachers.

Paradoxically, it is precisely these "dangerous discourses" that appeal to many students, particularly those who live daily with the realities that such discourses uncover. Encouraging these kinds of conversations is a message to students that the classrooms belong to them also because they are places where meaningful dialogue can occur around issues that are central to students' lives. And when students feel that the classrooms belong to them as well as to their teachers, they are free to learn. If teachers and students are prohibited from challenging the canon, we might well ask what education is for. As Benjamin Barber (1992) has stated cogently, "A canon that cannot be reinvented, reformulated, and thus reacquired by a learning community fails the test of truth as well as of pertinence, and is of no use to that community" (p. 214).

An example of information that challenges the canon is a test item from a "Multicultural Literacy Test" developed by Professor Bob Suzuki, my predecessor and mentor, who taught the first course in multicultural education at my university in 1975 (Suzuki, 1975a). The test, primarily on U.S. history, was always an eye-opener for students because it shattered some of the cherished myths they had learned through the official curriculum, and it made them reconsider some of the unchallenged truths they had accepted over the years. During one particular semester early in the 1980s I used the test with an undergraduate class of prospective teachers. Invariably, a number of answers surprised students, but I can still remember the look of shock on the face of a young woman of Italian American background when we reviewed the correct answer to the true/false question that read:

> In the 1920s the Ku Klux Klan was active in almost every state in the Union and directed most of its efforts to an anti-Catholic crusade to terrorize foreigners and to bring an end to immigration from Southern and Eastern Europe. (Suzuki, 1975a, p. 2)

The answer and explanation to the question were as follows:

> (true) Interestingly enough, such aspects of American history do not appear to be widely known and may have been repressed as a result of a curious "social amnesia" that seems to have affected many Americans. Some of the primary victims of the Ku Klux Klan were the Italians and the Jews. (Suzuki, 1975b, p. 2)

The young woman was astonished to discover that Italian Americans had been victims of this kind of oppression. All through school, she had never heard anything of the kind and nothing had ever been said about it in her family either because they themselves did not know it. Her shock was coupled with anger that she and others had been denied this information, and the realization changed the way that she was to look at curriculum and education from then on.

Another piece of data that I have used for many years in my introductory course to multicultural education was published in *Parade Magazine* (Wallace, Wallechinsky, & Wallace, 1983), as unlikely a source for this information as one could imagine. *Parade* printed an article titled "First U.S. City to be Bombed from the Air." It concerned the bombing of a Black community in Tulsa, Oklahoma, by the police, who commandeered private planes to drop dynamite on the city during a race riot. The article reads in part, "Before the riot, Tulsa blacks were so successful that their business district was called 'The Negro's Wall Street.' Envy bred hatred of the blacks, who accounted for a tenth of the segregated city's population." In 1921, when a mob of Whites gathered to lynch a Black man who had been accused of attacking a White woman, armed Blacks joined the fray and the riot began. Whites invaded the Black district, looting it, and eventually the National Guard was called in to restore order. The article concludes, "The police arrested more than 4000 blacks and interned them in three camps. All blacks were forced to carry green ID cards. And when Tulsa was zoned for a new railroad station, the tracks were routed through the black business district, thus destroying it."

I usually introduce the piece by asking if anybody knows which was the first U.S. city to be bombed from the air by the United States, and predictably I am greeted with blank stares. In all the years I have used this article, there have been just a handful of people who have known the answer to the question. People are genuinely dumbfounded when I read the article aloud; most have never imagined that something like this could happen in the United States (carrying identity cards, for instance, is associated not with the United States, but with apartheid in South Africa before 1992). But the reason I use this particular piece with my students is not to shock or appall, but to challenge their comfortable notions that "this could never happen here," or their taken-for-granted assumptions that Blacks have always done the looting during riots, or that there have been no examples of successful Black business communities. I have witnessed how this short article has managed to do all of this at once. Even among politically progressive, informed people who analyze every issue critically, this article has had an impact. A case in point is Tom Hidalgo, a progressive educator, former reporter, community activist, and all-around very informed citizen.

## REACTION TO THE ARTICLE

*By Tom Hidalgo*

The article about the bombing of the Black section of Tulsa absolutely blows my mind, although it shouldn't. I had never heard that story. It is similar to when one hears of some newly discovered atrocity committed by the Nazis. You always think this is the worst, nothing can top this. Then you read about or see some new example of cruelty or perversion and the cycle starts all over again. The more I think about it, the less it surprises me. Successful Blacks scared the hell out of Whites and they had to destroy them for it. The same thing is happening now. The same fear is leading to more hate. That explains much of the rejection and backlash against multiculturalism and diversity. What happened to the Tulsa Blacks could happen today and it probably will before too long. (2.9.94)

As I often tell my students, this particular occurrence need not substitute for more heroic and laudable events in U.S. history. But history needs to be more than celebrations; the Tulsa incident is also part of U.S. history, and it needs to be acknowledged and thought about.

### Students Transforming Schools

We need to remember that *learning begins when students begin to see themselves as competent, capable, and worthy of learning.* One way that students begin to see themselves in this way is when their voices and perspectives are included in the transformation of schools. Including students in school transformation is especially significant in multicultural education because of the inherent student-centeredness of the field. Moreover, attending to what students have to say about their experiences and listening to their suggestions can result in a more critical conception of multicultural education.

Although students have a lot to say about schools and learning, their perspectives frequently are not sought. Listening to students can reveal whether they perceive schools as responsive or unresponsive to them and why. Students' views have important implications for educational reform because their insights can prove to be important for developing meaningful, liberating, and engaging educational experiences. Through this process, students can become energized and motivated about schooling. The very act of speaking about their ideas can act as a catalyst for more critical thinking about their education in general. Young people often feel encouraged by the mere fact that somebody wants to listen to them and take their views seriously. Listening seriously to students is especially important for young people whose cultures and languages are invisible in the school setting and who may feel alienated due to their cultural, racial, social, class, linguistic, or other differences. Giving voice to the challenges they face in school and at home, and to the frustration of accommodating to an environment that may be hostile to their differences, can indeed be empowering for them.

In essence, educators lose a powerful opportunity to learn how schools could be better if they do not encourage the critical involvement of their students. Attending to students' questions and ideas for improving schools can reap important benefits for transforming schools. For example, how do students feel about the curriculum they must learn? What do they think about the books they read? Do they think of school as an engaging and exciting place? Are their own cultural, racial, gender, and other identities important considerations for them? Although these are key questions that affect their schooling, few students have an opportunity to discuss them. Even more important, students' views are often consistent with current thinking in education: Patricia Phelan, Ann Locke Davidson, and Hanh Thanh Cao (1992), in a 2-year research project designed to identify students' thoughts about school, discovered that their views on teaching and learning were notably consistent with learning theory, cognitive science, and the sociology of work.

Students can provide a great deal of food for thought for critical multicultural educators interested in transforming schools and classrooms. But in spite of the profound changes that can take place in the lives of students when their viewpoints are actively sought by educators, listening is not enough if it is not accompanied by profound changes in expectations of student learning and achievement. Listening to students should not be treated as a "touchy-feely" exercise or as therapy, nor should students' views be treated as if they were always correct. Instead, their opinions and views need to be used in tandem with those of teachers and families to help make their schooling more meaningful and positive.

Accounts of critical pedagogy in real-life classrooms are compelling examples of the positive and empowering influence it can have on student learning. For instance, Carmen Mercado (1993), working collaboratively with a middle school teacher and her students, designed a project in which students became researchers about conditions in their own neighborhood in the Bronx. Through dialogue with their teachers and among themselves, students selected topics to research that were important to them. They learned a variety of sophisticated academic skills at the same time that they learned to think more deeply about the reasons for such situations as drug abuse, homelessness, teenage pregnancy, and intergenerational conflicts. In many cases, they used their research skills in social action projects to improve their community. The most significant outcome of this project was that students became empowered both individually and collectively. The process of learning to define themselves as researchers had a profound impact on how students viewed themselves and their own capabilities as learners. In their school and in conferences where they presented the results of their work, students spoke and behaved as researchers; they described the exciting changes in their attitudes toward learning; and they developed an awareness of their collective responsibility and power.

Curriculum that draws on students' experiences can energize them because it focuses precisely on those things that are most important to them. In this way, curriculum can provide what María Torres-Guzmán (1992) has referred to as *cognitive empowerment*, encouraging students to become confident, active, and critical thinkers who learn to think about their background experiences as important tools for further learning. In a powerful example of cognitive empowerment, Torres-Guzmán reported on the case of an environmental science curriculum in El Puente Academy for Peace and Justice, a "New Visions" high school in New York City based on the principles of community involvement and social justice. In this project, students investigated the source of a chemical storage lot in their neighborhood. Taking the name *The Toxic Avengers*, the students observed, analyzed, and chronicled how the lot was used as a dump site, and they documented their findings through videotapes, charts, photographs, and maps. Their investigation eventually led to the cleanup of the toxic dump site, and in 1989 the students received the New Yorkers for New York Award from the Citizens' Committee (Torres-Guzmán, 1992).

A final example of critical pedagogy in action with young children is provided by Patty Bode. Patty, an art teacher who worked with children from grades 1 through 6 when she wrote the following, reflected on her experience with a first-grade child who was concerned about unfair representation in some of the books she was reading.

## A LETTER FROM KAELI

### By Patty Bode

A few weeks ago, I found this letter in my message box from one of my first-grade students:

*Dear !!!!!! mis Boudie*

> *Ples! halp. my moom was spcing to me abut wite piple leving bran and blak piple out of books.*

> *Love Kaeli*

*[Please help! My mom was speaking to me about White people leaving Brown and Black people out of books.]*

My response:

*Dear Kaeli,*

*Today I found your note in my message box. I was very interested to hear that you were speaking to your mom about White people leaving Brown and Black people out of books. I am glad you asked for help.*

*This is a problem that we need to help each other with. We need to ask our friends and teachers and families for help so we can work together.*

*I think we should work on this problem in art class. Maybe our class could design our own books which include all kinds of people of all colors, races, and all families. Maybe we could write some letters to book publishers and send them our artwork to give them some good ideas for improving their books.*

*See you in art class!*

*Love,*
*Ms. Bode*

As the art teacher, I was touched and moved that Kaeli came to me for help. There were dozens of adults in our school she could have gone to. Her call for help reinforced my classroom practices that have addressed institutionalized racism with all students from first through sixth grade. It was now March and I reflected back over the art lessons that the first grade had engaged in up to this point in the school year. It was powerfully revealing to me to witness my students addressing concerns in their personal and public lives that we had discussed, studied, and expressed through art since September. Their young 6-year-old minds had developed knowledge through a wide spectrum of art lessons: examining artists' work throughout history, interpreting various artists' messages, viewing our role in service to our community by creating images for our annual Dr. Martin Luther King Community Breakfast and other events, and painting self-portraits in a color theory lesson that directly explored dialogue about race and skin color. Kaeli's letter charged me with hope, but more importantly, with a sense of responsibility to teach my students to respond with direct action.

When Kaeli's class came to the art room, she read her letter aloud, and she showed her classmates the book that she had been reading at home which had attracted her attention to the inequities of racial representation. It was a fairly new book, published in 1993 by a prominent publishing house, about the human body. Out of

the hundreds and hundreds of pictures in the book, Kaeli counted
only 22 pictures of Brown and Black people.

The students discussed why this was a problem. In their first-
grade voices and 6-year-old vocabulary, they discussed "fair" and
"unfair," "discrimination," "stereotypes," and more. Through their
dialogue, they decided—without my prompting—that it was OK
for some books to exclusively depict Black people or Brown people
or White people or others if it was a story about a specific family or
event. But books that claimed to be about the "HUMAN BODY" or
about "PEOPLE OF THE WORLD" needed to be much more balanced to
pass the scrupulous eye of this first-grade class.

I provided some examples of various books for analysis by the
group. We decided which books were fair and which were unfair.
The class decided that the publishers needed to receive some letters
of information from them as well as some artwork to display good
examples of fair pictures. Then we launched into the art activity.

First, we learned a bit of color theory with our tempera paints.
We learned that the color brown is created by mixing red, yellow,
and blue, which are the primary colors that create all other colors
in the painted spectrum. With this knowledge, we realized that
every cup of brown paint is really a scoop of red, yellow, and blue
mixed together (or every color in the rainbow mixed together).
This gave importance to the color brown, and emphasized its key
role in our color theory.

We also discussed terminology and use of language. We discussed the words "Black" and "White" and learned a brief history of
the use of those terms. We discovered that none of our skin colors
were really black or white. We decided that using words like Black
or African American, White or European American, Latino or Hispanic, and Asian or Chinese American were important decisions
that required lots of thinking.

We also looked in mirrors at our own faces and saw that there
were many colors, tones, and shades among the children in the
class. At the same time, we studied and discussed many books. I
filled the walls of the art room with photographs of children's faces.
I spent a great deal of time choosing images of children to reflect
the enormous variety of ethnicity and race that our society holds.
One European American boy looked at the photo display and said,
"Ms. Bode, you left out the White people." I took him by the hand
and we studied the display together. I asked him to count the number of photos that he *thought* were "White" or European American
people and then to count the numbers of photos that he *thought*

were African American, Latino, Asian, and American Indian. One thing that he articulated was that "we can't always know someone's heritage by just looking at them," and his counting activity revealed that the photo display was actually a very balanced collection of many different groups of people. Together, we wondered why, at first glance, he had thought that European Americans were missing from the display. "Maybe it's 'cuz I'm used to seeing more of them," he said.

We spent our next art class drawing the facial features on the dry paint over the "face shapes" we had made the day before. As this unit of study unfolded, we added details to our artwork and clarified the big mission ahead of us. We enlisted the assistance of the classroom teacher to help us write letters. The librarian helped us find more examples of good books as well as decide which publishers needed to hear our message.

Here are two of the students' letters.

*Dear publisher,*

*Make your books faire! And if you don't me and my famyuliy will never by or read your unfaire books. we want fairenes.*

*From, Erika*

*[Make your books fair! And if you don't, me and my family will never buy or read your unfair books. We want fairness.]*

*Dear Publisher,*

*Pleas equalis african american aigin chinis japanis urapin americen pordaricin*

*sincerely, Caroline*

*[Please equalize African American, Asian, Chinese, Japanese, European American, Puerto Rican.]*

We will be sending our artwork and letters to any publishers who we believe need to hear our message, as well as to publishers who deserve our congratulations on a job well done.

This unit proved to be a good reminder to me that it is the responsibility of the entire community to work for social justice. One individual or one group should not be burdened to fight for their rights in solitude or exempt from the responsibility of democracy. It requires careful observation, attentive listening, and critical thought to facilitate sociopolitical consciousness effectively within a first grade classroom. (6.9.98)

Patty Bode's experience with her first-grade class reinforces that critical multicultural education need not be reserved for the college classroom, or just for classes in history or English. Even an art class for 6-year-olds is fertile ground for planting the seeds of critical thinking and social justice. Many other illustrations of critical pedagogy in action written by classroom teachers are included in publications by Rethinking Schools (Bigelow, Christensen, Karp, Miner, & Peterson, 1994) and the Network of Educators on the Americas (Lee, Menkart, & Okazawa-Rey, 1998). In these powerful accounts, critical multicultural pedagogy is the force behind student learning, and specific curricular and pedagogical innovations that promote learning are discussed.

## SUMMARY

Critical pedagogy, empowerment, and multicultural education are firmly interrelated concepts and approaches. As we have seen, multicultural education defined simply as the transmission of content is inconsistent with an approach that values critique and transformation, even if the content differs substantially from the traditional curriculum. Although changing the content of the curriculum may be a momentous shift because it represents a genuine challenge to a monolithic canon, if the new content is presented uncritically and unquestioningly, little change will occur in how students think and learn. Learning inevitably is enhanced when students are actively engaged, immersed in both the content and the context of their education.

# CHAPTER 6

# The Personal and Collective Transformation of Teachers

To teach in a manner that respects and cares for the souls of our students is essential if we are to provide the necessary conditions where learning can most deeply and intimately begin.

—bell hooks, *Teaching to Transgress*

ALTHOUGH TEACHING IS OFTEN approached as a technical activity—writing lesson plans, learning effective methods for teaching algebra, selecting appropriate texts, developing tests to assess student learning—anybody who has spent any time in a classroom knows that teaching and learning are primarily about relationships. What happens in classrooms is first and foremost about the personal and collective connections that exist among the individuals who inhabit those spaces. Consequently, teachers' beliefs and values, how these are communicated to students through teaching practices and behaviors, and their impact on the lives of students—these are the factors that make teaching so consequential in the lives of many people.

We can all recall inspirational or dreadful teachers, although we may have a hard time remembering exactly what they taught or the kinds of lessons they prepared. I cannot remember her name, but the remark of one of my first teachers that it was rude to speak Spanish in the classroom still stings. It may have been nothing more than an offhand comment on her part, but those words had a powerful impact on me. In the short term, they had the effect of invalidating my use of Spanish in school. In the long term, they were to influence for many years how I would view the value of my native language. Equally rooted in my memory is the image of Mr. Slotkin, a creative and nurturing eighth-grade science teacher whose classroom was always an exciting place that made going to school worthwhile. I do not recollect any of the specific lessons he taught and, except for this one successful encounter with science, I was never particularly a science enthusiast. The relationships I had with these teachers is what made a difference, and I suspect the same is true for most people. That is why the personal transformation of teachers is a necessary process that needs to go hand in hand with structural changes in schools.

Teaching and learning are not only about relationships, however. As Paulo Freire always insisted (1970a, 1970b, 1985), education is a *political* act. That is, it concerns decisions and actions that bear on *who* and *what* and *how* we teach, and also in *whose interest* we teach. Try as we might to separate it from the political sphere, education is always political because it focuses in a central way on questions of power, privilege, and access. As such, education is also about political commitment and social responsibility. Once teachers understand this, they no longer can point to others— the central office, the union, the principal, the prescribed basal reader— as the only or even the most important decision makers in the classroom. In spite of how teachers' actions are constricted by others, teachers still have enormous power to create enriching and empowering relationships with students, colleagues, and members of the community in which they teach.

Environments that are both critical and empowering are not created overnight; they are developed and sustained through the relationships formed in classrooms between and among teachers, students, and families. Building these relationships implies a profound transformation of the attitudes, beliefs, and behaviors of teachers concerning the nature of learning and intelligence, the role of diversity in learning, and, in fact, the ideological stance or world view they may have in general. The process of transformation is a personal and collective journey that teachers must travel. The transformation to which I refer begins as a political commitment on the part of teachers, individually and collectively, and it is demonstrated here through the stories of several teachers with whom I have had the privilege to work over the years.

If we understand teaching as consisting primarily of social relationships and as a political commitment rather than a technical activity, then it is unquestionable that what educators need to pay most attention to are their own growth and transformation and the lives, realities, and dreams of their students. This is not to take the responsibility off the shoulders of teacher education institutions or school systems, nor is it to say that it should not be an institutional odyssey as well. I also do not intend for this focus on teachers to be read as teacher bashing. On the contrary, I believe that most teachers enter the teaching profession because of a profound commitment to young people. Although some teachers lose their enthusiasm for teaching and their hope in children, many maintain their ideals, and they actively and consistently search for ways to create learning environments that are meaningful and engaging for their students. In what follows, we will consider some ways in which teachers do this.


## CONFRONTING ONE'S IDENTITY

Teachers in the United States, who are primarily White, middle-class, and monolingual, have had limited experiences with diverse populations, and they frequently perceive of diversity in a negative way. This was the conclusion reached by Kenneth Zeichner and Karen Hoeft (1996) after a thorough review of the literature concerning the role of teacher education in preparing educators for diverse classrooms. On the other hand, teachers who can call on their own experiences of marginalization, as well as those who have developed a bicultural identity and who have entered the teaching profession precisely because they see it as a way to serve their communities, find it easier to forge strong and meaningful relationships with their students. But being a member of a culturally or racially disempowered group does not guarantee that one can understand or identify with students of backgrounds different from one's own. That is, a Mexican American teacher will not necessarily be an effective teacher of Vietnamese students simply because she is Mexican American. In fact, she may not even necessarily be a better teacher of Mexican American students if her personal experiences and background differ markedly from those of her students and she has no immediate understanding of how to bridge these differences.

For teachers of the dominant culture who have little knowledge of the cultures, experiences, or feelings of their students from bicultural backgrounds, trying to understand them poses an even greater challenge. Sometimes teachers may use their ignorance of diversity to maintain that adjusting the curriculum and instruction to their students' backgrounds makes little sense; that is, teachers may reason that if students will need to assimilate anyway, why change the curriculum? The assumption is that learning is a one-way process in which students need to learn the culture and values of the school, but that teachers need not learn the culture and values of their students. Other teachers, whether from dominant or bicultural backgrounds, recognize that they first need to understand and accept their *own* diversity and delve into their *own* identities before they can learn about and from their students.

A good example of coming to terms with one's identity and all that it entails is the following journal entry by Ann Scott during her first semester in graduate school. In it, she confronted her fear of acknowledging a White identity rooted in privilege, and she mused about what it meant to go through this process as part of her personal and professional transformation.

## THE DISCOMFORT OF MY IDENTITY

*By Ann Scott*

I'm feeling a bit anxious as a result of this class. Looking at myself in this way can be quite uncomfortable, but I know how good it is for me to have this opportunity to develop as a human being. This is an aspect of graduate school that I had not expected—and for which I'm grateful even if it's painful at times. That is, I expected to be learning about education on an intellectual level, but I did not expect to be engaged so profoundly on an emotional and spiritual level, nor to be asked to look so closely at myself and to challenge myself this way. Hard work. But the kind of hard work that I'm willing to do. . . . Placing myself in various contexts, examining my privileges and all I take for granted because of my privileges, those things I did not earn but simply inherited; recognizing how much I lose as a result of my privileges; and, perhaps most disturbing of all, recognizing just a bit how others suffer because of my privileges.

Later in the same journal entry, Ann completely immersed herself in an exercise that I often ask students to do in my graduate class. First, I assign them Peggy McIntosh's (1988) groundbreaking article on White privilege in which the author analyzes in a detailed and candid way the numerous ways in which she benefits from her Whiteness. Reading this article is often an extraordinary experience for course participants: Many Whites, some for the first time, are forced to grapple with what it means to have unearned racial privilege; Black and other people of color are often grateful that a White person has articulated a reality of which they have been painfully aware for many years. After they have read it, we engage in a far-ranging discussion—Marilyn Cochran-Smith (1997) and some of the teachers with whom she has worked call these discussions "hard talk"—about race, racism, privilege, and the negative impact they have on bicultural children. I then extend the analogy used by McIntosh by asking course participants to reflect and write in their journals about unearned privilege that they may enjoy in another area of social identity. Everybody can write something, since everybody benefits from some kind of privilege, whether it is in terms of their race, gender, social class, sexual orientation, or some other way in which their status is rewarded by society.

I have found this exercise to be particularly helpful in helping people come face to face with the silent, insidious, and unacknowledged power of institutional racism and other forms of discrimination. It provides a key learning experience for many teachers in their long journey of transformation. Ann chose to enumerate many examples of her English-language privilege (only some of which I include here), and then she thought about this issue even more critically after she had finished.

### THE PRIVILEGE OF SPEAKING, READING, AND WRITING THE ENGLISH LANGUAGE

*By Ann Scott*

Being a "native" English speaker (and reader and writer) in the United States (even though English is *not* the native language of this place) bestows all kinds of privileges on me that are so ingrained and so hidden that it takes a great deal of effort just to see the most obvious ones. I'm not sure if I've been "carefully taught not to recognize privilege" of this sort, as Peggy McIntosh thinks, or if it's simply in the nature of privilege that it is invisible to the wearer of it. Perhaps if it was visible, it would quickly become intolerable in its ugly, undeserved unjustness.

In no particular order of importance, being an English speaker in the United States means

1. I can be confident that people will understand me wherever I go in the United States, and if they don't *they* will be seen as deficient, not me.
2. My language will be considered the essential, legal, primary, best, official, legitimate, or only way of communicating.
3. I can survive, even thrive, in my country without learning a second language.
4. I can negotiate pretty well in most places in the world with English, at least in the industrialized world, without ever learning a second language.
5. I will not be patronized because of my native language.

6. I will not be ignored or talked about as if I am not present because of my native language.
7. I will not be asked, told, or required by law or the ignorance of others to speak a language that is not native to me in the place I call home.
8. I will not suffer persecution or discrimination because my native language is other than English.
9. I will not have to worry about whether my accent will cause people to think I don't have command of English, even though I may have perfect command of English.
10. I need never become exhausted from the rigors of trying to communicate in a language that is foreign to me.
11. If I speak or write articulately in my native language, I will be considered intelligent and well educated. I will not be thought stupid or slow because of my accent or the way I speak English.
13. I will never feel ashamed of my native language.
14. I will not be pressured to forget or abandon my native language. On the contrary, I will be encouraged, even required, to study it and become more fluent in it.
15. If I learn a second language, this will be seen as an asset and a source of pride, whereas for the nonnative-English speaker, being bilingual is a detriment and a source of shame.
16. I do not have to be pulled in two directions in terms of language—between my loyalties and pride in my own language and my desire to survive and belong in the dominant culture of the place I call home.
17. I do not have to feel ashamed of my parents or other family members because of the language they speak or because of their language proficiency.
18. Growing up in the United States as a native-English speaker, I have a lot of choices about educational attainment. I can be pretty lazy in school; I can do the minimum amount of work; I can even drop out of school in my early teens and still be able to speak, read, and write the dominant language adequately. (I'm not entirely sure about this one; it was true in the 1960s when I was in high school.)

About halfway through this exercise, I realized how faulty my assumptions about privilege are when I think about all the native-English speakers who are people of color, are disabled, have strong southern or rural or city accents, or are otherwise not in the dominant, Anglocentric mold. So many of the privileges I listed were also attached to my Whiteness, my WASPness. I can see gender discrimination with ease because I'm not one of the preferred people. To some extent I can recognize class privilege, but mainly I see the privileges of the classes above me. So anyway, I went back and tried to revise a lot of my list to reflect privilege specifically related to language, but many of them could be contested from the point of view of a non-Anglo native-English speaker. Perhaps then, I should specify, when I talk about language privilege, that I mean the language spoken by Whites with specific kinds of accents or dialect, that is, a much more strictly defined language.

Wow, this stuff is really hard to do. (10.2.93)

As Ann indicated, this is hard work, but it is a process that opens up worlds of understanding that otherwise might remain closed. Courageous teachers who take this journey find, as did Ann, that it pays off in many ways both personally and professionally.

Identification with one's culture does not stop at the point of just recognizing privilege, however; if it did, then it would result only in shame and guilt. Most teachers, like most human beings in general, do not wish to remain feeling bad about themselves; they need something more positive upon which to build. This is the case with Debbie Habib, a former doctoral student who reflected deeply about her background and experiences to understand how these had affected her teaching and her life and to analyze how White privilege had influenced her differently from other White students. As a Sephardic Jew with Turkish roots, Debbie often is mistaken for Arabic, Latina, biracial, or Iranian. People who try to figure out her background often make comments such as, "You're *something*, right?" This *something*, as Debbie explains below, is seen as "a little too ethnic."

### A KID FROM JERSEY: WHITE PRIVILEGE AND "A LITTLE TOO ETHNIC"

*By Deborah Leta Habib*

Visiting the "Mainline" Philadelphia home of a college friend's family was an interesting cultural experience for a kid from Jersey who thought boarding schools only truly existed in Louisa May Alcott's *Little Women.* I did not lead a sheltered life, mind you. My first-generation, middle-class, lefty liberal Jewish family frequented plays and peace marches, and I was nourished on a diet of discourse and library books. In my Italian, Jewish, Black, Greek, and

Catholic New Jersey community of upbringing, we just didn't do boarding schools. And so, as I was recovering from the shock of learning about a boarding school for girls where they played a game called "lacrosse" and from where my new rebellious best friend had emerged, I soon faced another challenge: I was "a little too ethnic."

Years later, I can name the emotions and experiences that shaped my sense of self with phrases like White privilege, anti-Semitism, and internalized anti-Semitism. But 15 years ago I didn't have these terms, or the reflective ability or support to make sense of it all. In middle and high school, we all hung out together, shared snacks and smokes, and visited each other's houses. But when racial violence consumed the school, I was White. I was Jewish at home, but only White at school. Everybody had to choose one, White or Black. So, a few years later, when I walked into my friend's parents' house on "The Mainline" (which had plastic coated furniture, as did my aunt's, only hers held the smells of the kitchen and the Bronx air, whereas the Mainline plastic had no smell at all), I was a little taken aback by the coldness of the greeting. I introduced myself in what I thought was a polite manner; it had always worked for my friends' parents in Jersey, who seemed to think I was nice enough. Part of me just thought these Mainline-parents had been sitting on plastic for too long, but my heart and somewhat nauseous stomach detected something else.

After a few more meetings spread over several years, I finally commented to my friend that her parents didn't seem to like me too much. "It's not that they don't like you," she said. "It's just that you're a little too ethnic for them." I thought about standing in their kitchen, me with my curly dark hair, wide nose, olive skin, and peasant build, them with their fair hair, blue eyes, and fine bones. I remembered the time that my friend and I were leaving for Europe, and her mother suggested we visit the churches and cathedrals . . . "and I'm sure there are some lovely temples too," she added, not quite knowing what to say. Considering I had rarely stepped foot in a temple before, I thought it unlikely that I would make it a focus of my trip. Was I the first Jewish person they had ever met, ever spoken with? My friend had told me that their club had an unwritten "No Jews Allowed" policy. I knew that Jews as a group were often made to feel invisible in this society and at times blatantly discriminated against or threatened. As a child, I believe I once wondered why the school calendar was organized around holidays that my family did not celebrate, and I had heard numerous stories of flight from persecution and arrival in a less than welcoming new land. But I had never been so personally aware of anti-Semitism until it seared my soul in my friend's kitchen and I experienced a form of judgment that those who do not have White privilege probably feel on a regular basis.

Fifteen years after our first meeting, I received a card from my friend's parents (she is still my close friend, so they have probably realized that I am not just a passing ethnic fad), appreciating my support in helping her coordinate her wedding and taking care of logistics so she could have time with her family. So perhaps they are beginning to accept me. Has my skin lightened, hair uncurled, ancestry changed? Or am I "one of the nice ones, not like the others"? Have they done some soul searching, examined their biases, made conscious changes in their attitudes? I would love to be sure this is it, but I am a bit skeptical.

Since that first meeting, I have learned that boarding schools not only exist, but that they serve the specific purpose of maintaining privilege in this society, and that lacrosse is a game that was first played by Native Americans. My Italian, Jewish, Black, Greek, Catholic community of upbringing now includes many Asian Americans and East Indians, one of whom owns the Dunkin' Donuts which he made kosher. My parents are active on a race relations committee which, among other things, is negotiating with the town to pave a road that would link, physically and symbolically, two neighborhoods separated by race and class. I now have the vocabulary to describe the experiences and emotions that shaped and still shape my identity. Some of these words are White privilege, anti-Semitism, and internalized anti-Semitism. They are useful as I try to unlayer and heal my ethnic identity and internalized racism with honesty and integrity. Here I sit in reflection: educator, activist, spiritual being, that kid from Jersey, the one with White privilege who is "a little too ethnic." (March 1994)

Debbie's reflections are especially useful because they help to deconstruct the White/Black dichotomy so often associated with difference. As she mentioned, in her high school you were either Black or White; there was nothing else. Given the growing presence of students from backgrounds that cannot be categorized so easily, as well as the increasingly biracial and biethnic identities of the students in U.S. classrooms, it is essential to acknowledge the complicated nature of diversity. But this recognition should not diminish the power of racial and other kinds of privilege.

A growing number of scholars are writing critically and convincingly about the need for White teachers to acknowledge and "own" their White identity if they are to become effective teachers of all students (O'Donnell & Clark, 1999; Howard, 1999). This process requires that Whites recognize their complicity in maintaining injustice if they choose to do nothing about it. Although the process of recognizing, confronting, and learning from one's unearned privileges is indispensable, it also can be tremendously painful and discouraging. To become transformative, it needs to be complemented by hopeful beliefs and actions. For many teachers, this means finding out about and becoming a White ally. Beverly Daniel Tatum (1994) speaks of this process as "the restoration of hope."

Patty Bode, the art teacher who described in Chapter 5 the process of confronting unfair representation in books with her first graders, has engaged in just such a journey. Always known as a gifted art teacher, Patty had won many accolades and awards from students, parents, co-teachers, and local and national organizations for her sensitive and inclusive teaching. But she felt that "something was missing." When she started her graduate studies, she began to rethink her ideas and her classroom practices. The following is an excerpt from Patty's reflections.

## ON BECOMING A WHITE ALLY

### By Patty Bode

Before I started my graduate studies, I was proudly practicing multicultural education in my classroom, but I knew I still had an enormous amount to learn. As an art teacher, my curriculum drew from world art throughout history. I developed cross-cultural comparisons of folk artists from traditional societies throughout the globe and I researched contemporary artists who made statements about current events and social status and identity. I developed curriculum to encourage student dialogue about skin color in what I hope was a respectful way and in a safe educational environment.

I noticed an inordinate number of students of color in special education. I hoped I was doing a good job, but I knew something was missing. I was not certain what it was. I grappled with my position as a European American teacher and my place in multicultural education. I worried that somehow my practice would not be viewed as valid in a realm of study that grew out of the Civil Rights Movement with African American educators asserting the right to be accurately represented in curriculum and with concerns about the achievements of students of color.

This is why knowledge and identification of other White allies became so empowering to me. Reading the articles by Peggy McIntosh [1988] and Christine Sleeter [1994] were turning points. Their writing was not surprising or revelatory, just confirming. Their scholarship reinforced and validated my beliefs. Naming my position as a White ally underscored my role in multicultural education and provided me with a forum for dialogue among my students. When my third-grade Latino student asks me, "Ms. Bode, if you are not Latina, why do you care so much about Latino art and culture?" I am able to respond with more self-assurance and certainty. Together my students and I frame a context for Dr. Martin Luther King's words, "Injustice anywhere is a threat to justice everywhere." We talk about privilege and responsibility. We read stories about cooperation to create change. We become partners who trust each other. We promise to work together to fight racism. It all begins to make sense in the mind of a third grader. (11.12.97)

Patty Bode's is the story of a White teacher who is finding the way to honor her own identity and her role in the quest for social justice in teaching. Teachers who can identify with their students culturally, racially, in terms of social class origin, or in other ways, may find that the process is not quite as difficult because they can draw on and reflect about their own experiences with difference and consequently they are able to more readily understand the feelings and perspectives of their students. I have seen this happen time and again in my own classes. For instance, when I ask my graduate students to discuss their identity and why it is important to them or not, I have found consistently that those who identify with their culture and ethnicity are more easily able to identify with their students of diverse backgrounds. I present two examples to illustrate this. First, Tom Hidalgo, the grandson of Spanish immigrants who worked in the coal mines of West Virginia, relates how he developed his identity as a Spaniard, and how it has profoundly influenced his work as a community organizer and his interest in oral history and multicultural education as transformative processes.

*ENRICHING DIFFERENCES*

*By Tom Hidalgo*

My ethnic background is critical to me. The first time I really remember noticing my Spanishness I was in first grade. I remember going home and asking my parents why we had a name like Hidalgo. Nobody else in my class did. Everybody else had names like Hylton and Parsons and Jones and Green. They explained to me that their names came from England and mine came from Spain. I felt different, but also special. In fact, my sister and I were the only "ethnics" in the school of more than 800 kids! From then on I always felt special being Spanish. And lucky.

I believe that because I was different, I have always been interested in other cultures and peoples and places. I have always valued and tried to learn from differences in people. I have always noted ethnic or racial or cultural differences in people and even at a young age I remember feeling that these differences were very enriching to the environment. I'm sure this has driven much of my work and interests. (1.26.94)

In the second example, David Ruiz, a former graduate student who was a counselor for students of color in an independent school in Massachusetts, wrote simply, "I guess that being Puerto Rican is as important to me as being alive is" (9.16.94). He found it curious, but understandable, that most Whites in our class did not identify with their ethnic backgrounds. In his journal, he mused about why this might be so.

## BEING ON THE WINNING TEAM

By David Ruiz

That the United States is characterized by Anglo-conformity seems to be apparent based on the responses given by many of the Euro-Americans in class on Wednesday. It is quite easy to be on the winning team and not ask how it is that you're winning. Most White Americans are comfortable in their dominant roles and are not really concerned about whether or not the scales of justice were tilted. Few would trade places with those other people and most would deny any wrongdoing on their part or on the part of their ancestors.

It seemed like they had conveniently forgotten their roots. Maybe it doesn't matter when you're on the barrel edge, looking into the barrel, watching all the other crabs trying to get out. . . . It is quite easy to be on the winning team and not ask how it is that you're winning. (9.21.94)

As we can see from the foregoing examples, the failure to identify with their own identity can prevent teachers from identifying more closely with their students. In conjunction with this, teachers need to develop identities as learners.

## BECOMING A LEARNER OF STUDENTS

As Paulo Freire (1970b) proposed many years ago, teaching and learning need to be thought of as reciprocal processes in which students become teachers and teachers become students. If this is the case, then teachers no longer simply deposit knowledge into students' minds; rather, teachers become actively engaged in learning through their interactions with students. This is an especially timely consideration if we think about the wide gulf that currently exists in the United States between teachers, who are overwhelmingly White, middle-class, and monolingual English speakers, and their students, who are increasingly diverse in culture, ethnicity, social class, and native language. Historically in this situation, the conventional approach has been to instruct students in the ways of White, middle-class, English-speaking America and, in the process, to rid them of as many of their differences as possible.

Without denying the need to teach students the cultural capital that they need to help them negotiate society, it is also important that teachers make a commitment to become *students of their students*. This implies at least two kinds of processes. First, teachers need to learn *about* their students, a change from the one-way learning that usually takes place in classrooms. For this to happen, teachers need to become researchers. In the words of Ira Shor (Shor & Freire, 1987):

> The first researcher, then, in the classroom is the teacher who investigates his or her students. This is one basic task of the liberatory classroom, but by itself it is only preparatory because the research process must animate students to study themselves, the course texts, and their own language and reality. (pp. 9–10)

Second, as implied by Shor, teachers need to create spaces in which teachers can learn *with their students,* and in which students are encouraged to learn about themselves and one another.

The assertion that teachers can and should become learners is in no way meant to lessen their duty to teach. Nor is it to imply that there are equal power relations between teachers and students in the classroom, or that students' and teachers' knowledge have equal status in society. These are romantic notions that, taken to an extreme, relieve educators of their responsibility to teach. Years ago, for instance, I heard a teacher remark that his students were so "street smart" that they really did not need to be instructed in the academic content of the schools, something that he surely would not have said of his own children. This condescending attitude does little to help students. In fact, such comments often have more to do with teachers' feelings that their students are unable to learn or unworthy of learning academic knowledge.

Teachers have a grave responsibility to prepare students to become effective and critical participants in the world, and this is particularly true for their bicultural students, who consistently have been denied this access. Teachers need to be authoritative—that is, knowledgeable, clear, and direct—rather than authoritarian in their interactions with students. They need to teach students the kinds of skills they must have in order to make a difference in the world. This means, among other things, that students need to learn the language of power (Delpit, 1988).

Going through the paces of learning about one's students is not enough. It is not simply about learning a technical strategy, or picking up a few cultural tidbits. It is impossible, for example, to become culturally responsive simply by taking a course in which cultural responsiveness is reduced to a strategy. This does not mean that teaching is always an intuitive undertaking, although it certainly has this quality at times. But more important are the *attitudes* of teachers when they are in the position of learners. In discussing the specific case of African American students, Jacqueline Jordan Irvine (1990) has suggested that learning can be improved if the interpersonal context that exists between students and their teachers is a positive one. She developed the concept of *cultural synchronization* to describe this relationship. Cultural synchronization assumes both integrity and humility; it cannot be either deceptive or an artificial donning of cultural values. Rather, it means that teachers need to learn what can help their students learn, and then change their teaching accordingly.

Students are very perceptive, no matter how young they are, and they can spot negative attitudes or false intentions a mile away. David Corson (1995) has asserted that teachers, being human beings, are just as susceptible to the influence of negative attitudes as anybody else; however, because they have enormous power over children, their attitudes can become particularly harmful because they can be put into action in the classroom. Frances Kendall (1996) cites the appalling case of a White teacher who, in a videotape of her teaching, was found to wash her hands after every time she touched a Black child. In this case, no matter what this teacher might say, her negative beliefs were communicated unequivocally to her young students. This is not to imply that teachers who hold these beliefs cannot change, but it is to suggest that beliefs and attitudes need to change before any specific strategies can help.

In journal responses to an assignment that participants analyze the pros and cons of culturally responsive pedagogy, Lizette Román, a bilingual teacher, was critical of what she clearly saw as superficial cultural learning, but she also reflected on the necessity for teachers to learn more about their students in order to be effective with them.

## CULTURAL KNOWLEDGE AND CULTURALLY RESPONSIVE PEDAGOGY

*By Lizette Román*

To have knowledge of another culture does not mean to be able to repeat one or two words in a student's language, nor is it to celebrate an activity or sing a song related to their culture. To acknowledge and respect is to be able to understand and apply this knowledge to everyday classroom activities. It is to be able to make changes or modifications in one's curriculum or pedagogy when the needs of the students have not been served. It is to be patient, tolerant, curious, creative, eager to learn, and, most important, nonauthoritarian with students.

In order for a teacher to promote excellence in education, there has to be a real and honest connection between the needs and cultural values of teachers and students. This is culturally responsive education. It was not until I thought more about it that I realized that both multicultural education and cultural congruency are simply *means* by which minority students will gain a better future. Students cannot learn outside of their cultural context. Factors such as achievement, dropout rates, even students' behavior and attendance are affected when schools as a whole do not take into consideration students' cultures and learning styles. All students, regardless of their ethnic group, need to feel connected with their schools, their homes, and their communities.

There are cons to culturally responsive pedagogy when teachers do not understand or acknowledge their students' culture and insist on teaching according to their own values. There are cons when a teacher stereotypes or generalizes about her students. This often has the effect of lowering expectations of the students, consequently affecting students' performance. There are cons when a teacher does not recognize a student's individuality and sees him only as part of the group. Knowledge of a particular cultural learning style is useful and serves as a guideline, but it does not necessarily represent the learning styles of all members of that culture. (11.13.96; 11.20.96)

Defining the teacher as a learner is a radical departure from the prevailing notion of the educator as repository of all knowledge, a view that is firmly entrenched in society. Ira Shor (Shor & Freire, 1987) critiqued this conventional portrait of teachers vis-à-vis their students: "The students are not a flotilla of boats trying to reach the teacher who is finished and waiting on the shore. The teacher is also one of the boats" (p. 50). Yet in spite of how terrifying it may be for teachers to act as all-knowing sages, this conception of teacher is a more familiar and, hence, less threatening one than teacher as learner. Once teachers admit that they do not know everything, they make themselves as vulnerable as their students. It is this attitude of learner on the part of teachers that is needed, first, to convey to students that nobody is above learning; and second, to let students know that they also are knowers and that what they know can be an important source of learning for others as well. It follows from this perspective that teachers need to build on what their students bring with them to the classroom.

What exactly should teachers know about their students? In the case of bicultural students specifically, teachers would do well to learn about their lives outside of school, including their families and cultures, how they see the world, what is important to them, and their values and dreams for the future. They also can learn at least one of the languages of the students whom they teach. Engaging in this kind of learning, which needs to be approached with both humility and energy, represents nothing less than a political commitment on the part of teachers. But because this learning can be done *with*, and not only *for* or *about*, students, it is neither overwhelming nor impossible. The following excerpt is a powerful example of this kind of learning.

Bill Dunn is a high school English teacher in a small urban school system. A few years ago, he decided that it was time he "came out of the closet" as a Spanish speaker, so he asked me to sponsor an independent research study in which he could document his experience. From a working-class Irish family, Bill was born, was raised, and still lives in the town in which he teaches, and he cares deeply about it. He had taught for 20 years in the same school district and he had seen it change from a mostly working-class Irish and European American school system to one that was over two-thirds Puerto Rican. He had heard a great deal of Spanish spoken over those 20 years, and when he became a doctoral student, he decided this was the perfect opportunity to explicitly learn the language.

The independent research project he did allowed him to design his game plan: He would take a course in our university Spanish department and another at a local community center; he would sit in on bilingual classes at his high school; and he would keep a journal of all of these activities. Following is an extensive excerpt from the eloquent journal that was a result of Bill's immersion into the Spanish language and the lives of his students (Dunn, 1994).

*MI SEMESTRE DE ESPAÑOL:*
*A CASE STUDY ON THE CULTURAL DIMENSION OF*
*SECOND-LANGUAGE ACQUISITION*

*By Bill Dunn*

I've searched for a word to describe the cultural complexities of acquiring a second language, and eventually I settled on the word "stance." By stance I mean many things: the reason why I desire to learn a second language, my attitude toward my community and the people who speak the "target" language, and many confrontations with my own cultural identity and the cultural identities of others. Stance also has a pugilistic connotation. I believe that there is an element of risk involved in living in a multicultural community. You have to be willing to take the heat. In *Pedagogy of the Oppressed* Paulo Freire [1970b] points to risk as the essence of being human. . . . To acquire a second language you must assume an attitude that reaches out to people, and to do that you must be able to see beyond your own culture.

The cultural conflicts of second-language acquisition came to me in a vivid way one day while I was involved in a totally unrelated activity. I had been aware for quite a while of the cultural turmoil of living in a language-rich environment. In fact, I don't think anyone could teach in a situation like my town without being aware of the troubled cultural waters in which we are engulfed on a daily basis. Much of the conflict is caused by language because language is in many ways culture. But the phrase which brought the cultural dimension of second-language acquisition to the surface for me occurred one day while I was working on a carpentry project. . . . I was thinking of the word for wood in Spanish, *madera,* and I wondered whether it could be used like in English to mean forest or woods. I thought to myself, "One of these days I have to come out of the closet with my Spanish." It was that particular phrase which drove home the cultural implications for second-language acquisition. Like the risks involved in revealing a homosexual orientation, there are risks involved in acquiring a second language as well. Americans are particularly poor at second-language acquisition; the dominant culture demands "English only." When you acquire a second language, you put yourself at odds with the dominant culture, and any time you go against the flow you have to be willing to take some heat for it. In a working-class town like mine you have to be willing to breach some very turbulent cultural waters. There is bound to be personal conflict on the psychic level as well because in order to acquire a second language you also have to be willing to acquire some of the habits and cultural attitudes of those who speak the language. These conflicts can be very subtle and just being aware of them can be a major first step in the right direction.

To acquire a second language, you must also acquire a second culture, and that is going to cause problems. There will be a resentment among members of your own cultural group, and occasionally suspicion among members of the target language group. (I must add, though, that my experience with native-Spanish speakers in my town has been extremely positive.) Despite these cultural barriers there are wonderful rewards and gains in letting one's cultural attitudes melt and mix with different currents. First, there is the insight into an alternate reality or perspective on the world and your environment, and second, there is a freedom in distancing yourself from the inhibiting ties of your own culture.

In my work, I often act as a bridge between different cultures. Part of my evolution as a teacher has been in self-defense: I have learned to make my life easier by making life easier for my students; but another, greater part of my experience has been a deep curiosity and yearning to understand the lives of my students. In my struggle to understand, I have learned not only a great deal about my students, but also about myself.

One thing that I have learned is that language carries a lot of cultural baggage with it. The distinctions that are made on the basis of language in my town are fascinating. We are a sort of walking, living, and breathing language lab. Obviously there exists the English–Spanish cultural distinction. There are also economic distinctions. . . . On any given day in my classroom and in the hallways of my school, I witness remarkable language interactions which often go unnoticed and are not valued, or worse, are devalued. . . . If the third floor of my school were the language wing of a prestigious boarding school, we would be answering questions for

Morley Safer on *Sixty Minutes* as to why we are so successful at language acquisition when the rest of America fails so dismally. Instead we are called on by the school board to answer why our students perform so poorly on standardized tests.

I hope that you will enjoy [the following] cultural scenes. They are not the dramatic headlines that we are all too familiar with in our town. These are scenes from everyday life which in this town can be very complex.

[Dos] Escenas de cultura [Two cultural scenes]

Scene One: *A few years ago I was busy with some paper work during homeroom. Four or five students were chatting in Spanish and I found this to be very distracting. I asked them to be quiet, but they kept on talking. A little later I asked them again more forcefully. One of the students pointed out to me that there were other students speaking in English and I was not chastising them. I thought about that later in the day and I realized that this student was right. I began to wonder what it was that bothered me about the Spanish. I didn't think they were talking about me or anything like that, but I was annoyed. Shortly after that incident I began to realize that there were cultural collisions occurring beneath the surface, and I also began to understand that most people are not aware of the source of these collisions.*

Scene Two: *I'm in my classroom about a month ago. It is a senior class and there is no seating arrangement. I like to think of them as mature enough to sit where they want. There are two very attractive, well-dressed girls who always sit together. One is Black and the other is Puerto Rican. They chat a lot, and I have to constantly get their attention. On this particular day I ask them to be quiet several times. Finally the Black girl informs me that she is not going to be quiet as long as* they can talk. *With her head she motions toward the corner of the room where the bilingual kids sit. . . . I have been practicing Spanish with the bilingual kids, and in this kid's statement I sense a kind of "you like them better than us" attitude. El círculo ha cerrado (The circle has closed).*

When I decided to do this project, I was apprehensive because I was not sure how far I could get in 3 months of trying to teach myself Spanish. Puedo comunicar en español pero mi lenguage no es muy bueno [I can communicate in Spanish but my language is not very good]. Yet I feel that I have made some progress. I have also made some wonderful friends that I probably would not have met otherwise. One thing that I have noticed is that people who speak more than one language really like to talk, and I have learned a great deal just by talking to people.

In the beginning I got very excited about learning Spanish. I hadn't felt that way about learning anything in a long time. I borrowed some Spanish-language tapes and I listened to them. . . . I also worked in several different Spanish-language books. . . . Perhaps the most interesting aspect of my second-language learning was the use of television. . . . I like talk shows like *Christina* and *The Nuevo Paul Rodríguez Show* and news programs like *Noticias y Más*.

My hall duty at school is outside a Spanish One class, and I listen to what goes on in there. It seems to be a very traditional class. It also seems to me that the teacher could be using the talents of her students much more creatively. . . . Sometimes it almost seems like she is devaluing the language of her students. I have heard this from other Spanish teachers too. They put down the Spanish of the kids in this town. If I were teaching this class I would be looking for ways in which I could use the language talents of my students as a vehicle to help the monolingual students.

About a month into my study I noticed something very peculiar. I had been very excited, as I mentioned, about my project. Then everything just sort of slowed down. I found this to be very puzzling. I am guessing that things occurred on the subconscious level that caused the shutdown. My theory is that my own cultural identity was struggling to reassert itself. It was kind of like I was pushing my mind into places that it just didn't want to go. . . . As a teacher this impressed me very much. I have witnessed similar responses in my students when they come into class and just want to put their head on the desk. Again, you don't really understand this until you have experienced it for yourself. Too often we dismiss this sort of thing as laziness. It is very easy to draw the wrong conclusion. This was one of my most powerful insights into second-language acquisition. It was almost like my mind was saying, "enough with all this Spanish."

In terms of where I am now with the Spanish language, it is difficult to say. It took me a long time to get over what [Stephen] Krashen calls "the silent period." I don't know. I tend to be very inhibited to begin with so it was really difficult for me to begin to speak in Spanish. I did notice that it was very important whom I was speaking to. It is still very difficult for me to speak to a native-Spanish speaker. I'm more comfortable with someone whose second language is Spanish. I think this is a valuable insight as a teacher because many students may be very inhibited with me because I'm a native English speaker. Again, this is an insight that you don't understand until you undergo the process. . . . Another peculiarity of speaking involves who else is around. There are certain colleagues that I am very inhibited from speaking Spanish if they walk by. They tend to be teachers who are very biased in their views. This is insightful for students too. If a teacher is continually putting down a student's language and culture, that would probably be the least desirable conversationalist for the students.

When I finally came out of my "silent" period, I again got very excited about this aspect of learning a second language. Again though, it was a "roller coaster" sort of experience. One thing I can definitely point out about this aspect is that it is very hard to function in a second language when you are tired or your mind is preoccupied with other problems. Some days when I was alert the words came easily, and on other days when I was tired I just drew a blank. I think I have a greater understanding of my students because many of them come to school tired or with severe problems.

As part of my study I have been speaking with nonnative-Spanish speakers. I found them to be very sympathetic. I think they understand how difficult it is to acquire a second language when you are older. I noticed too that the [kids in the bilingual program] were more receptive toward me. I covered a class for a bilingual teacher, and the students were quite hospitable. I feel that because they are trying to accomplish a similar feat, they are more understanding. Sometimes when I speak Spanish to the mainstream [Spanish-speaking] kids they can be very critical.

I thought that it would be interesting to sit in on a bilingual class and observe. Anne, a bilingual teacher, gave me permission. . . . I knew a few of the kids and they said hello. I returned the greetings and thanked them in Spanish for allowing me to participate in their class. . . . Anne passed out a test, and I was very disappointed. I only answered a question or two, but what shocked me was I didn't understand two-thirds of the questions. I had no idea what was being asked, and I thought of all those kids in the lower tracks who are condemned to answering questions that they don't understand at the end of countless chapters that they don't comprehend. At first I felt a tremendous need to occupy myself. I reached over and took a book on the history of Puerto Rico from the bookshelf, and I started to read. . . . I knew that if I had been a student I would have been chastised for reading the book so I put it down. . . . After a while of sitting there feeling stupid and kind of neglected, I had the urge to talk to someone. I think if I had been a kid, I would have acted up or talked to someone near me even if they couldn't understand me. Then, because I wasn't really doing anything I got very, very tired. I really wanted to put my head down on the desk. I know that if I had been a student, I would have been sleeping. . . .

I came away from this class with a much deeper understanding of what it feels like to be alienated. I really felt lonely in there. I didn't feel angry, but I could certainly understand how a kid could get angry in that kind of situation. Most teachers because of their own experience of school have never dealt with these kinds of feelings, and I think they would have a hard time understanding this. I also felt that bilingual program kids tend to get isolated in most schools. They spend a good deal of the day in small groups apart from the rest of the school.

[There] are things about Puerto Rican people and culture that I admire very much. I would also have to admit that I did not always admire these things because I did not understand them at first. This is a good lesson not only for second-language learning but for any situation where different cultures come in contact. It takes time to build understanding. . . . Another aspect of my study has been a combination craft and cultural project. With my friend and colleague, Edgar Rodríguez, I have started a project to build a *cuatro* [a Puerto Rican stringed instrument]. It has been a fun undertaking, and I am looking forward to playing it. I think there has to be room in the curriculum for these kinds of things. They have to be valued as a learning experience. It is hard to describe the absolute joy that I have witnessed in many of my students' eyes when they see my project. Many of them have told me that their grandfathers play the cuatro. . . .

I now know from personal experience that second-language acquisition is a slow and difficult process, yet in most American schools we demand that nonnative-English speakers achieve fluency in a short period of time. Multiculturalism is a reality in places like my town, and I guess it comes down to whether you view it as a loss or a gain. There is a lot of conflict in my community, but there is also a lot of potential. As a nation, we cannot afford to continue to drift farther and farther apart. The trend in America over the past 2 decades has been to move away from problems. It has led to two nations, one White, affluent, and scared, and the other non-White, poor, and angry. We need to begin to reach out and understand one another. That is happening in places like my town. People are beginning to communicate. As Edgar says, "I have learned that the greatest thing in the world is to communicate." In our town, that communication is often in two languages.

As we see from his journal, Bill Dunn got more from the project than he ever imagined. Not only did he learn Spanish (he could understand most things and speak pretty well after one semester, although he is still studying it, by now having made a lifelong commitment to become bilingual), but he also learned a great deal about himself and his students in the process. Bill had always been a fine teacher because he cared about and got along with his students, and because he saw their diversity as a strength to build on. But he became an even better teacher and he developed a newfound respect for his students after he learned the energy and hard work it takes to learn academic content in a second language. His teaching practices also changed as a result of the project. For example, in his field notes he explored how many of the mistakes his students made in English were related to Spanish. Not only could he explain things to them in Spanish, but he could use examples from the Spanish language itself.

Probably the most powerful testimony to the changes he underwent as a result of learning Spanish came from his students. At the end of his journal, Bill wrote:

> At one point I asked one of my students, Julie, how she felt about an Anglo teacher trying to teach himself Spanish. Her reply was, "A lot of these teachers around here are know-it-alls. They think they know everything. When you try to learn Spanish, you are showing me that you are a learner too." I thought about Paulo Freire's theory of forming a dialogue with students and that authentic education is not A *for* B, or A *about* B, but A *with* B. My undertaking to teach myself Spanish clearly places me with my students.

## IDENTIFYING WITH STUDENTS

If, as we have seen throughout this book, students are empowered as learners when they can identify with school and with their teachers, it follows that the process needs to be a mutual one. As we saw in the case of Bill Dunn, it happens when teachers make a specific commitment to identify with the everyday realities of their students. No amount of school reform or restructuring can accomplish this kind of identification. In the words of Jim Cummins (1996), implementing true educational reform that has a goal of turning around deep-seated and long-term discrimination requires "*personal redefinitions* of the ways in which *individual educators* interact with the students and communities they serve" (p. 136).

In my own research, I have found that this kind of redefinition is longed for by students (Nieto, 1996). Ron, a student who had experienced little success in school until he reached an alternative high school that was based on a model of genuine relationships with students, explained the problem eloquently:

> When a teacher becomes a teacher, she acts like a teacher instead of a person. She takes her title as now she's mechanical, somebody just running it. Teachers shouldn't deal with students like we're machines. You're a person, I'm a person. We come to school and we all [should] act like people. (p. 268)

Educational research provides compelling examples of what can happen when teachers begin to identify with their students. In a study of an ongoing collaborative research project with Yup'ik teachers in southwest Alaska, Jerry Lipka (1991) wrote about how identifying with students can create a positive classroom climate. Lipka analyzed a lesson that was seemingly about art, but a closer look revealed that the lesson was actually about subsistence and survival and therefore based on values and skills important to this community. Lipka discovered that when Yup'ik teachers are teaching Yup'ik children and relating to them in culturally compatible ways in familiar settings, many of the factors that have been characterized as creating school failure are absent. He concluded that cultural and social *relationships* were the key to explaining the success of the teacher and students he studied.

In the case cited above, the teacher and students shared the same cultural understandings and experiences. As a consequence, the cultural congruence of the curriculum and pedagogy appeared effortless and natural. Can the same happen with teachers who do not share the same background as their students? Although it certainly takes more work, developing a strong identification with students from a different culture is possible. Research by Frederick Erickson and Gerald Mohatt (1982) reported on two classrooms of American Indian children, one taught by an Indian teacher and the other by a non-Indian. The classroom organization of these teachers differed markedly at the beginning of the school year, but by the end of the year, they were much more similar than different. How did this occur? According to the researchers, the non-Indian teacher used what they termed "teacher radar" to pick up cues from children about what strategies might be effective in teaching them. By the end of the year, the non-Indian teacher, just as his colleague, also had table groups rather than rows, and he spent more time working with small groups and tutoring rather than in whole-class instruction.

Writing more than 25 years ago, Mildred Dickeman (1973) posited that the most valuable resources available for teachers to relate classroom goals to the cultural diversity of their students were those that most often were overlooked: their students, the members of the local community, and the teachers themselves. She called on teachers to uncover their own untold stories, their ethnic heritages, and "family tragedies and achievements" (p. 24) that resulted from immigration, as a way of identifying with their culturally diverse students. Further, she suggested that teachers had available, "however forgotten, repressed, or ignored, the experiences of self and family" in the context of pressure for assimilation and upward mobility" (pp. 23–24). Accordingly, Dickeman suggested that it was only when teachers learned to recognize their own alienation that they could best relate to their students.

The process that Dickeman proposed was to build on the experiences of teachers not as teachers but as people with particular histories and strengths. This process can result in a profound transformation of how teachers view their past and even their role as teachers. The purpose of identifying with one's students is not to dabble in other people's cultures, but to use the relationships that ensue to change classroom practices to be more effective with a wider range of students. It is a process that is as empowering and enriching for teachers as it is for the students with whom they work. Learning from one's students means that teachers predictably become more multicultural in their outlook and world view. As such, it implies a profound shift in attitudes and values toward students and what they have to offer. In the final analysis, it means not just talking about multicultural education as an educational program or strategy, but putting into practice a multicultural view of the world.

## BECOMING MULTICULTURAL

I have argued elsewhere (Nieto, 1996) that to become a multicultural teacher, one needs to become a multicultural person first. Young people are especially keen observers of the verbal and nonverbal messages of the adults around them, and they are usually adept at spotting inconsistencies between what their teachers say and what they do. For example, teachers can talk on and on about the value of knowing a second language, but if they themselves do not attempt to learn another language, their words may sound hollow to their students. Even if their curriculum is outwardly multicultural, if teachers do not demonstrate through their actions and behaviors that they truly value diversity, students often can tell.

Becoming a multicultural person implies, as we have seen previously, that teachers need to learn more about their students and about the world in general. This means stepping out of our own world and learning to understand some of the experiences, values, and realities of others. It is sometimes an exhilarating experience, but it also can be uncomfortable and challenging because it decenters us and our world, forcing us to focus on the lives and priorities of others who are different from us. It also helps us to empathize with others whom we ordinarily might not have included within our circle of humanity. Karen Donaldson, now a well-known re-searcher and teacher in multicultural education, went through this very process when she began her doctoral studies with me a decade ago.

## BEING BLACK AND MULTICULTURAL

*By Karen McLean Donaldson*

I can remember coming into the doctoral program in 1989 with one major question in mind: Would I be able to stay true to my cultural commitment of addressing the racial oppression of Black Ameri-cans? At the time, I didn't care much about looking into gender or class issues, although I was female and in a disadvantaged economic class. I believed that being Black caused more hardship for me, my family, community, and my racial ethnic group in general. Going into that first course in multicultural education, I was angry to see racism being tossed into the bowl of "isms." I thought, "Surely the injustices of racism far outweigh and are much more venomous than all of the other 'isms' put together." Before taking the course I saw racism as a Black and White issue. This is how I had been groomed all of my life: "Whites were against us and hated us." This was my total socialization experience.

As far back as I can remember, my parents taught my siblings and me about our mixed heritage, but "Negro" and later "Black American" is how we identified. It was a funny thing for me be-cause I was the lightest one in the whole family, but there was never any doubt of who I was. My father helped with this because he taught me that being Black didn't mean what shade you were, but rather how our inner soul connected to its ancestors; being Black was a state of mind. Yet all of my life I have been asked, "What are you?" I could have passed for Jewish, Italian, Latina,

Arab, and so on, but my parents instilled Black pride and knowledge in me that would never allow that.

My mother is biracial. Her father came from the Cabo Verde islands and her mother was Sicilian. When my grandmother got ill and was hospitalized, none of her Italian relatives would take the children because they were considered Black. They therefore became wards of the state and were separated into various foster homes. My mother and youngest aunt were sent to Boston and lived with Black foster parents. The other six siblings stayed in the Cape Cod area and held onto their Cape Verdean culture and language. My father, on the other hand, was born and raised in North Carolina and was Black and Indian, along with some other European mixtures; he was, that is, a product of the institution of slavery. He would often share sad stories of segregation in the South. Sometimes I would sneak out of my bed when there was company and listen to the appalling stories of racism that he had experienced as a child and adult. To know of my parents' suffering and the suffering of Black people in general made me bitter and distrustful toward Whites.

When I began the doctoral program, I asked myself why I was getting ready to take this multicultural education journey, and then I realized that all of my life I had loved learning about cultures. I had shrugged off some of the most wonderful experiences because they were so few and far between: my visits to the synagogue on the hill to learn about Jewish culture; my fifth-grade teacher from Ireland who taught me so much about Irish culture; my yearly summer visits to Cape Cod where I not only learned about my Cape Verdean heritage but about the Mashpee Indian heritage. This course brought all of that back for me. I began releasing the anger I felt, and opening up to understand that my race was not the only race that suffered in America. I opened myself to understand the intersection of race, class, and gender as well as exceptionality, ageism, language, and so on. I began to understand more of the human connection and the need to address all of these issues.

I am still dedicated to reducing racism in schools and in society, but I do this with a well-rounded view. And though I still concentrate on the continued progress of my people, I realize we all must become versed in one another's experiences and cultures if the young are to succeed in our diverse world. I think of myself now as a human rights educator and activist and I work with others in advocating for peace and justice for all human beings.

As a professor, in addition to my scholarship, I share firsthand experiences. I speak about the racial prejudice that I had toward Whites in general. In my classes, we talk about identity, conditioning, and the role power plays with regard to oppression. I teach and continue to learn about the numerous cultures in the United States and abroad. I often use the arts as a way of giving students hands-on experiences in understanding other peoples' cultures. Although I now spend much of my time doing research and writing books, teaching is still a big part of who I am. My students let me know how much they appreciate my open and nontraditional style of teaching. That first multicultural course helped in my transformation as a true humanitarian and it made me a much better teacher and individual, which in turn has enhanced my students' learning.

## CHALLENGING RACISM AND OTHER BIASES

If teachers simply follow the decreed curriculum as handed down from the central office, or if they go along with standard practices such as rigid ability tracking or high-stakes testing that result in unjust outcomes, they are unlikely ever to question the fairness of these practices. But when they engage in a personal transformation through such actions as described above—that is, when they become learners with, of, and for their students and forge a deep identification with them; when they build on students' talents and strengths; and when they welcome and include the perspectives and experiences of their students and families in the classroom—then they cannot avoid locking horns with some very unpleasant realities inherent in the schooling process, realities such as racism, sexism, heterosexism, classism, and other biases.

A compelling instance of this kind of learning happened when Youngro Yoon Song, a college teacher of Korean, took the introductory course in multicultural education with me several years ago. Many international students who have taken the course with me, especially those from Asia, initially believe that multicultural education is not an issue in their societies. That is, they do not believe that a multicultural education course will be very useful to them if they expect to teach English back in their own countries, or their native language here in the United States. Youngro began to change her mind early in the semester when she first experienced videos, discussions, and readings about racism. In a word, she began to see racism around her that she had not seen in quite the same way before. By the end of the semester, Youngro wrote about her new sense of responsibility concerning racism.

## RACISM

*By Youngro Yoon Song*

This course has given me a chance to be concerned about various kinds of prejudice (racism, sexism, ethnic stereotyping . . .). I used to consider these things as just a form of social injustice, not as my concern.

The books, films, and articles awoke me to realize the importance of the issues that I face everyday. I began to realize that I also had prejudice and I was trained to be blind to all kinds of injustice. I began to realize that I have to do something about the issues we talked about in the class. As an educator, woman, and member of a minority people, I want to share the burden of this society. The issue is how I should do so.

One thing I can do right now is to help the young generation of Koreans whom I work with at the college level to establish and be proud of their own identity as Koreans. Fortunately, I have the opportunity to teach them Korean and to share these thoughts with them. Of course, I am afraid of how much I will be able to do. But looking back on what I have learned, doing something is better than doing nothing. (12.12.90)


An almost unavoidable consequence of working closely and collaboratively with students, students' families, and other teachers is that teachers begin to discover the biased and racist ideologies behind some of the practices that they previously had overlooked. Consequently, they have no alternative but to begin to question how equitable such practices really are. This pedagogical stance, what Cherry McGee Banks and James Banks (1995a) have called an *equity pedagogy,* challenges the very structure of schools, including seemingly natural and neutral practices such as tracking and disciplinary policies.

Facing and challenging racism and other biases is both an inspiring and a frightening prospect. It means upsetting business as usual, and this can be difficult even for committed and critical teachers. Kathe Jervis (1996), for example, has documented how even in a progressive middle school in New York City where teachers were solidly committed to equity and diversity, students' questions about race and racism often were greeted with silence on the part of the staff. Paradoxically, the school was consciously designed to be diverse and equitable. Yet through numerous anecdotes, Jervis demonstrated how commitment to diversity frequently remained at an abstract level, rarely making itself felt in the actual conversations that go on in classrooms or in the planned or unplanned curriculum. As often is the case, it was only through the actions of a Black teacher that racism was discussed at all. Jervis concluded, "When Whites in power don't hear the boiling lava that lies below the surface, they perpetuate silences around race. Then they are surprised when racial feelings erupt, although it is they who have paid no attention to the volcano" (p. 575).

Confronting racism and other biases means, among other things, carefully analyzing schools' policies and practices as well as the ideologies behind them, and attempting to change those that are unfair. It does not mean that teachers need to position themselves as charismatic, solitary figures, as the Don Quixotes of schools engaged in an impossible but romantic quest. If this is the stance they take, teachers are likely to end up either completely burned out by the effort, or so alienated from their peers that they can have no appreciable impact on the general life of the school. Charismatic teachers do not last long, nor do they usually make substantive changes outside their classrooms. Because they often consider their colleagues to be hopelessly backward or racist or ignorant, these teachers refuse to do the hard work it takes to develop alongside them. This behavior, rather than a collaborative struggle with colleagues, becomes little more than a reflection of the overly individualistic and narcissistic culture that they tend to criticize. In the end, their stance is both arrogant and self-defeating. In some ways, these teachers become just like their ineffective peers who prefer to close their doors to the outside world. And classroom hermits accomplish precious little by themselves.

When I first became a teacher educator, I often told my preservice teachers to mind their own business if they wanted to be effective with their students: I encouraged them to stay out of the faculty lunchroom (where as a neophyte teacher, I had heard many damaging and racist comments about children) and to close their classroom doors. Now my advice is just the opposite: I ask them to go to the faculty lunchroom and engage in conversations so that they can change the discourse about the students they teach, and to *open* their doors rather than close them. Opening their doors is a fitting metaphor for the kinds of collective relationships that teachers need to forge in order to make meaningful change in schools.

What I am arguing for is a stance as a *critical colleague,* that is, as teachers who can develop respectful but critical relationships with peers. In the long run, teachers who work collaboratively in a spirit of solidarity and critique will be better able to change schools to become more equitable and caring places for more students. Although we have been considering the *personal* transformation of teachers, I would submit that *even personal transformation is best accomplished as a collective journey that leads to change in more than just one classroom.*

## DEVELOPING A COMMUNITY OF CRITICAL FRIENDS

Working in isolation, no teacher can singlehandedly effect the changes that are needed in an entire school, at least not in the long term. Time and again, teachers in my classes have spoken about the need to develop a cadre of peers to help them and their school go through the process of transformation. But what is needed is not simply peers who support one another—important as this may be—but also peers who debate, critique, and challenge one another to go beyond their current ideas and practices. Developing a community of critical friends is one more step in the journey of transformation.

In the excerpt below, Mary Ginley wrote about why she had returned to graduate school. Although in a doctoral program, she was not really interested in earning a doctorate. Actually, she wanted to continue to work with second graders for the rest of her career. But what she wanted from graduate school was a group of critical friends and colleagues to help her develop as an even better teacher. Mary is a gifted and caring teacher; she is also very self-critical, a combination that makes teaching both incredibly difficult and enormously rewarding.

### WHY I WENT BACK TO SCHOOL

*By Mary Ginley*

I decided to go back to school for two reasons. One was that I
needed someone to talk to. Dora [the principal of her school, who
had been a close friend and died that year] was gone and Rocío
[a friend and colleague who had returned to Puerto Rico] was
gone. There were so few people to talk to about what we are trying
to do, what we might be doing right and where we are going
wrong. I take a lot of risks in regard to curriculum and pedagogy
and I needed to find people who were doing the same thing and
running into the same problems—people I could trust to say, "I'm
not sure this is the way to go. . . . It's not working." Without them
saying, "See, I told you we need a basal reading program and a spell-
ing book."
    The other reason I returned to school was to figure out how to
do it right. Why did the kids who failed to learn to read in my class,

year after year, have last names like Vega, Lopez, and Rivera, while the kids who sailed along were named Moriarty, Cavanaugh, and Schwartz? Why were the kids who were constantly in trouble—on the playground, on the bus, in the classroom—always from the same part of town? I'd like to say I couldn't have done anything differently, that I did my best but it wasn't good enough, that there were too many other factors. But that would be an easy out. Dora used to say I was too hard on myself. But I'm not . . . not really. I look for excuses and find them because I hate to admit that I've failed these kids. The other reason I wanted to go back to school is to try to discover how to make school successful for all kids—not just the Moriartys, Cavanaughs, Schwartzes, and Ginleys—because so far, I haven't done it right. This course is helping; others will too. I know they will.

## SUMMARY

Individual and collective stories of teachers are a useful reminder that, just as schools need to undergo an institutional transformation if they are to become places where all students learn, teachers too need to experience a similar transformation. Specifically, teachers need to learn *about* their students, *identify* with them, *build* on their strengths, and *challenge* head-on the many displays of privilege and inherent biases in the schools in which they teach. This is arduous work because it requires paying attention to many different arenas of school life, and it is inevitably accompanied by conflict. Yet as we are reminded by Paulo Freire (Shor & Freire, 1987), conflict is necessary for change to take place: "In the last analysis, conflict is the midwife of consciousness" (p. 176).

# CHAPTER 7

# Creating Learning Communities: Implications for Multicultural Education

The task of creating environments where all kids can experience the power of their ideas requires unsettling not only our accepted organization of schooling and our unspoken and unacknowledged agreement about the purposes of schools. Taking this task seriously also means calling into question our definitions of intelligence and the ways in which we judge each other.

—Deborah Meier, *The Power of Their Ideas*

IF IT IS TRUE that student learning cannot take place without the transformation of teachers and schools, then what is needed are learning communities that include all students and their teachers in a meaningful way. Consequently, a focus on discrete skills or specific techniques, or a change of curriculum, is inadequate in suggesting conditions that can improve learning. As we have seen throughout this book, learning is a complex issue and it cannot be reduced to a consideration of psychological processes or individual styles or predispositions. We also must pay attention to relationships among students, teachers, and families; to the identification and connection that students feel with schools; to the cultural and social realities of students' lives; and to the economic and political context in which schools exist. There are lessons to be learned from the many stories about student learning, teacher transformation, and school change that I have presented in this book, lessons that might serve as models for other teachers and schools committed to developing demanding, caring, and inclusive learning communities.

In this chapter we will reflect on some of these lessons. First, I will consider the principal themes that have emerged throughout the book that have implications for student learning and teacher transformation. Then I will suggest five conditions that appear to be necessary to improve student learning and that need to be part of comprehensive school reform efforts. These interrelated conditions ultimately redefine schooling, the role of teachers, and the very nature of teaching and learning. Although it is somewhat arbitrary to consider them separately because they are so intimately connected, for the purpose of expediency they will be described in turn.

As we shall see, when it is conceptualized as broad-based school reform, multicultural education can have a decisive impact on how and to what extent students learn. A comprehensive approach of this kind fosters the creation and practice of successful learning environments for a larger number of students, especially those who have been denied access to a high-quality education due to the barriers of structural inequality.

## PRINCIPAL THEMES

Throughout this book, four major interrelated themes have become evident. I will briefly describe each of them and explain how they are connected to the main idea of the book, that is, that student learning and teacher transformation need to be at the very heart of multicultural education.

### Theme One: Learning Is a Complex Process That Cannot Be Explained Simply by Focusing on Culture and Language, or on Changes in Pedagogy and Curriculum

Multicultural education has failed to have an immediate and direct connection to student learning because for the most part it has not broken out of a rather shallow "holidays and heroes" mold. This is no doubt the case because the emphasis in most schools has been to develop multicultural education primarily through curriculum integration, a far easier task than to dismantle tracking or challenge an entrenched racist ideology, for example. That is, it is more likely that additions will be made to the curriculum than to the process of learning itself; or to the nature of the interactions between teachers and students and their families; or to teachers' basic attitudes and beliefs about their students' abilities; or even to how students from diverse backgrounds actually learn. Yet multicultural education is much more than just curriculum integration. James Banks

(1995) has suggested that multicultural education is composed of five dimensions, with content integration just one of them. Further, he suggests that the other four dimensions—knowledge construction, prejudice reduction, an equity pedagogy, and an empowering school culture and social structure—are at least equally important.

Although students' cultural, linguistic, and social class backgrounds need to be taken into account in developing a multicultural perspective on learning, even these must be viewed according to the particular context of the individual student, and the school and community in which learning takes place. Accordingly, language, culture, and social class differences in and of themselves are not enough to describe successful student achievement. The curriculum (the *what*) and pedagogy (the *how*) of education also must be acknowledged as influencing student learning. In tandem with changes in curriculum and pedagogy, a critical perspective about school policies and practices such as rigid ability grouping, retention, and disciplinary rules is needed. But changing school policies and practices, if decontextualized from broader issues, also will be ineffective. For example, a school may decide to dismantle tracking, but if teachers do not believe in their hearts that all students are capable of high levels of achievement, detracking by itself will do little good because societal attitudes toward certain groups of people have a profound effect on how schools and teachers interact with students. Consequently, it is not simply cultural and linguistic differences that explain the success or failure of students to learn, but how those differences relate to school policies and practices, and how school policies and practices are at least partly a result of societal attitudes.

As we have seen, developing a multicultural perspective concerning learning is made even more difficult because multicultural education as a field of inquiry is informed by and builds on diverse academic fields that are sometimes conceptually at odds, including psychology, anthropology, sociology, linguistics, history, and economics. Of course, the boundaries between and among diverse disciplines are not as impermeable as the above would suggest. Yet it is also true that many disciplines are blurring boundaries and cross-fertilization is becoming more commonplace. Perhaps as a result of this interdisciplinary perspective, we will gain a fuller understanding of learning.

### Theme Two: Student Learning and Academic Achievement Must Be Understood Within the Sociopolitical Context of Education

A key assumption that underlies this book is that education is an inherently political enterprise. Macro-level issues regarding structural inequality such as institutional racism, sexism, and similar biases unquestionably influence student learning. That is why it is impossible to separate the sociopolitical context in which education takes place from education itself. For example, a political climate in which serious consideration, not to mention massive media attention, is given to the assumption that Whites are inherently superior to and more intelligent than Blacks (Herrnstein & Murray, 1994)—inconceivable as this notion may seem in the late twentieth century—is bound to affect how students of different races are treated and what is expected of them, not just in schools but in society in general. When such ideas are repeated in different forms from generation to generation, they result in a widely accepted societal ideology about the connection between intelligence and race (Gould, 1981). The major victims of such thinking are the children in our schools.

Likewise, the fact that a student speaks a language other than English might be considered a benefit in a setting where bilingualism is valued, but a detriment where it is devalued or feared. Further, the language itself, or the variant of the language, influences a community's reaction to students who speak it. Parisian French, for instance, often is considered a cultured and high-status language, but Haitian Creole rarely is accorded the same rank. As a result, students who speak Haitian Creole are predictably treated differently from those who speak Parisian French, in spite of the fact that both languages are rule-governed systems of communication perfectly appropriate for expressing speakers' thoughts. Needless to say, power, race, and social class are significant complicating factors in this case. It is probably safe to say that if middle-class Black Haitians spoke Parisian French and poor White Parisians spoke Haitian Creole, the status of the two languages in all probability would be reversed.

As we have seen throughout this book, a strictly psychological orientation to learning can be quite limited. We need to avoid an exclusive focus on individual students and how they might be assisted in their learning—a noble and important effort, but an incomplete one—and consider also the specific conditions and climate in the educational environment that promote student learning. The psychologist's frame of reference on the individual reveals a substantial truth: that individuals, not groups, learn. Still, it is equally true that individuals are members of groups and some groups have been the victims of widespread educational failure *not as individuals but because of their membership in particular groups.* The review of educational inequality in Chapter 2 made this point clear. Although the field of psychology is essential in explicating learning, it is limited by its very nature, that is, by its singular focus on the individual. Along with individual characteristics and dispositions, learning also is heavily influenced by social, cultural, and political forces that are largely beyond the control of individuals. These factors sometimes are not taken into account when a psychological frame of reference is used. A welcome change in this regard in recent years has been the consideration of Vygotskian perspectives that demonstrate that learning is a social and cultural endeavor (Vygotsky, 1978).

When sociocultural and sociopolitical frames of reference, rather than just a psychological one, are used to explain and understand learning, unequal outcomes among students of diverse backgrounds can be better understood. Decisions concerning such practices as tracking, testing, curriculum, pedagogical approaches, and what language to use in instruction are thus placed in a broader context. Moreover, social policies that affect schools and schooling also become more understandable.

### Theme Three: Multicultural Education Is a Progressive Force Within the Larger Educational Reform Movement

Multicultural education began as a movement to transform schools (Banks & Banks, 1995b; Perry & Fraser, 1993; Sleeter, 1996). Because it is rooted in the civil rights movement, multicultural education sought to improve education for students who had not had, in the words of Meyer Weinberg (1977), "a chance to learn." Nevertheless, multicultural education is vastly different from the increasingly conservative educational reform platform, with its calls for more standardized testing, vouchers to subsidize private schools, and "choice" as primary slogans. All educational philosophies or pedagogical approaches that claim to be worthwhile—including multicultural education—need to be evaluated in terms of whether, how, and to what extent student learning is promoted. As we have seen, without this kind of scrutiny, educational reforms can become just empty exercises in bureaucratic shuffling or the external imposition of city, state, and federal policies that have little to do with the actual learning, or lack of learning, that takes place in classrooms.

Educational reforms—whether smaller schools, site-based management, increased parent involvement, culturally relevant pedagogy, or native-language instruction—are all potentially good ideas that may in fact substantially improve educational outcomes for many more students than is currently the case, but given the complex nature of schooling and society, simply calling for educational reform is not enough. In spite of this caveat, because of the historically liberatory and critical theoretical stance of multicultural education, it cannot be dismissed as simply another palliative to widespread failure.

### Theme Four: The Nature of Teacher–Student Relationships Is Central to Student Learning

The fourth major theme in this book is that the nature and extent of the relationships between teachers and their students are crucial in promoting student learning. Put another way, *the way students are thought about and treated by society and consequently by the schools they attend and the educators who teach them is fundamental in creating academic success or failure.*

We should not magnify the role or importance of individual teachers; doing so simply reinforces the caricature of teachers as charismatic figures, an image that is both unreachable and unreasonable for the vast majority of mere mortals. Neither can we place the blame for student failure simplistically at the feet of teachers as if teachers somehow were disconnected from the society in which we all live. However, the straightforward conclusion reached by Michael Fullan and Suzanne Stiegelbauer (1991) after many years of researching educational reform bears repeating: "Educational change depends on what teachers do and think— it's as simple and as complex as that" (p. 117). As we have seen, teachers' attitudes, beliefs, and actions, within the broader context of the society in which these take place, are fundamental to understanding student learning.

The role of teachers is a complicated matter because they are not solitary agents of change. But the inescapable truth that has emerged in this book is that teachers' attitudes and behaviors *can* make an astonishing difference in student learning. Martin Haberman (1995) has suggested, based on innumerable interviews and interactions with what he calls "star teachers," that chief among the qualities of such teachers is their approach to students who have been labeled "at risk": Rather than blaming students for failure to learn, "star" teachers look beyond individuals to such conditions as irrelevant curriculum, poor teaching, and cumbersome bureaucracies. Haberman's conclusion reinforces the tremendous impact that teachers have on student learning.

## CONDITIONS THAT PROMOTE STUDENT LEARNING: SYSTEMIC SCHOOL REFORM WITH A MULTICULTURAL PERSPECTIVE

Educational reform cannot be envisioned without taking into account both micro- and macro-level issues that may affect student learning. Micro-level issues include the cultures, languages, and experiences of students and their families, and how these are taken into account in determining school policies and practices. Macro-level issues include the racial, social class, and gender stratification that helps maintain inequality, and the resources and access to learning that are provided or denied by schools. In addition, the way that students and their families view their status in schools and society also needs to be considered.

Conditions such as inequitable school financing (Darling-Hammond, 1995), unrepresentative school governance (Meier & Stewart, 1989), and large class size (Glass, 1982) may play a powerful role in promoting student underachievement. Yet reform strategies such as longer school days, more rigorous graduation standards, and increased standardized testing often do not take inequitable funding or class size into account. Equalizing just these two conditions of schooling probably would result in a dramatic improvement in the learning of students who have not had the benefit of smaller classes and better-endowed schools. School reform efforts that do not acknowledge such macro-level disparities are sometimes little more than pie-in-the-sky endeavors because they assume that all schools begin with a level playing field. The conditions described below, while acknowledging that disparities such as these exist, nevertheless provide hope for school systems where such changes as equitable funding or small class size may not happen anytime in the near future. Rather than wait for these changes to occur, schools can begin by changing the climate in which learning takes place.

Five kinds of school reform can substantially improve student learning:

1. School reform that is antiracist and antibias
2. School reform that reflects an understanding of all students as having talents and strengths that can enhance their education
3. School reform that is based on the notion that those most intimately connected with students need to be meaningfully involved in their education
4. School reform that is based on high expectations and rigorous standards for all learners
5. School reform that is empowering and just

## School Reform That Is Antiracist and Antibias

An antiracist and antibias perspective is at the very heart of multicultural education. Although some educators may believe that having a multicultural education approach will automatically take care of racism, this is far from the case. In fact, multicultural education without a clear antiracist focus may end up maintaining rigid stereotypes if it focuses on only superficial aspects of culture or the addition of ethnic tidbits to the curriculum. In contrast, being antiracist means paying attention to all areas in which some students may be favored over others, including the curriculum, choice of materials, sorting policies, and teachers' interactions and relationships with students and their communities.

Teachers' knowledge, experiences, attitudes, and beliefs play a crucial role in promoting antiracist and antibias school reform. A case in point is the story of Margaret Harris (1995), a high school history teacher who has defined herself as a "multiculturalist in training," and who described how she got to become one:

> As a teacher and department chairperson, I don't know when I first became interested in developing a more inclusive, multicultural curriculum. I think a lot of pieces started to come together for me at different moments: students' voices, political and historical reading, life's experiences, conversations. A look at my bookshelf tells me that I always was a muliculturalist in training, but just didn't know it. I love to learn as much as I love to teach. In fact, I'm not sure how an educator can separate the two. (p. 276)

When teachers, especially those of European American heritage, place themselves in the position of learner, they invariably need to confront difficult and uncomfortable issues concerning their own biases and privilege. Harris described this process in her own transformation:

> I have found that the more I am invested in a subject, the tougher it is to admit that I have to relearn it. I wear my commitment, service, and hard-learned knowledge and experience on my sleeve as a badge of honor. "I'm not a racist!" "I don't see color—everyone is the same to me!" "I am colorblind." This belief kept me from recognizing that I, too, had been indoctrinated in that racist institutional lexicon of the established curriculum. (p. 284)

Educators committed to multicultural education with an antiracist perspective need to closely examine both school policies and the attitudes and behaviors of the staff to determine how these might be complicitous in causing academic failure. The kinds of expectations held for students, whether using their native language is permitted or punished, how sorting takes place, and how classroom organization, pedagogy, and curriculum might influence student learning all need to be considered. For example, during her graduate studies, Ann Scott's reactions to films, readings, and class discussions concerning White privilege were, as she said, "hard work." But it is only when teachers undergo this kind of hard work, whether in their schools or through personal encounters or professional development, that they can learn to identify how racism and other kinds of institutional discrimination operate in schools and society to the detriment of some students and the advantage of others.

*Institutional power* is a significant consideration here because discussions of racism tend to focus on individual biases and negative perceptions toward members of other groups. This perception conveniently skirts the issue of how institutions themselves, which are far more powerful than individuals, develop harmful policies and practices that victimize American Indians, African Americans, Latinos, immigrants, poor European Americans, females, gay and lesbian students, and others from powerless groups. The major difference between individual and institutional discrimination is precisely the wielding of power, because it is primarily through the power of the people who control institutions such as schools that oppressive policies and practices are reinforced and legitimated (Tatum, 1992; Weinberg, 1990). That is, when racism and other forms of discrimination are understood as *systemic* problems, not just as individual dislikes for a particular group of people, we can better understand their negative and destructive effects.

The transformation of Patty Bode as a White ally is a case in point. Although she had developed a thoughtful multicultural perspective in her teaching years before, it was only when she reflected more carefully on her role as a White teacher that her practice underwent a profound transformation. Not only did she learn to analyze every aspect of the teaching and learning process and the implications of these for student learning, but she also understood the crucial role that White teachers could play in the struggle for equitable education.

### School Reform That Reflects an Understanding of All Students as Having Talents and Strengths That Can Enhance Their Education

As we have seen in the many examples of research and personal testimony in this book, even many well-meaning educators approach their role in teaching bicultural students with the assumption that these students bring little of value to their education. Too often, they are considered to be deficient for social, cultural, or genetic reasons. The potential inherent strengths of many students may be overlooked when teachers feel that they need to begin educating students by first doing away with their prior learning. The role of "teacher as missionary" is the unfortunate result.

Beginning with a more positive view of students' strengths is in the long run not only a better policy, but indeed a more hopeful strategy. Teachers who begin by first learning about their students and then building on their students' talents and strengths change dramatically the nature of the teaching/learning dynamic and the climate in which education takes place. Rather than feeling that their students have nothing to give, the perspective that students are active, engaged, and motivated co-constructors of learning is the result. A compelling example of this approach was provided by Maria Botelho's letter to Ms. Curry, her first-grade teacher, who had assumed that Maria's knowledge of Portuguese was a detriment to her education.

## School Reform That Is Based on the Notion That Those Most Intimately Connected with Students Need to Be Meaningfully Involved in Their Education

Research on involvement by parents, students, and teachers in decisions affecting education has indicated consistently that such involvement can dramatically improve student learning (Henderson & Berla, 1995). Yet the people who are closest to learners and learners themselves frequently are excluded from discussions, policy implications, and implementation of school reform measures. Although schools give lip service to parent, teacher, and student involvement, schools usually are not organized to encourage the involvement of these groups.

For instance, Jim Cummins (1996) reviewed programs that included student empowerment as a goal and concluded that students who are encouraged to develop a positive cultural identity through interactions with their teachers experience a sense of control over their own lives and develop the confidence and motivation to succeed academically. In the case of teachers, a study of secondary schools reported that teachers who had more control over classroom conditions considered themselves more efficacious (Lee, Bryk, & Smith, 1993). Regarding parents, an analysis of a number of programs stressing effective parent involvement found that all of the programs reviewed shared, among others, the following components: a commitment to involve low-income parents, family empowerment as a major goal, and a stated desire to reduce the gap between home and school cultures by designing programs that respond to and build on the values, structures, languages, and cultures of students' homes (Fruchter, Galletta, & White, 1993).

School reform measures that stress the meaningful involvement of students, teachers, and families look quite different from traditional approaches to school improvement. Rather than thinking of ways to circumvent the ideas of students, teachers, and parents, school reformers actively seek their involvement in developing, for instance, disciplinary policies, curriculum development, and decisions concerning ability grouping and the use of tests. As we have seen in many examples throughout this book, including teachers in school reform can be a powerful way to reflect the realities of the classroom in school-based reform. But if teachers' involvement is noncritical, or if students and parents are not part of the mix, the result can be the empowerment of teachers at the expense of students and families.

There are many ways in which parents and students can be involved, and governance is only one of them. Helping to make decisions about curriculum content, the hiring of new staff, or grouping policies is an important role, but not all parents or students feel equally comfortable, nor do they have the time, to be involved in this way. Even the simple process of listening to, respecting, and affirming families' ideas can be a big step in involving them. Mary Ginley's questions to parents about their children is an example of this. Although seemingly basic, the mere act of bringing parents into their children's education through questions about the children proved to be a powerful mechanism for letting families know that their insights and ideas were valued. Similarly, when students' viewpoints are seriously considered, they may feel more connected to schools, which in turn may help them to define themselves as capable and worthy of learning.

### School Reform That Is Based on High Expectations and Rigorous Standards for All Students

Many young people struggle on a daily basis with tremendous odds, concerning not only their school lives, but their very existence. These odds include personal, family, and social problems such as poverty, racism, violence, drug abuse, and lack of health care and appropriate housing. As we reach the start of the twenty-first century, these problems are becoming even more severe and complicated as families experience great distress and our society undergoes monumental structural changes. Add to this the fact that the very identities of some students are thought to be a barrier to their learning—including their social class, race, ethnicity, and native language—and many teachers feel themselves at a loss to teach their students effectively.

As we have seen, in many cases students' identities and the conditions in which they live are used as a justification for having low expectations, or as a reason for "watering down" the curriculum. I maintain that just the opposite should happen. That is, because schools in our society historically have been expected to provide an equal and equitable education for all students, not just for those who are White or middle-class, or who speak English fluently, it is with even greater urgency that the mission of schools needs to be redefined to support students who might not be identified as potentially academically capable. If schools are purposeful about giving all students more options in life, particularly students from communities that do not have the necessary resources with which to access these options, then we need to begin with the assumption that these students are academically able, individually and as a group.

I am not suggesting that it is easy to have equally high standards for all students. I have seen many examples of young people for whom teachers and schools seem to be doing the very best they can, and yet these young people face such massive personal and family problems that the situation seems hopeless. But as educators, we have no other choice than to believe that school conditions *can* be created in which all students can become successful learners. As we have seen throughout this book, there have been too many examples of academic success in the face of tremendous adversity to conclude that intelligence and ability are handed out sparingly or based on only genetic endowments, or that they cannot be affected by educational environments. These examples are powerful reminders that great potential exists in all students. What needs changing first are the attitudes, beliefs, and values with which teachers approach their students, and the conditions in schools to support the high-level learning of all students. As stated simply by Mary Ginley, "Being nice is not enough." Although being nice to students may be a good start, if unaccompanied by a deep belief and trust that bicultural students are capable and worthy, it will not necessarily lead to improved learning. Forging a deep and committed connection to their students, as Lizette Román wrote about so convincingly, is the key to motivating students to become learners.

## School Reform That Is Empowering and Just

When educational reform is perceived to be a bureaucratic procedure, or when technical processes take precedence in school restructuring, then crucial questions related to social justice and student empowerment are swept aside. But school reform that has as its primary goal the improvement of learning for all students needs to concern more than just changing schedules, or buying new textbooks, or adding ethnic content to curriculum. While these reforms in fact may improve conditions for learning among a greater number of students, they will not by themselves change the nature of learning that takes place in classrooms. A case in point is the educational reform known as *block scheduling*, the realignment of school schedules in middle and secondary schools from 40-minute slots to 1-½-, 2- or 3-hour-long segments. Block scheduling has become a popular reform and it makes sense for a lot of reasons: Students have more time to tackle important issues in greater depth; teachers can build significant relationships with students when they work closely and intensively with them; and teachers have the opportunity to work collaboratively with one another. However, if the content of what students learn in their blocks does not change, or if the way in which they are expected to learn is not affected, then block scheduling may not provide the improvements promised.

School reform measures that have as their underlying focus both the empowerment of students and the creation of socially just learning environments are based on the view that critical reflection and analysis are fundamental to the development and maintenance of a democratic society. Without this perspective, learning can be defined as simply "banking education," or as the depositing of knowledge in otherwise empty receptacles. But if we expect schools to be living laboratories for democracy, where all students know that they are worthy and capable of learning and where they develop a social awareness and responsibility to their various communities, then classrooms and schools need to become just and empowering environments for all students.

Throughout this book, we have seen how the thrill of learning can make a dramatic difference in the lives of students and teachers alike. We saw in "Looking from the Edge," the poem by Elizabeth Capifali, that even as an adult, learning about her heritage was empowering; it provided "a boost of adrenaline" that helped her as both a teacher and a learner. In the case of Youngro Yoon Song, confronting racism in the United States for the first time had an equally moving result: It caused her to think more critically about her responsibility as a teacher of Korean to second- and third-generation Korean American college students. And what Ann Scott described as "hard work" was also exhilarating because in her graduate studies she was challenged as a learner not only on an intellectual level but also in emotional terms. It was this combination of affect and intellect that helped her grow immensely as a teacher. Whether we are referring to teachers, students, teacher educators, or administrators, personal and institutional transformations need to occur at the same time for schools to change in meaningful ways.

## CONCLUSION

I began this book by reflecting on how student learning sometimes has been a secondary consideration in multicultural education because the field has emphasized such issues as improving students' self-esteem, incorporating cultural content into the curriculum, and fostering interethnic friendships. Although these are indeed significant goals in multicultural education, the question, *But can they do math?* has gnawed at me for years because it underscores the lack of access of bicultural students to high levels of learning and thus to expanded options for the future.

If there is one thing that has become apparent throughout this book, it is that there is no simple formula for increasing student learning. A step-by-step blueprint for school reform is both inappropriate and untenable because each school differs from all others in its basic structure, goals, and human dimensions. Nevertheless, it is also evident that there are a number of *levels,* societal, institutional, personal, and collective, in which changes need to take place to promote student learning. At the societal level, conditions such as school funding and the inequitable distribution of resources for learning are major factors that influence academic failure or success. At the institutional level, school policies and practices based on deficit explanations of diversity alienate many students. In addition, when schools function as a collection of individuals rather than as models of collaboration and support among teachers, little substantive change can take place in the learning of all the students who go there. And at the personal level, the beliefs, values, and attitudes that teachers have about their students can be decisive in helping or hindering learning.

At the core of this book is my powerful belief in the effect, positive or negative, that teachers can have on students through their interactions with them, their families, and their communities. Along with my own practice as a teacher, this belief is based on my experiences with many remarkable educators with whom I have had the privilege to work over the years, some of whose words are written in this book. Fighting institutional norms that grant unearned privileges to some students over others, challenging ideologies that insist that some children are inherently superior to others, and uniting with other activists both inside and outside of school who believe that all children are capable of high levels of achievement and therefore deserve the very best, these educators make a significant difference in the lives of the children they touch.

In the end, if teachers believe that students cannot achieve at high levels, that their backgrounds are riddled with deficiencies, and that multicultural education is a frill that cannot help them to learn, the result will be school reform strategies that have little hope for success. On the other hand, if teachers begin by challenging societal inequities that inevitably place some students at a disadvantage over others; if they struggle against institutional policies and practices that are unjust; if they begin with the strengths and talents of students and their families; if they undergo a process of personal transformation based on their own identities and experiences; and, finally, if they engage with colleagues in a collaborative and imaginative encounter to transform their own practices and their schools to achieve equal and high-quality education for all students, then the outcome is certain to be a more positive one than is currently the case. A critical and comprehensive approach to multicultural education can provide an important framework for rethinking school reform, and it is a far more promising scenario for the effective learning of students. When teachers understand the light in the eyes of their students as evidence that they are capable and worthy human beings, then schools can become places of hope and affirmation for students of all backgrounds and all situations.

# References

Aaronsohn, E., Carter, C. J., & Howell, M. (1995). Preparing monocultural teachers for a multicultural world: Attitudes toward inner-city schools. *Equity and Excellence in Education, 28*(1), 5–9.

Abi-Nader, J. (1993). Meeting the needs of multicultural classrooms: Family values and the motivation of minority students. In M. J. O'Hair & S. J. Odell (Eds.), *Diversity in teaching: Teacher education yearbook 1* (pp. 212–236). Fort Worth, TX: Harcourt Brace Jovanovich.

Adams, D., Astone, B., Nuñez-Wormack, E., & Smodlaka, I. (1994). Predicting the academic achievement of Puerto Rican and Mexican-American ninth-grade students. *The Urban Review, 26*(1), 1–14.

Alva, S. A. (1991). Academic invulnerability among Mexican-American students: The importance of protective resources and appraisals. *Hispanic Journal of Behavioral Sciences, 13*(1), 18–34.

American Association of University Women Educational Foundation and Wellesley College Center for Research on Women. (1992). *How schools shortchange girls: The AAUW report.* Washington, DC: AAUW.

Anyon, J. (1981). Social class and school knowledge. *Curriculum Inquiry, 11*(1), 3–41.

Apple, M. W. (1993). The politics of official knowledge: Does a national curriculum make sense? *Teachers College Record, 95*(2), 222–241.

Apple, M. W., & Christian-Smith, L. K. (1991). *The politics of the textbook.* New York: Routledge & Chapman Hall.

Appleton, N. (1983). *Cultural pluralism in education: Theoretical foundations.* New York: Longman.

Arias, M. B., & Casanova, U. (Eds.). (1993). *Bilingual education: Politics, practice, research.* Chicago: University of Chicago Press.

Arvizu, S. F. (1994). Building bridges for the future: Anthropological contributions to diversity and classroom practice. In R. A. DeVillar, C. J. Faltis, & J. P. Cummins (Eds.), *Cultural diversity in schools: From rhetoric to reality* (pp. 75–97). Albany: State University of New York Press.

Ascher, C. (1990). *Testing students in urban schools: Current problems and new directions.* New York: Teachers College, Columbia University. (ERIC Clearinghouse on Urban Education)

Ascher, C., & Burnett, G. (1993). *Current trends and issues in urban education.* New York: Teachers College, Columbia University. (ERIC Clearinghouse on Urban Education)

Au, K. (1980). Participation structures in a reading lesson with Hawaiian children. *Anthropology and Education Quarterly, 11*(2), 91–115.

Bachman, J. G., Green, S., & Wirtanen, I. D. (1971). Dropping out: Problem or symptom? *Youth in transition* (Vol. 3). Ann Arbor: University of Michigan, Institute for Social Research.

Báez, T., Fernández, R. R., Navarro, R. A., & Rice, R. I. (1986). Litigation strategies for educational equity: Bilingual education and research. *Issues in Education, 3*(3), 198–214.

Baker, D. P., & Riordan, C. (1998). The "eliting" of the common American Catholic school and the national education crisis. *Phi Delta Kappan, 80*(1), 16–23.

Banks, C. A. M., & Banks, J. A. (1995a). Equity pedagogy: An essential component of multicultural education. *Theory into Practice, 34*(3), 152–158.

Banks, J. A. (1995). Multicultural education: Historical development, dimensions, and practice. In J. A. Banks & C. A. M. Banks (Eds.), *Handbook of research on multicultural education* (pp. 3–24). New York: Macmillan.

Banks, J. A. (Ed.). (1996). *Multicultural education, transformative knowledge, and action: Historical and contemporary perspectives.* New York: Teachers College Press.

Banks, J. A. (1997). *Teaching strategies for ethnic studies* (6th ed.). Boston: Allyn & Bacon.

Banks, J. A., & Banks, C. A. M. (Eds.). (1995b). *Handbook of research on multicultural education.* New York: Macmillan.

Barber, B. R. (1992). *An aristocracy of everyone: The politics of education and the future of America.* New York: Oxford University Press.

Bartolomé, L. I. (1994). Beyond the methods fetish: Toward a humanizing pedagogy. *Harvard Educational Review, 64,* 173–194.

Belenky, M. F., Clinchy, B. M., Goldberger, N. R., & Tarule, J. M. (1986). *Women's ways of knowing: The development of self, voice, and mind.* New York: Basic Books.

Bennett, C. I. (1995). *Comprehensive multicultural education: Theory and practice* (3rd ed.). Boston: Allyn & Bacon.

Bennett, K. P. (1991). Doing school in an urban Appalachian first grade. In C. E. Sleeter (Ed.), *Empowerment through multicultural education* (pp. 27–47). Albany: State University of New York Press.

Berliner, D. C. (1997). Educational psychology meets the Christian Right: Differing views of children, schooling, teaching, and learning. *Teachers College Record, 98*(3), 381–416.

Bigelow, B., Christensen, L., Karp, S., Miner, B., & Peterson, B. (Eds.). (1994). *Rethinking our classrooms: Teaching for equity and justice.* Milwaukee: Rethinking Schools.

Bigler, E., & Collins, J. (1995). *Dangerous discourses: The politics of multicultural literature in community and classroom* (Report Series 7.4). Albany: State University of New York at Albany, National Research Center on Literature Teaching and Learning.

Boateng, F. (1990). Combating deculturalization of the African-American child in the public school system: A multicultural approach. In K. Lomotey (Ed.), *Going to school: The African-American experience* (pp. 73–84). Albany: State University of New York Press.

Bourdieu, P. (1986). The forms of capital. In J. G. Richardson (Ed.), *Handbook of theory and research for the sociology of education* (pp. 241–248). Westport, CT: Greenwood Press.

Bowles, S., & Gintis, H. (1976). *Schooling in capitalist America: Educational reform and the contradictions of economic life.* New York: Basic Books.

Boykin, A. W. (1994). Afrocultural expression and its implications for schooling. In E. R. Hollins, J. E. King, & W. C. Hayman (Eds.), *Teaching diverse populations: Formulating a knowledge base* (pp. 225–273). Albany: State University of New York Press.

Bruner, J. (1996). *The culture of education.* Cambridge, MA: Harvard University Press.

Bryk, A. S., Lee, V. E., & Holland, P. B. (1993). *Catholic schools and the common good.* Cambridge, MA: Harvard Educational Review Press.

Cassidy, J. (1995). Who killed the middle class? *The New Yorker, 71*(32), 113–124.

Chomsky, N. (1965). *Aspects of the theory of syntax.* Cambridge, MA: MIT Press.

Christian, D. (1994). *Two-way bilingual education: Students learning through two languages.* Santa Cruz: University of California, National Center for Research on Cultural Diversity and Second Language Learning.

Churchill, W. (1992). *Fantasies of the master race: Literature, cinema and the colonization of American Indians* (M. A. Jaimes, Ed.). Monroe, ME: Common Courage Press.

Cochran-Smith, M. (1991). Learning to teach against the grain. *Harvard Educational Review, 61,* 279–310.

Cochran-Smith, M. (1997). Knowledge, skills, and experiences for teaching culturally diverse learners: A perspective for practicing teachers. In J. J. Irvine (Ed.), *Critical knowledge for diverse teachers and learners* (pp. 27–87). Washington, DC: American Association of Colleges for Teacher Education.

Cohen, E. G. (1994). *Designing groupwork: Strategies for the heterogeneous classroom* (2nd ed.). New York: Teachers College Press.

Cohen, E. G., & Lotan, R. A. (Eds.). (1997). *Working for equity in heterogeneous classrooms: Sociological theory in practice.* New York: Teachers College Press.

Cole, M. (1985). The zone of proximal development: Where culture and cognition create each other. In J. Wertsch (Ed.), *Culture, communication, and cognition: Vygotskian perspectives* (pp. 146–161). Cambridge: Cambridge University Press.

Cole, M., Gay, J., Glick, J. A., & Sharp, D. W. (1971). *The cultural context of learning and thinking: An exploration in experimental anthropology.* New York: Basic Books.

Cole, M., & Griffin, P. (1983). A socio-historical approach to re-mediation. *The Quarterly Newsletter of the Laboratory of Comparative Human Cognition, 5*(4), 69–74.

Collier, V. P. (1995). *Promoting academic success for ESL students: Understanding second language acquisition at school.* Elizabeth: New Jersey Teachers of English to Speakers of Other Languages—Bilingual Educators.

Commins, N. L. (1989). Language and affect: Bilingual students at home and at school. *Language Arts, 66*(1), 2–43.

Corbett, D., & Wilson, B. (1995). Make a difference *with,* not *for,* students: A plea to researchers and reformers. *Educational Researcher, 24*(5), 12–17.

Corson, D. (1995). Realities of teaching in a multiethnic school. In O. García & C. Baker (Eds.), *Policy and practice in bilingual education: Extending the foundations* (pp. 70–84). Clevedon, England: Multilingual Matters.

Council of Great City Schools. (1992). *National urban education goals: Baseline indicators, 1990–1991.* Washington, DC: Author.

Crawford, J. (1992). *Hold your tongue: Bilingualism and the politics of "English only."* Reading, MA: Addison-Wesley.

Cross, W. E., Jr. (1995). Oppositional identity and African American youth: Issues and prospects. In W. D. Hawley & A. W. Jackson (Eds.), *Toward a common destiny: Improving race and ethnic relations in America* (pp. 185–204). San Francisco: Jossey-Bass.

Cuban, L. (1993). *How teachers taught: Constancy and change in American classrooms, 1880–1990* (2nd ed.). New York: Teachers College Press.

Cummins, J. (1986). Empowering minority students: A framework for intervention. *Harvard Educational Review, 56,* 18–36.

Cummins, J. (1996). *Negotiating identities: Education for empowerment in a diverse society.* Ontario, CA: California Association for Bilingual Education.

Darder, A. (1991). *Culture and power in the classroom: A critical foundation for bicultural education.* New York: Bergin & Garvey.

Darling-Hammond, L. (1994). Performance-based assessment and educational equity. *Harvard Educational Review, 66,* 5–30.

Darling-Hammond, L. (1995). Inequality and access to knowledge. In J. A. Banks & C. A. M. Banks (Eds.), *Handbook of research on multicultural education* (pp. 465–483). New York: Macmillan.

Darling-Hammond, L. (1996). The right to learn and the advancement of teaching: Research, policy, and practice for democratic education. *Educational Researcher, 25*(6), 5–17.

Delgado-Gaitán, C. (1992). School matters in the Mexican-American home: Socializing children to education. *American Educational Research Journal, 29*(3), 495–513.

Delgado-Gaitán, C., & Trueba, H. (1991). *Crossing cultural borders: Education for immigrant families in America.* London: Falmer Press.

Delpit, L. D. (1988). The silenced dialogue: Power and pedagogy in educating other people's children. *Harvard Educational Review, 58,* 280–298.

Derman-Sparks, L., & A.B.C. Task Force. (1989). *Anti-bias curriculum: Tools for empowering young children.* Washington, DC: National Association for the Education of Young Children.

Dewey, J. (1916). *Democracy and education.* New York: Free Press.

Deyhle, D. (1992). Constructing failure and maintaining cultural identity: Navajo and Ute school leavers. *Journal of American Indian Education, 31,* 24–47.

Deyhle, D., & Swisher, K. (1997). Research in American Indian and Alaska Native education: From assimilation to self-determination. In M. W. Apple (Ed.),

*Review of research in education* (Vol. 22, pp. 113–194). Washington, DC: American Educational Research Association.

Díaz, E., Flores, B., Cousin, P. T., & Soo Hoo, S. (1992, April). *Teacher as sociocultural mediator.* Paper presented at the annual meeting of the American Educational Research Association, San Francisco.

Díaz, E., Moll, L. C., & Mehan, H. (1986). Sociocultural resources in instruction: A context-specific approach. In *Beyond language: Social and cultural factors in schooling language minority students* (pp. 187–230). Los Angeles: Office of Bilingual Education, California State Department of Education, Evaluation, Dissemination, and Assessment Center.

Dickeman, M. (1973). Teaching cultural pluralism. In J. A. Banks (Ed.), *Teaching ethnic studies: Concepts and strategies* (43rd Yearbook; pp. 4–25). Washington, DC: National Council for the Social Studies.

*Digest.* (1995, August). School dropouts: New information about an old problem. (ERIC Clearinghouse on Urban Education, No. 109)

Dilworth, M. E. (Ed.). (1992). *Diversity in teacher education: New expectations.* San Francisco: Jossey-Bass.

Dolson, D. P. (1985). The effects of Spanish home language use on the scholastic performance of Hispanic pupils. *Journal of Multilingual and Multicultural Education, 6*(2), 135–155.

Dolson, D. P., & Mayer, J. (1992). Longitudinal study of three program models for language-minority students: A critical examination of reported findings. *Bilingual Research Journal, 16* (1 & 2), 105–157.

Donaldson, K. (1996). *Through students' eyes.* New York: Bergin & Garvey.

Donato, R. (1997). *The other struggle for equal schools: Mexican Americans during the civil rights era.* Albany: State University of New York Press.

Duffy, T. M., & Jonassen, D. H. (1992). *Constructivism and the technology of instruction: A conversation.* Hillsdale, NJ: Erlbaum.

Dunn, B. (1994). *Mi semestre de español: A case study of the cultural dimension of second language acquisition.* Unpublished independent study journal, University of Massachusetts, Amherst.

Dyson, A. H. (1992). *"Whistle for Willie," lost puppies, and cartoon dogs: The sociocultural dimensions of young children's composing or toward unmelting pedagogical pots.* Berkeley: National Center for the Study of Writing and Literacy.

Educational Testing Service. (1991). *The state of inequality.* Princeton, NJ: Author.

Erickson, F. (1987). Transformation and school success: The politics and culture of educational achievement. *Anthropology and Education Quarterly, 18*(4), 335–356.

Erickson, F. (1990). Culture, politics, and educational practice. *Educational Foundations, 4*(2), 21–45.

Erickson, F. (1993). Transformation and school success: The politics and culture of educational achievement. In E. Jacob & C. Jordan (Eds.), *Minority education: Anthropological perspectives* (pp. 27–51). Norwood, NJ: Ablex.

Erickson, F. (1997). Culture in society and in educational practices. In J. A. Banks & C. A. M. Banks (Eds.), *Multicultural education: Issues and perspectives* (3rd ed.; pp. 32–60). Boston: Allyn & Bacon.

Erickson, F., & Mohatt, G. (1982). Cultural organization of participation structures in two classrooms of Indian students. In G. Spindler (Ed.), *Doing the ethnography of schooling: Educational anthropology in action* (pp. 132–174). New York: Holt, Rinehart & Winston.

Fine, M. (1991). *Framing dropouts: Notes on the politics of an urban high school.* Albany: State University of New York Press.

Finn, J. D., & Achilles, C. M. (1990). Answers and questions about class size: A statewide experiment. *American Educational Research Journal, 27,* 557–577.

Flores, B., Cousin, P. T., & Díaz, E. (1991). Transforming deficit myths about learning, language, and culture. *Language Arts, 68*(5), 369–379.

Foley, D. E. (1991). Reconsidering anthropological explanations of ethnic school failure. *Anthropology and Education Quarterly, 22,* 60–86.

Ford, D. Y. (1996). *Reversing underachievement among gifted black students: Promising practices and programs.* New York: Teachers College Press.

Fordham, S. (1990). Racelessness as a factor in black students' school success: Pragmatic strategy or pyrrhic victory? In N. M. Hidalgo, C. L. McDowell, & E. V. Siddle (Eds.), *Facing racism in education* (Reprint Series No. 21; pp. 232–262). Cambridge, MA: Harvard Educational Review.

Fordham, S., & Ogbu, J. U. (1986). Black students' school success: Coping with the "burden of acting White." *Urban Review, 18*(3), 176–206.

Forman, E. A., Minick, N., & Stone, C. A. (Eds.). (1993). *Contexts for learning: Sociocultural dynamics in children's development.* New York: Oxford University Press.

Forray, K. R., & Hegedüs, A. T. (1989). Differences in the upbringing and behavior of Romani boys and girls, as seen by teachers. *Journal of Multilingual and Multicultural Development, 10*(6), 515–528.

Fossey, R. (1996). Missing children: Kidding ourselves about school dropout rates. *The Harvard Education Letter, 12,* 5–7.

Foster, M. (1996). Introduction. In J. I. Irvine & M. Foster (Eds.), *Growing up African American in Catholic schools* (pp. 1–7). New York: Teachers College Press.

Freire, P. (1970a). *Cultural action for freedom.* Cambridge, MA: Harvard Educational Review.

Freire, P. (1970b). *Pedagogy of the oppressed.* New York: Seabury Press.

Freire, P. (1973). *Education for critical consciousness.* New York: Continuum.

Freire, P. (1985). *The politics of education: Culture, power, and liberation.* New York: Bergin & Garvey.

Freire, P., & Macedo, D. (1995). A dialogue: Culture, language, and race. *Harvard Educational Review, 65,* 377–402.

Fruchter, N., Galletta, A., & White, J. L. (1993). New directions in parent involvement. *Equity and Choice, 9*(3), 33–43.

Fullan, M. G., with Stiegelbauer, S. (1991). *The new meaning of educational change* (2nd ed.). New York: Teachers College Press.

Fulwood, S. (1991, January 1). Attitudes on minorities in conflict. *Los Angeles Times,* p. A1.

Gamoran, A., Nystrand, M., Berends, M., & LePre, P. (1995). An organizational analysis of the effects of ability grouping. *American Educational Research Journal, 32*(4), 687–715.

Gándara, P. (1995). *Over the ivy walls: The educational mobility of low-income Chicanos.* Albany: State University of New York Press.

García, E. E. (1993). Language, culture, and education. In L. Darling-Hammond (Ed.), *Review of research in education* (19th Yearbook of the American Educational Research Association, pp. 51–98). Washington, DC: AERA.

García, E. E. (1994). *Understanding and meeting the challenge of student cultural diversity.* Boston: Houghton Mifflin.

García, E. E. (1995). Educating Mexican American students: Past treatment and recent developments in theory, research, policy, and practice. In J. A. Banks & C. A. M. Banks (Eds.), *Handbook of research on multicultural education* (pp. 372–387). New York: Macmillan.

García, H. S. (1995). Toward a postview of the Chicano community in higher education. In R. V. Padilla & R. Chávez Chávez (Eds.), *The leaning ivory tower: Latino professors in American universities* (pp. 151–163). Albany: State University of New York Press.

García, J. (1993). The changing image of ethnic groups in textbooks. *Phi Delta Kappan, 75*(1), 29–35.

Gardner, H. (1983). *Frames of mind: The theory of multiple intelligences.* New York: Basic Books.

Gates, H. L., Jr. (1992). *Loose canons: Notes on the culture wars.* New York: Oxford University Press.

Gay, G. (1990). Achieving educational equality through curriculum desegregation. *Phi Delta Kappan, 72*(1), 56–62.

Gay, G. (1995a). Bridging multicultural theory and practice. *Multicultural Education, 3*(1), 4–9.

Gay, G. (1995b). Mirror images on common issues: Parallels between multicultural education and critical pedagogy. In C. E. Sleeter & P. L. McLaren (Eds.), *Multicultural education, critical pedagogy, and the politics of difference* (pp. 155–189). Albany: State University of New York Press.

Gay, G. (1996, April). *Multicultural education effects on student achievement.* Paper prepared for the Carnegie Foundation Project on Design Principles for Multicultural Education, Center for Multicultural Education, University of Washington, Seattle.

Gee, J. P. (1990). *Social linguistics and literacies: Ideologies in discourse.* Bristol, PA: Falmer Press.

George, P. S., & Shewey, K. (1993). *New evidence for the middle school.* Columbus, OH: National Middle Schools Association.

Gibson, M. A. (1987). The school performance of immigrant minorities: A comparative view. *Anthropology & Education Quarterly, 18*(4), 262–275.

Gibson, M. A. (1991). Minorities and schooling: Some implications. In M. A. Gibson & J. U. Ogbu (Eds.), *Minority status and schooling: A comparative study of immigrant and involuntary minorities* (pp. 357–381). New York: Garland.

Gibson, M. A. (1995). Perspectives on acculturation and school performance. *Fo-*

*cus on Diversity* (Newsletter of the National Center for Research on Cultural Diversity and Second Language Learning), 5(3), 8–10.

Gibson, M. A., & Ogbu, J. U. (Eds.). (1991). *Minority status and schooling: A comparative study of immigrant and involuntary minorities.* New York: Garland.

Giroux, H. A. (1983). *Theory and resistance in education: A pedagogy for the opposition.* Hadley, MA: Bergin & Garvey.

Glass, G. V. (1982). *School class size: Research and policy.* Beverly Hills, CA: Sage.

Goodlad, J. I. (1984). *A place called school.* New York: McGraw-Hill.

Gordon, M. (1964). *Assimilation in American life: The role of race, religion, and national origins.* New York: Oxford University Press.

Gould, S. J. (1981). *The mismeasure of man.* New York: Norton.

Grant, C. A., & Millar, S. (1992). Research and multicultural education: Barriers, needs and boundaries. In C. A. Grant (Ed.), *Research in multicultural education: From the margins to the mainstream* (pp. 7–18). London: Falmer Press.

Greene, M. (1988). *The dialectic of freedom.* New York: Teachers College Press.

Greenfield, P. M. (1994). Independence and interdependence as developmental scripts: Implications for theory, research, and practice. In P. M. Greenfield & R. R. Cocking (Eds.), *Cross-cultural roots of minority child development* (pp. 1–37). Hillsdale, NJ: Erlbaum.

Greenfield, P. M., & Cocking, R. R. (Eds.). (1994). *Cross-cultural roots of minority child development.* Hillsdale, NJ: Erlbaum.

Haberman, M. (1991). The pedagogy of poverty versus good teaching. *Phi Delta Kappan, 73*(4), 290–294.

Haberman, M. (1995). Selecting "star" teachers for children and youth in urban poverty. *Phi Delta Kappan, 76*(10), 777–781.

Hall, W. S., Reder, S., & Cole, M. (1979). Story recall in young black and white children: Effects of racial group membership, race of experimenter, and dialect. In A. W. Boykin, A. J. Franklin, & Y. F. Yates (Eds.), *Research directions of black psychologists* (pp. 253–265). New York: Russell Sage Foundation.

Hamovitch, B. A. (1996). Socialization without voice: An ideology of hope for at-risk students. *Teachers College Record, 98*(2), 286–306.

Harris, Louis, & Associates. (1994). *Dropping out or staying in high school: Pilot survey of young African American males in four cities.* New York: Commonwealth Fund.

Harris, M. (1995). Multiculturalist in training: A high school teacher's experience in developing a multicultural curriculum. *Teaching and Change, 2*(3), 275–292.

Heath, S. B. (1983). *Ways with words.* New York: Cambridge University Press.

Heath, S. B. (1995). Race, ethnicity, and the defiance of categories. In W. D. Hawley & A. W. Jackson (Eds.), *Toward a common destiny: Improving race and ethnic relations in America* (pp. 39–70). San Francisco: Jossey-Bass.

Heath, S. B., & McLaughlin, M. W. (Eds.). (1993). *Identity and inner-city youth: Beyond ethnicity and gender.* New York: Teachers College Press.

Henderson, A. T., & Berla, N. (1995). *A new generation of evidence: The family is crucial to student achievement.* Washington, DC: Center for Law and Education.

Herrnstein, R. J., & Murray, C. (1994). *The bell curve: Intelligence and class structure in American life.* New York: Free Press.

Hilliard, A. (1989). Teachers and cultural style in a pluralistic society. *NEA Today,* 7(6), 65–69.

Hirsch, E. D. (1987). *Cultural literacy: What every American needs to know.* Boston: Houghton Mifflin.

Hodgkinson, H. L. (1989). *The same client: The demographics of education and service delivery systems.* Washington, DC: Center for Demographic Policy, Institute for Educational Leadership.

Hollins, E. R., King, J. E., & Hayman, W. C. (1994). *Teaching diverse populations: Formulating a knowledge base.* Albany: State University of New York Press.

Hollins, E. R., & Spencer, K. (1990). Restructuring schools for cultural inclusion: Changing the schooling process for African American youngsters. *Journal of Education, 172*(2), 89–100.

hooks, bell. (1994). *Teaching to transgress: Education as the practice of freedom.* New York: Routledge.

Howard, G. R. (1999). *You can't teach what you don't know: White teachers, multiracial schools.* New York: Teachers College Press.

Igoa, C. (1995). *The inner world of the immigrant child.* New York: St. Martin's Press.

Irvine, J. J. (1990). *Black students and school failure: Policies, practices, and prescriptions.* Westport, CT: Greenwood Press.

Irvine, J. J. (1992). Making teacher education culturally responsive. In M. E. Dilworth (Ed.), *Diversity in teacher education: New expectations* (pp. 79–92). San Francisco: Jossey-Bass.

Irvine, J. J. (Ed.). (1997). *Critical knowledge for diverse teachers and learners.* Washington, DC: American Association of Colleges for Teacher Education.

Irvine, J. J., & Foster, M. (Eds.). (1996). *Growing up African American in Catholic schools.* New York: Teachers College Press.

Irvine, J. J., & York, D. E. (1995). Learning styles and culturally diverse students: A literature review. In J. A. Banks & C. A. M. Banks (Eds.), *Handbook of research on multicultural education* (pp. 484–497). New York: Macmillan.

Jensen, A. R. (1969). How much can we boost I.Q. and scholastic achievement? *Harvard Educational Review, 39,* 1–123.

Jervis, K. (1996). "How come there are no brothers on that list?" Hearing the hard questions all children ask. *Harvard Educational Review, 66,* 546–576.

Kalantzis, M., Cope, B., & Slade, D. (1989). *Minority languages.* London: Falmer Press.

Katz, M. B. (1971). *Class, bureaucracy, and the schools: The illusion of educational change in America.* New York: Praeger.

Kendall, F. E. (1996). *Diversity in the classroom: New approaches to the education of young children* (2nd revised ed.). New York: Teachers College Press.

Kiang, P. N. (1995). Bicultural strengths and struggles of Southeast Asian Americans in school. In A. Darder (Ed.), *Culture and difference: Critical perspectives on the bicultural experience in the United States* (pp. 201–225). Westport, CT: Bergin & Garvey.

Kinchloe, J. L., & Steinberg, S. R. (1993). A tentative description of post-formal thinking: The critical confrontation with cognitive theory. *Harvard Educational Review, 63,* 296–320.

Kleinfeld, J., & Nelson, P. (1991). Adapting instruction to Native Americans' learning styles: An iconoclastic view. *Journal of Cross-Cultural Psychology, 22,* 273–282.

Kohl, H. (1994). *"I won't learn from you" and other thoughts on creative maladjustment.* New York: New Press.

Kozol, J. (1978). *Children of the revolution: A Yankee teacher in the Cuban schools.* New York: Delacorte Press.

Kozol, J. (1991). *Savage inequalities: Children in America's schools.* New York: Crown.

Kreisberg, S. (1992). *Transforming power: Domination, empowerment, and education.* Albany: State University of New York Press.

Labov, W. (1972). *Language in the inner city: Studies in the black English vernacular.* Philadelphia: University of Pennsylvania Press.

Ladson-Billings, G. (1992). Culturally-relevant teaching: The key to making multicultural education work. In C. A. Grant (Ed.), *Research and multicultural education: From the margins to the mainstream* (pp. 106–121). Bristol, PA: Falmer Press.

Ladson-Billings, G. (1994). *The dreamkeepers: Successful teachers of African American children.* San Francisco: Jossey-Bass.

Ladson-Billings, G. (1995a). Multicultural teacher education: Research, practice, and policy. In J. A. Banks & C. A. M. Banks (Eds.), *Handbook of research on multicultural education* (pp. 747–759). New York: Macmillan.

Ladson-Billings, G. (1995b). Toward a theory of culturally relevant pedagogy. *American Educational Research Journal, 32*(3), 465–492.

Lambert, W. E. (1975). Culture and language as factors in learning and education. In A. Wolfgang (Ed.), *Education of immigrant students* (pp. 55–83). Toronto: Ontario Institute for Studies in Education.

Lee, C. D., & Slaughter-Defoe, D. T. (1995). Historical and sociocultural influences on African American education. In J. A. Banks & C. A. M. Banks (Eds.), *Handbook of research on multicultural education* (pp. 348–371). New York: Macmillan.

Lee, E., Menkart, D., & Okazawa-Rey, M. (1998). *Beyond heroes and holidays: A practical guide to K–12 anti-racist, multicultural education and staff development.* Washington, DC: Network of Educators on the Americas.

Lee, S. J. (1996). *Unraveling the "model minority" stereotype: Listening to Asian American youth.* New York: Teachers College Press.

Lee, V. E., Bryk, A. S., & Smith, J. B. (1993). The organization of effective secondary schools. In L. Darling-Hammond (Ed.), *Review of research in education* (19th Yearbook of the American Educational Research Association, pp. 171–267). Washington, DC: AERA.

Lee, V. E., & Ekstrom, R. B. (1987). Student access to guidance counseling in high school. *American Educational Research Journal, 24*(2), 287–310.

Leistyna, P., Woodrum, A., & Sherblom, S. A. (Eds.). (1996). *Breaking free: The transformative power of critical pedagogy* (Reprint Series No. 27). Cambridge, MA: Harvard Educational Review.

Levine, A., & Ndiffer, J. (1996). *Beating the odds: How the poor get to college.* San Francisco: Jossey-Bass.

Lewis, O. (1965). *La vida: A Puerto Rican family in the culture of poverty — San Juan and New York.* New York: Random House.

Lipka, J. (1991). Toward a culturally based pedagogy: A case study of one Yup'ik Eskimo teacher. *Anthropology and Education Quarterly, 22*(3), 203–223.

Lipman, P. (1997). Restructuring in context: A case study of teacher participation and the dynamics of ideology, race, and power. *American Educational Research Journal, 34*(1), 3–37.

Loewen, J. W. (1995). *Lies my teacher told me: Everything your American history textbook got wrong.* New York: New Press.

Lomawaima, K. T. (1994). *They called it Prairie Light: The story of Chilocco Indian School.* Lincoln: University of Nebraska Press.

Lomawaima, K. T. (1995). Educating Native Americans. In J. A. Banks & C. A. M. Banks (Eds.), *Handbook of research on multicultural education* (pp. 331–347). New York: Macmillan.

Lomotey, K. (1990). *Going to school: The African-American experience.* Albany: State University of New York Press.

Louis, K. S., Marks, H. M., & Kruse, S. (1996). Teachers' professional community in restructuring schools. *American Educational Research Journal, 33*(4), 757–798.

Lucas, T., Henze, R., & Donato, R. (1990). Promoting the success of Latino language minority students: An exploratory study of six high schools. *Harvard Educational Review, 60*(3), pp. 315–340.

Margolis, R. J. (1968). *The losers: A report on Puerto Ricans and the public schools.* New York: ASPIRA.

May, S. (Ed.). (1999). *Rethinking multicultural and antiracist education: Towards critical multiculturalism.* London: Falmer Press.

McCaslin, M., (1996). The problem of problem representation: The Summit's conception of student. *Educational Researcher, 25*(8), 13–15.

McCaslin, M., & Good, T. L. (1992). Compliant cognition: The misalliance of management and instructional goals in current school reform. *Educational Researcher, 21*(3), 4–17.

McDermott, R. P. (1977). The cultural context of learning to read. In S. F. Wanat (Ed.), *Papers in applied linguistics* (Linguistics and Reading Series 1, pp. 10–18). Arlington, VA: Center for Applied Linguistics.

McGoldrick, M., Pearce, J. K., & Giordano, J. (Eds.). (1982). *Ethnicity and family therapy.* New York: Guilford Press.

McIntosh, P. (1988). *White privilege and male privilege: A personal account of coming to see correspondences through work in women's studies* (Work Paper No. 189). Wellesley, MA: Wellesley College Center for Research on Women.

McLaren, P. L. (1995). White terror and oppositional agency: Towards a critical multiculturalism. In C. E. Sleeter & P. L. McLaren (Eds.), *Multicultural educa-*

*tion, critical pedagogy, and the politics of difference* (pp. 33–70). Albany: State University of New York Press.

Means, B., & Knapp, M. S. (1991). Cognitive approaches to teaching advanced skills to educationally disadvantaged students. *Phi Delta Kappan, 73*(1), 282–289.

Mehan, H. (1991). *Sociological foundations supporting the study of cultural literacy* (Research Report No. 1). Santa Cruz: University of California, National Center for Research on Cultural Diversity and Second Language Learning.

Mehan, H., Datnow, A., Bratton, E., Tellez, C., Friedlaender, D., & Ngo, T. (1992). *Untracking and college enrollment* (Research Report No. 4). Santa Cruz: University of California, National Center for Research on Cultural Diversity and Second Language Learning.

Meier, D. (1995). *The power of their ideas: Lessons from a small school in Harlem.* Boston: Beacon.

Meier, K. J., Stewart, J., Jr., & England, R. E. (1989). *Race, class, and education: The politics of second-generation discrimination.* Madison: University of Wisconsin Press.

Mercado, C. I. (1993). Caring as empowerment: School collaboration and community agency. *Urban Review, 25*(1), 79–104.

Moll, L. D. (1992). Bilingual classroom studies and community analysis: Some recent trends. *Educational Researcher, 21*(2), 20–24.

Montero-Sieburth, M., & Pérez, M. (1987). *Echar palante,* moving onward: The dilemmas and strategies of a bilingual teacher. *Anthropology and Education Quarterly, 18*(3), 180–189.

Mosteller, F. (1995). The Tennessee study of class size in the early school grades. *The Future of Children, 5*(2), 113–127.

NABE No-Cost Study on Families. (1991). *NABE News, 14*(4), 7, 23.

National Center for Education Statistics. (1995). *The educational progress of Hispanic students.* Washington, DC: U.S. Department of Education, Office of Educational Research and Improvement.

National Coalition of Advocates for Students. (1988). *New voices: Immigrant students in U.S. public schools.* Boston: Author.

National Commission on Excellence in Education. (1983). *A nation at risk: The imperative for educational reform.* Washington, DC: Author.

Nelson-Barber, S., & Estrin, E. T. (1995). Bringing Native American perspectives to mathematics and science teaching. *Theory into Practice, 34*(3), 174–185.

Nieto, S. (1994). What are our children capable of knowing? *Educational Forum, 58*(4), 434–440.

Nieto, S. (1995). A history of the education of Puerto Rican students in U.S. mainland schools: "Losers," "outsiders," or "leaders"? In J. A. Banks & C. A. M. Banks (Eds.), *Handbook of research on multicultural education* (pp. 388–411). New York: Macmillan.

Nieto, S. (1996). *Affirming diversity: The sociopolitical context of multicultural education* (2nd ed.). White Plains, NY: Longman.

Nieto, S. (1998). From claiming hegemony to sharing space: Creating community in multicultural courses. In R. Chávez Chávez & J. O'Donnell (Eds.), *Speaking the unpleasant: The politics of non-engagement in the multicultural education terrain* (pp. 16–31). Albany: State University of New York Press.

Nieto, S. (forthcoming). *Affirming diversity: The sociopolitical context of multicultural education* (3rd ed.). White Plains, NY: Longman.

Nieto, S., & Rolón, C. (1997). Preparation and professional development of teachers: A perspective from two Latinas. In J. J. Irvine (Ed.), *Critical knowledge for diverse teachers and learners* (pp. 93–128). Washington, DC: American Association of Colleges for Teacher Education.

Oakes, J. (1985). *Keeping track: How schools structure inequality.* New Haven, CT: Yale University Press.

Oakes, J. (1990). *Multiplying inequalities: The effects of race, social class, and tracking on opportunities to learn mathematics and science.* Santa Monica, CA: Rand Corporation.

Oakes, J. (1992). Can tracking research inform practice? *Educational Researcher, 21*(4), 12–21.

Oakes, J., Well, A. S., Jones, M., & Datnow, A. (1997). Detracking: The social construction of ability, cultural politics, and resistance to reform. *Teachers College Record, 98*(3), 482–510.

O'Donnell, J., & Clark, C. (1999). *Becoming and unbecoming White: Owning and disowning a racial identity.* Westport, CT: Bergin & Garvey.

Ogbu, J. U. (1987). Variability in minority school performance: A problem in search of an explanation. *Anthropology and Education Quarterly, 18*(4), 312–334.

Ogbu, J. U. (1992). Understanding cultural diversity and learning. *Educational Researchers, 21*(8), 5–14.

Olsen, L. (1988). *Crossing the schoolhouse border: Immigrant students and the California public schools.* San Francisco: California Tomorrow.

Olsen, L., & Mullen, N. A. (1990). *Embracing diversity: Teachers' voices from California's classrooms.* San Francisco: California Tomorrow.

Orfield, G. F. (1994). *The growth of segregation in American schools: Changing patterns of segregation and poverty since 1968.* Alexandria, VA: National School Boards Association.

Orfield, G., Bachmeier, M.D., James, D.R., & Eitle, T. (1997). *Deepening Segregation in American Public Schools.* Cambridge, MA: Harvard University Project of School Desegregation.

Ovando, C. J., & Collier, V. P. (1998). *Bilingual and ESL classrooms: Teaching in multicultural contexts.* Boston: McGraw-Hill.

Ovando, C. J., & Gourd, K. (1996). Knowledge construction, language maintenance, revitalization, and empowerment. In J. A. Banks (Ed.), *Multicultural education, transformative knowledge, and action: Historical and contemporary perspectives* (pp. 297–322). New York: Teachers College Press.

Pallas, A. M., Natriello, G., & McDill, E. L. (1989). The changing nature of the disadvantaged population: Current dimensions and future trends. *Educational Researcher, 18*(5), 4, 16–22.

Pang, V. O. (1995). Asian Pacific Americans: A diverse and complex population. In J. A. Banks & C. A. M. Banks (Eds.), *Handbook of research on multicultural education* (pp. 412–424). New York: Macmillan.

Perry, T., & Fraser, J. W. (1993). Reconstructing schools as multiracial/multicultural democracies: Toward a theoretical perspective. In T. Perry & J. W. Fraser (Eds.), *Freedom's plow: Teaching in the multicultural classroom* (pp. 3–24). New York: Routledge.

Persell, C. H. (1997). Social class and educational equality. In J. A. Banks & C. A. M. Banks (Eds.), *Multicultural education: Issues and perspectives* (3rd ed.; pp. 87–107). Boston: Allyn & Bacon.

Peterson, R. E. (1991). Teaching how to read the world and change it: Critical pedagogy in the intermediate grades. In C. E. Walsh (Ed.), *Literacy as praxis: Culture, language, and pedagogy* (pp. 156–182). Norwood, NJ: Ablex.

Phelan, P., Davidson, A. L., & Cao, H. T. (1992). Speaking up: Students' perspectives on school. *Phi Delta Kappan, 73*(9), 695–704.

Philips, S. U. (1982). *The invisible culture: Communication in classroom and community on the Warm Springs Indian Reservation*. White Plains, NY: Longman.

Phinney, J. S. (1993). A three-stage model of ethnic identity development in adolescence. In M. E. Bernal & G. P. Knight (Eds.), *Ethnic identity: Formation and transmission among Hispanics and other minorities* (pp. 61–79). Albany: State University of New York Press.

Piaget, J. (1951). *The child's conception of the world*. New York: Humanities Press.

Poplin, M., & Weeres, J. (1992). *Voices from the inside: A report on schooling from inside the classroom*. Claremont, CA: Claremont Graduate School, Institute for Education in Transformation.

Ramirez, M., & Castañeda, A. (1974). *Cultural democracy, bicognitive development and education*. New York: Academic Press.

Ramírez, R. (1974). Culture of liberation and the liberation of culture. In Centro de Estudios Puertorriqueños, *Taller de cultura: Cuaderno 6, Conferencia de historiografía* (pp. 81–99). New York: City University of New York, Puerto Rican Studies Research Center.

Ramsey, P. G. (1998). *Teaching and learning in a diverse world: Multicultural education for young children* (2nd ed.). New York: Teachers College Press.

Reissman, F. (1962). *The culturally deprived child*. New York: Harper & Row.

Reyes, M. de la L. (1992). Challenging venerable assumptions: Literacy instruction for linguistically different students. *Harvard Educational Review, 62*(4), 427–446.

Riggs, M. (Producer). (1987). *Ethnic notions* [Film]. (Available from California Newsreel, 149 Ninth Street, San Francisco, CA 94103)

Ríos, F. (Ed.). (1994). *Teacher thinking in cultural contexts*. Albany: State University of New York Press.

Roderick, M. (1995). *Grade retention and school dropout: Policy debate and research questions*. Bloomington, IN: Center for Evaluation, Development, and Research.

Rodríguez, C. E. (1995). Puerto Ricans in historical and social science research. In J. A. Banks & C. A. M. Banks (Eds.), *Handbook of research on multicultural education* (pp. 223–244). New York: Macmillan.

Ruiz, R. (1991). The empowerment of language-minority students. In C. E.

Sleeter (Ed.), *Empowerment through multicultural education* (pp. 217–227). Albany: State University of New York Press.

Rumbaut, R. G., & Ima, K. (1987). *The adaptation of Southeast Asian refugee youth: A comparative study.* San Diego: Office of Refugee Resettlement.

Sadker, M., & Sadker, D. (1994). *Failing at fairness: How America's schools cheat girls.* New York: Scribner's.

Scanzoni, J. H. (1972). *The black family in modern society.* Rockleigh, NJ: Allyn & Bacon.

Schofield, J. W. (1991). School desegregation and intergroup relations: A review of the literature. In G. Grant (Ed.), *Review of research in education* (Vol. 17). Washington, DC: American Educational Research Association.

Scribner, S., & Cole, M. (1981). *The psychology of literacy.* Cambridge, MA: Harvard University Press.

Sheets, R. H. (1995). From remedial to gifted: Effects of culturally centered pedagogy. *Theory into Practice, 34*(3), 186–193.

Sheets, R. H. (1996). Urban classroom conflict, student-teacher perception: Ethnic integrity, solidarity, and resistance. *The Urban Review, 28*(2), 165–183.

Shor, I., (1992). *Empowering education: Critical teaching for social change.* Chicago: University of Chicago Press.

Shor, I., & Freire, P. (1987). *A pedagogy for liberation: Dialogues on transforming education.* New York: Bergin & Garvey.

Sleeter, C. E. (1992). *Keepers of the American dream: A study of staff development and multicultural education.* London: Falmer Press.

Sleeter, C. E. (1994). White racism. *Multicultural Education, 1*(4), 5–8, 39.

Sleeter, C. E. (1996). *Multicultural education as social activism.* Albany: State University of New York Press.

Sleeter, C. E., & Grant, C. A. (1993). *Making choices for multicultural education: Five approaches to race, class and gender* (2nd ed.). New York: Merrill.

Sleeter, C. E., & McLaren, P. L. (1995). Introduction: Exploring connections to build a critical multiculturalism. In C. E. Sleeter & P. L. McLaren (Eds.), *Multicultural education, critical pedagogy, and the politics of difference* (pp. 1–32). Albany: State University of New York Press.

Smitherman, G. (1977). *Talkin and testifyin: The language of black America.* Boston: Houghton Mifflin.

Smitherman, G. (1994). The blacker the berry, the sweeter the juice: African American student writers. In A. H. Dyson & C. Genishi (Eds.), *The need for story: Cultural diversity in classroom and community* (pp. 80–101). Urbana, IL: National Council of Teachers of English.

Soto, L. D. (1993). Native language school success. *Bilingual Research Journal, 17*(1 & 2), 83–97.

Spring, J. (1989). *The sorting machine revisited: National educational policy since 1945.* White Plains, NY: Longman.

Spring, J. (1995). *The intersection of cultures: Multicultural education in the United States.* New York: McGraw-Hill.

Spring, J. (1997). *Deculturalization and the struggle for equality: A brief history of the education of dominated cultures in the United States* (2nd ed.). New York: McGraw-Hill.

Stanton-Salazar, R. D. (1997). A social capital framework for understanding the socialization of racial minority children and youth. *Harvard Educational Review, 67*, 1–40.

Steele, C. M. (1992, April). Race and the schooling of Black Americans. *The Atlantic Monthly*, pp. 68–78.

Suzuki, B. H. (1975a). *Multicultural Literacy Test*. Unpublished course materials, University of Massachusetts, Amherst.

Suzuki, B. H. (1975b). *Answers to Multicultural Literacy Test*. Unpublished course materials, University of Massachusetts, Amherst.

Tatum, B. D. (1992). Talking about race, learning about racism: The application of racial identity development theory in the classroom. *Harvard Educational Review, 62*, 1–24.

Tatum, B. D. (1994). Teaching white students about racism: The search for white allies and the restoration of hope. *Teachers College Record, 95*(4), 462–475.

Thomas, W. P., & Collier, V. (1997). *School effectiveness for language-minority students*. Washington, DC: National Clearinghouse for Bilingual Education.

Torres-Guzmán, M. E. (1992). Stories of hope in the midst of despair: Culturally responsive education for Latino students in an alternative high school in New York City. In M. Saravia-Shore & S. F. Arvizu (Eds.), *Cross-cultural literacy: Ethnographies of communication in multiethnic classrooms* (pp. 477–490). New York: Garland.

Treisman, P. U. (1992). Studying students studying calculus: A look at the lives of minority mathematics students in college. *The College Mathematics Journal, 23*(5), 362–372.

Trueba, H. T. (1989). *Raising silent voices: Educating the linguistic minorities for the 21st century*. Cambridge, MA: Newbury House.

Tyack, D. (1995). Schooling and social diversity: Historical reflections. In W. D. Hawley & A. W. Jackson (Eds.), *Toward a common destiny: Improving race and ethnic relations in America* (pp. 3–38). San Francisco: Jossey-Bass.

U.S. Bureau of the Census. (1993, July). *Monthly News*.

U.S. Department of Justice. (1993). *1992 statistical yearbook of the Immigration and Naturalization Service*. Washington, DC: U.S. Government Printing Office.

Vasquez, O. A., Pease-Alvarez, L., & Shannon, S. M. (1994). *Pushing boundaries: Language and culture in a Mexicano community*. New York: Cambridge University Press.

Villegas, A. M., & Watts, S. M. (1992). Life in the classroom: The influence of class placement and student race/ethnicity. In *On the right track: The consequences of mathematics course placement policies and practices in the middle grades* (Report to the Edna McConnell Clark Foundation). Princeton & New York: Educational Testing Service and National Urban League.

Vygotsky, L. S. (1978). *Thought and language*. Cambridge, MA: MIT Press.

Wallace, I., Wallechinsky, D., & Wallace, E. (1983, March 13). First U.S. city to be bombed from the air. *Parade Magazine*, p. 26.

Walker, E. V. S. (1993). Caswell County Training School, 1933–1969: Relationships between community and school. *Harvard Educational Review, 63,* 161–182.

Walsh, C. E. (Ed.). (1991). *Literacy as praxis: Culture, language, and pedagogy.* Norwood, NJ: Ablex.

Wang, M. C., & Gordon, E. W. (1994). *Educational resilience in inner-city America: Challenges and perspectives.* Hillsdale, NJ: Erlbaum.

Weinberg, M. (1977). *A chance to learn: A history of race and education in the U.S.* Cambridge: Cambridge University Press.

Weinberg, M. (1990). *Racism in the United States: A comprehensive classified bibliography.* Westport, CT: Greenwood Press.

Weinberg, M. (1994). Diversity without equality = oppression. *Multicultural Education, 1*(4), 13–16.

Wells, A. S., & Serna, I. (1996). The politics of culture: Understanding local political resistance to detracking in racially mixed schools. *Harvard Educational Review, 66,* 93–118.

Welner, K. G., & Oakes, J. (1996). (Li)ability grouping: The new susceptibility of school tracking systems to legal challenges. *Harvard Educational Review, 66,* 451–470.

Wheelock, A. (1992). *Crossing the tracks: How "untracking" can save America's schools.* New York: New Press.

Witkin, H. A. (1962). *Psychological differentiation.* New York: Wiley.

Wong Fillmore, L. (1991). When learning a second language means losing the first. *Early Childhood Research Quarterly, 6,* 323–346.

York, D. E. (1996). The academic achievement of African Americans in Catholic schools: A review of the literature. In J. I. Irvine & M. Foster (Eds.), *Growing up African American in Catholic schools* (pp. 11–46). New York: Teachers College Press.

Zanger, V. V. (1993). Academic costs of social marginalization: An analysis of Latino students' perceptions at a Boston high school. In R. Rivera & S. Nieto (Eds.), *The education of Latino students in Massachusetts: Issues, research, and policy implications* (pp. 167–187). Boston: Gastón Institute.

Zeichner, K. M., & Hoeft, K. (1996). Teacher socialization for cultural diversity. In J. Sikula, T. Buttery, & E. Guyton (Eds.), *Handbook of research on teacher education* (2nd ed.; pp. 525–547). New York: Macmillan.

Zinn, H. (1980). *A people's history of the United States.* New York: Harper & Row.

# Index

# About the Author

SONIA NIETO is Professor of Language, Literacy, and Culture in the School of Education, University of Massachusetts, Amherst. Her books include *Affirming Diversity: The Sociopolitical Context of Multicultural Education*, and *Puerto Rican Students in U.S. Schools*, as well as many book chapters and articles. She is an advisor to several national organizations that focus on educational equity and social justice, and she has received many awards for her community service, advocacy, and scholarly activities. In 1998, she was awarded an Annenberg Institute Senior Fellowship in Urban Education.

UNIVERSITY COLLEGE WINCHESTER
LIBRARY